Is Life Sacred?

Is Life Sacred?

GEOFFREY G. DRUTCHAS

THE PILGRIM PRESS
Cleveland, Ohio

The Pilgrim Press, Cleveland, Ohio 44115
© 1998 by Geoffrey G. Drutchas

Pages 199–200 constitute an extension of this copyright page.

Biblical quotations are from the New Revised Standard Version of the Bible,
© 1989 by the Division of Christian Education of the National Council of the
Churches of Christ in the U.S.A., and are used by permission

Printed in the United States of America on acid-free paper

03   02   01   00   99   98   5   4   3   2   1

Library of Congress Cataloging-in-Publication Data

Drutchas, Geoffrey G. (Geoffrey Gilbert), 1952–
     Is life sacred? / Geoffrey G. Drutchas.
        p.   cm.
     Includes bibliographical references and index.
     ISBN 0-8298-1275-X (pbk. : alk. paper)
     1. Abortion—Religious aspects—Christianity.   2. Euthanasia—
Religious aspects—Christianity.   3. Assisted suicide—Religious aspects—
Christianity.   I. Title.
     HQ767.25.D78   1998
     241'.697—dc21   98-36257
                                                             CIP

To my parents;
my parents-in-law;
my wife, Eileen;
and my son, Griffin,
with thanks for your
constancy and support

Contents

Preface

On June 2, 1990, Janet E. Adkins, a fifty-four-year-old woman diagnosed with Alzheimer's disease, flew into the Detroit Metro Airport and checked into a nearby Romulus, Michigan, motel for an appointment with Dr. Jack Kevorkian, a local pathologist known to assist in suicides. Two days later, Janet Adkins was dead, after being hooked up to an intravenous apparatus, which Dr. Kevorkian called the "Mercitron," and then pressing a button releasing into her body a lethal dose of potassium chloride.[1]

Only a little more than two months later, another woman, Virginia "Ginger" Harper, also flew to Detroit to end her life. Suffering from a metastasizing breast cancer that had spread to her liver, she was already experiencing acute pain. Because of the national publicity surrounding Janet Adkins and Dr. Kevorkian, Ginger Harper and her husband, Bob, were under the impression that Michigan was the only state where assisted suicide was entirely legal.[2] After checking into the Comfort Inn in Romulus on August 18, 1990, Harper—with the assistance of her husband and daughter—committed suicide using a combination of drugs and a plain plastic bag pulled over her head by her husband.[3]

The two Romulus, Michigan, motels where, respectively, Janet Adkins stayed and Ginger Harper met her chosen fate are within three or four miles of the congregation I serve as a United Church of Christ pastor and literally in the backyards of some of my parishioners. If assisted suicide was not an open topic of discussion among my parishioners before summer 1990, it quickly became one after the successive deaths of Adkins and Harper.

Still, my parishioners' concern with end-of-life issues did not begin with Adkins's and Harper's deaths. Nor did it evaporate as some of the initial notoriety surrounding Dr. Kevorkian and assisted suicide began to subside. In fact, my fellow church members have been dealing with end-of-life issues all along. They continue to do so.

I have been consistently impressed by the practical moral intelligence of parishioners addressing end-of-life issues for themselves. Again and again, I have heard my fellow congregants affirm life as a good. Many are either ambivalent or critical towards the work of Dr. Kevorkian. At the same time, when they or a loved one has been at life's edge and faced with a respirator or artificial hydration and nutrition without prospect of recovery, I have also heard them remark to me: "Pastor, I know they say that life is sacred, but this isn't living." Unfortunately, it is not possible for most Christian laypeople to say this without some measure of guilt, because the idea that life should be preserved at all costs and regardless of circumstances still intellectually captivates us as an ideal and holds emotional sway, even if less clearly and resolutely than before.

It was this dilemma that prompted me to explore the whole notion of life's sacredness as it pertains to both the beginning and the end of human life. What I found is that the sanctity of life is literally an incoherent moral principle for Christians. More simply explained, a belief in the sacredness of human life does not *cohere* with biblical teaching, church tradition, or even current belief and practice among many, perhaps a majority of, Christian theologians and laypeople. Instead, it is a more modest, nonsacralizing respect for life that deserves and largely commands the genuine support of Christians—no matter how loudly a sometimes well-placed minority may otherwise insist. This conclusion may sound radical. Yet it is not, as the profuse evidence, presented in almost pedantic but purposeful detail, will show.

Acknowledgments

Although any errors or mistakes of judgment in what I have researched and written are strictly mine alone, I am deeply indebted to many who have lent me their support and encouragement over the years that have preceded this volume. At an earlier time, I benefited greatly from the teaching and example of scholarship provided by two history professors, William O. McCagg and Norman Pollack, both of Michigan State University. Subsequently, as my vocation led me through a stint in law school, graduate studies in theology and ethics at the Harvard Divinity School, Syracuse University, and Lancaster Theological Seminary, and nearly twenty years of ministry in hospital, campus, and parish settings, I have counted myself fortunate to be able to also include among my mentors, teachers, and guides such men and women as James Luther Adams, William Barnett, Lee Barrett, Hugo Bedau, Alice Berry, Gregory Drutchas, Mason Fernald, Ivan Galantic, Joyce Galantic, Howard Hunter, Robert Marshall, Jean Mayer, Richard R. Niebuhr, Ralph Potter, Charles Reed, Franklyn Reeves, Mary P. Rutkowski, Karen Steere, Richard F. Suhrheinrich, and Conrad Wright.

Most of the research for the present work on the sanctity of life was pursued over a five-year period. Leonard Weber and Howard Brody of the Medical Ethics Resource Network of Michigan (MERN) and the Center for Ethics and Humanities in the Life Sciences at Michigan State University were helpful as I was first starting out: my attendance at a week-long seminar, which they coordinated in East Lansing in August 1991 with James F. Childress as the keynote speaker, provided me with a better orientation to the current field of medical ethics.

At Lancaster Theological Seminary, where I subsequently began investigating the history of the sanctity of life in earnest, I was at various times blessed to have the good counsel of Donald Freeman, Lee Barrett, Ann Schoup, and seminary president Peter Schmiechen. Professor Barrett provided the greatest assistance. Besides proposing some additional avenues of research, he twice reviewed the original manuscript and made various editorial suggestions prior to its submission in final form to Pilgrim Press editor Timothy G. Staveteig, associate managing editor Ed Huddleston, and editorial assistant Kelley Baker.

In the earliest research phase the shelves of the Lancaster Theological Seminary library proved to be a boon to my work. Yet I soon delved into the resources of numerous other libraries. Beyond the Lancaster Seminary, I am deeply indebted to the library staffs and resources of the Detroit Public Library, Georgetown University, Harvard University, the Library of Congress, Michigan State University, the University of Detroit–Mercy, and Wayne State University.

Fortunately, in the thick of research and writing, often punctuated by interruptions caused by the demands of parish ministry, there were many professional colleagues who by words of interest or concern gave my work an extra boost when it was most needed. Fellow clergy Lawrence Cameron, Donald Lintelman, Raymond Lord, and Lowell Schrupp especially come to mind. But so too does the administrative and ministerial staff of the congregation which I serve as senior pastor, namely, Jeannette Wackro, Eugene Wackro, Dorothy Wakeling, Vernagene Schafer, and associate pastor Anna Souto. Each of these fellow staff members and good friends did their best to make sure that my free time really was free so that I could persist with my research and writing unimpeded. Our church's administrative assistant, Jeannette Wackro, was especially considerate and vigilant on my behalf, fending off unnecessary interruptions on my Monday "sabbath," usually devoted to research and writing. For this, she has my enduring gratitude.

Simultaneously, throughout the process of research and writing I found myself constantly refreshed and inspired by members of my congregation at St. Paul United Church of Christ, Taylor, Michigan, who, learning about the focus of my work through a series of sermons I delivered on Sunday mornings, further shared their own experiences, insights, and Christian faith with me. In this regard, our church's ongoing Tuesday morning Bible study group proved to be a wonderfully instructive forum. Week to week, as our group joined in prayer and reflection over scripture and sought to relate our troubled times to holy writ and vice versa, I had the opportunity to hear and learn what "ordinary" lay Christians—fellow ministers from the pew—were thinking and feeling about some of the controversial beginning-of-life and end-of-life issues that were regularly making headlines and which I was already investigating from a more academic perspective.

Finally, I remain profoundly conscious of the fact that none of my work could have been accomplished without the constructive influence, sacrifice, and moral support of my family—immediate and extended. My father, Gilbert H. Drutchas, died just as I was beginning the doctoral studies leading up to this work. But the memory of the stalwart battle that he and my mother waged against the grim and devastating illness which ultimately felled him was never far from mind. Without question, this memory, along with my experiences as a pastor, contributed to my own outlook on life and death and lent special impetus and momentum to the task of assessing from a Christian perspective whether claims about the sacredness of life were historically and theologically valid.

Meanwhile, as I actually got down to my research and writing on the subject, both my mother, Elaine M. Drutchas, and my parents-in-law, Bruce and Patricia Vernor, were helpful in the most tangible and practical ways. They were particularly gracious about making their own homes available as places of retreat when I most needed solitude to assimilate my research and pursue writing.

Even more significantly, however, my wife, Eileen, and my son, Griffin, rather cheerfully accepted the crimp in so much of our own time together, including summer vacations. Indeed, showing incredible patience and putting up with one inconvenience after another as the research and writing went on and on, they kept faith and never lost hope that one day the work would get done. For these reasons and more, this book is especially dedicated to them.

1

Is Human Life "Sacred in All Its Forms"?

In the mid-1980s Richard John Neuhaus made an uncanny prophecy. The Lutheran theologian—a subsequent convert to Catholicism—predicted that the Roman Catholic Church in America would step forward to fill a leadership vacuum created as other, more liberal Protestant Christian groups, not wanting to impose their faith on others, effectively removed themselves from the "public square."[1] In March 1995, Pope John Paul II issued an encyclical which signaled that Neuhaus's prophecy was rapidly being realized.

Titled *The Gospel of Life,* the encyclical offered a highly particular understanding of the purpose and significance of human life. Reiterating one of the major themes and preoccupations of John Paul II's entire papacy, it affirmed human life as sacred in all its forms.[2] It also insisted that a commitment to the sacredness or sanctity of life represented a fundamental moral norm for Christianity. The encyclical expressed alarm about the growing violation of human life by men and women enthralled with personal freedom and technological convenience.[3]

Reflecting the Roman Catholic Church's interest in exercising public influence, as well as its willingness to make use of the mass media to this end, *The Gospel of Life* was published almost from the start in a paperback edition. Within weeks after being officially issued by the Vatican, this papal encyclical could be found on display near the checkout counters of grocery and discount stores.

No doubt the encyclical's largest and most immediate audience was the pope's own Roman Catholic flock. Yet the leadership vacuum left by liberal Protestants, coupled with the pope's personal charisma and the increased blurring of all denominational lines, virtually assured John Paul II of a Protestant audience as well. Indeed, as the boldest public statement on human sanctity or sacredness issued by any Christian leader, John Paul II's encyclical could not help but garner the sym-

1

pathy and support of conservative Protestants who, doctrinal differences notwithstanding, share many of the pope's intense concerns about the moral degradation of modern society and the disregard for human life.[4] Today, thanks to the *Gospel of Life* encyclical, which stands as the definitive statement on the sanctity of life, Pope John Paul II presides over a Roman Catholic Church that is uniquely positioned to provide ecumenical leadership on behalf of the right to life and to profoundly shape, if not determine, the ethical course of Christianity as a whole.

DANGER OF A DIVIDE

Jesus, according to John 17:21, prayed "that they may all be one." However, the prominence of the pope as a Christian moral leader, the political clout of the Roman Catholic Church, and the growing cooperation between Roman Catholics and conservative Protestant evangelicals on the sanctity of life issue—all enhanced by the *Gospel of Life* encyclical—are not without hazards for the future of Christianity's wider communion. These could well be the basis for a new, pernicious divide within Christianity between those churches or communities which embrace a sanctity of life perspective and those which do not.

The potential severity of the divide is underscored by the sheer passion with which some have already taken up sanctity of life as a Christian cause. In his encyclical and other pronouncements, for instance, the pope has virtually argued that sanctity of life is an issue over which good Christians cannot disagree. His position has been echoed by other Roman Catholic and Protestant leaders and seconded by rank-and-file laity.

Although the geographical distance between the papal palace in Rome and a bombed-out abortion clinic in Atlanta is great, the pope's absolutist sanctity of life rhetoric has carried far, becoming a definite boon to the so-called prayer warriors who believe that trespass against property and even human life is entirely justified for the protection of innocent life. Conservative Protestant divines have further abetted these prayer warriors with comfort and encouragement.[5]

Not surprisingly, then, protest vigils outside clinics and hospitals that engage in abortion and other termination-of-life procedures have become the order of the day among sanctity of life advocates, often leading to violence.[6] In the existing sanctity of life movement, opponents are constantly vilified and demonized. If Christian, they are regarded as apostates.[7]

This kind of vituperation has traditionally fomented religious separatism and outright schisms. It could do so now. Thus, in spite of the great strides in ecumenism that have taken place in the latter half of the twentieth century, there is reason to fear for the future of peace and unity among the Christian churches. Ecumenicity could readily be short-circuited over the sanctity of life issue.

Another ready casualty of the divide over the sanctity of life could be the peace of mind of ordinary men and women faced with life-and-death decisions in emergency rooms and intensive-care wards of hospitals, even if they belong to denominational faith communities that do not espouse the sanctity of life. Already, the statements and claims of sanctity of life advocates, so adamantly pronounced, afflict the consciences of many with unnecessary doubt, anguish, and guilt. The result has sometimes been a merciless prolongation of human life not warranted by Christian faith. This is a situation of great pathos that needs to be challenged and remediated.

SOME DEFINITIONS

In his book *After Virtue,* philosopher Alasdair MacIntyre remarks on the extent to which those engaged in public moral discourse within modern society are increasingly talking past each other. Even more pointedly, MacIntyre suggests that in the guise of dialogue a kind of uncivil war is under way.[8] Perhaps no issue better illustrates MacIntyre's thesis than the debate over sanctity of life.

Owing to the considerable controversy it has engendered, sanctity of life as both a phrase and a principle has become part of common parlance. Despite its widespread invocation and use, however, there is no consensus on how it should be defined. Particular definitions of the sanctity of life abound both among its advocates, who are either religiously or secularly oriented, and among its critics or detractors. Christian ethicist Arthur Dyck sees in sanctity of life claims a statement about life's "supreme value," a sentiment echoed by former U.S. Surgeon General C. Everett Koop.[9] Not too dissimilarly, a secularist such as Leon Kass defines sanctity of life in terms of dignity of life.[10] The editorialists for *Christianity Today* go a little further, equating the sanctity of life with a "high regard for life."[11] Meanwhile, J. H. Channer, a British ethicist and the editor of a volume on abortion and the sanctity of life, understands the sanctity or sacredness of life to mean that human life has "inherent value" or is "ultimately meaningful."[12] For Joseph Fletcher, a critic and skeptic, the statement that life is sacrosanct translates into an affirmation that it is "intrinsically good" and valuable.[13] Similarly, for feminist theologian Beverly Wildung Harrison to speak of the sacredness of life is to affirm its "intrinsic worth."[14] Upping the ante, Jewish rabbi and scholar Immanuel Jakobovits ascribes to life in its sacredness "an infinite value."[15]

Other writers, however, believe that sanctity of life as a phrase carries even more specific normative content. John J. Haldane, for example, identifies sanctity of life as an affirmation of the inviolability of innocent life.[16] On a similar note, Helga Kuhse, who has attacked the concept of sanctity of life altogether on several grounds, also associates the sanctity or sacredness of life with its inviolability. Kuhse contends that those who subscribe to a sanctity of life position believe that "it is absolutely prohibited intentionally to terminate life because all human life, irrespective of its quality or kind, is equally valuable and inviolable."[17] Kuhse adds, "What the sanctity-of-life doctrine prohibits is the intentional termination of innocent human life."[18]

While the elements Kuhse identifies with the sanctity of life position may not be embraced by all sanctity of life proponents, they do seem to reflect the perspective of many contemporary Christians who view human life as sacred. For these Christians, all human life is to be regarded as equal in value, without distinction or discrimination as to differing physical or mental capacities. Moreover, these same Christians insist that nothing should be willfully done to threaten or harmfully intrude upon a human life, let alone terminate it. The only exception arises in those instances where the innocence of a person has been lost because of his or her personal involvement in a criminal act or in war, and retribution of some kind is held to be warranted.

Such an exception deserves to be discussed in detail. For now, however, as we consider definitions of sanctity, it is simply appropriate to acknowledge that even the sterner Christian advocates of human sanctity can take a less than absolutist stance in the protection and preservation of human life when it serves their own ideological purposes.

In the end, given the multiplicity of meanings ascribed to the sanctity or sacredness of life, a certain wariness—perhaps even a full-fledged caveat emptor—is justified. As a principle or doctrine, the sanctity of life can be arbitrary and idiosyncratic to the point of incoherence. Nonetheless, in spite of these shaky definitional foundations, the sanctity of life has become the theological cause célèbre of our times and a major Christian dogma claiming the warrant of holy writ, Christian theology, and a long ecclesiastical history.

EMBRACED FROM THE BEGINNING?

Pope John Paul II claims in *The Gospel of Life* that Christianity has always embraced the sanctity of life, an assertion buttressed not only by conservative Protestants but also by a host of secularists. All, whether advocates or critics, regard a sanctity of life posture as a historic Christian doctrine, intrinsic to Christianity. This unanimity of opinion is impressive.

Nevertheless, we need to be cautious. In fact, a fair and balanced scrutiny of the historical record suggests that the sanctity of human life is not a historic Christian doctrine at all. As a principle, it is certainly not consistent with other teachings of most Christian churches.

Admittedly, the sweep of history for the Christian churches is vast. It is not easy to apply a two-thousand-year heritage to contemporary issues in an intelligible and meaningful way. Under the circumstances some latitude should be given to differing historical perspectives. Still, it is not unreasonable to ask for evidence when it is claimed that a dogma has an emphatic historical basis and deep Christian roots.

Yet, in spite of all the pronouncements made, neither the pope nor anyone else—whether Roman Catholic, Protestant, or secular—has put forth credible evidence to substantiate that the sanctity of life position has a biblical basis or was even a widespread concern for the Christian churches before the nineteenth century. Indeed, the greatest impetus for the sanctity of life doctrine, as currently promulgated by the pope and others, came in all likelihood from secular, rather than religious, sources. The entire sanctity of life doctrine may actually represent a divergence from traditional Christian teachings.

Sanctity of life doctrine—promoted and embraced as a heteronomous principle—would appear to be at odds with the emphasis on love and compassion, the rejection of legalism, and the overarching concern for eternal life that have together stood at the heart of the gospel message as traditionally interpreted. An incompatibility between the sanctity of life and such major gospel themes, coupled with a lack of clear and specific rootedness in the Judeo-Christian tradition, could explain why a number of very eminent Christian theologians of this century have not rushed to join the chorus in favor of a so-called right to life.

Sanctity of life doctrine has implications for a whole host of moral decisions, including those concerning capital punishment and war. What follows, however, will focus primarily on the sanctity of life doctrine as it is most commonly embraced in the realm of bioethical discussion today. The intention is to (1) trace the emergence of the sanctity of life doctrine; (2) review and assess the various contemporary arguments that have been propounded on behalf of the sanctity of human life in bioethical decision-making; and (3) propose an alternative Christian stance which is more consonant with actual Christian tradition and perhaps more realistic and responsible in light of human circumstances today.

Although the challenge is immense, the purpose herein is to at least call into question a modern dogma whose merits have never been sufficiently critiqued from a Christian perspective. In a sense, the genealogy that follows is a prolegomenon. If nothing more, it establishes a framework for further inquiry and reflection on the wisdom, viability, and orthodoxy of the sanctity of life doctrine. Such a framework may be of particular help to pastors, chaplains, denominational policy makers, and participants in ecumenical dialogue.

PART 1

What Are the Sources for the Sanctity of Life?

2
The Biblical Origins

One of the arguments marshaled in support of contemporary sanctity of life doctrine is that it has origins of great antiquity within the Judeo-Christian tradition. Sanctity of life doctrine, it has been claimed, has emerged directly from express biblical commandments—"I am the Lord your God. . . . You shall not kill" (Exod. 20:2, 13)—or is an immediate outgrowth of particular theological and anthropological statements embodied by scripture. Yet rarely, if ever, has this claim about the biblical origins of the sanctity of life been examined in depth. In fact, if pursued, such an examination reveals that even though particular scriptural passages can be invoked by Roman Catholics and Protestants to elaborate and defend a sanctity of life principle today, the Bible does not presuppose or specify such a principle itself. Moreover, there is much content within biblical scripture that would seem to contradict a sanctity of life perspective.

ROMAN CATHOLIC AND PROTESTANT CLAIMS

Both Roman Catholics and Protestants have been earnest in their efforts to show that the sanctity of life principle originates in Holy Scripture. Perhaps reflecting the new concern for scriptural authority within the post–Second Vatican Roman Catholic Church, Pope John Paul II has been at the forefront of the initiative to biblically legitimate the sanctity of life. But his Protestant counterparts have never been far behind. Separately and together, they have cited a variety of biblical passages as sources for the sanctity of life doctrine, especially emphasizing Genesis 1:27 and 5:1–2, where there are pronouncements about human beings created in the image of God, and Exodus 20:13, which, as a part of the Sinai covenant, admonishes its audience not to kill.

For the current Roman Catholic pontiff, Genesis 1:27 and 5:1–2 are compelling affirmations of the sacredness of human life. According to Pope John Paul II, both passages, properly grasped, make clear that "man . . . possesses life as a gift, of which he cannot consider himself the owner." For this reason too, "he cannot feel that he is the arbiter of life, whether his own or that of others."[1] Instead, God is the owner and arbiter of human life, which must be respected and honored accordingly. Furthermore, in the pope's view, the "deep content" of Genesis 1:27 and 5:1–2, upholding the sacredness and inviolability of human life created in the divine image, is powerfully reinforced by the sixth commandment from Mt. Sinai with its emphatic prohibition on killing.[2]

"Of course," the pope concedes, "we must recognize that in the Old Testament this sense of the value of life, though already quite marked, does not yet reach the refinement found in the Sermon on the Mount." Nevertheless, he adds, "the over-all message, which the New Testament will bring to perfection, is a forceful appeal for respect for the inviolability of physical life and the integrity of the person."[3]

The pope's general line of argument and reasoning has been more than echoed by Protestant Christians.[4] For example, J. Kerby Anderson, a Protestant evangelical, joins Pope John Paul II in insisting that Genesis 1:27 and 5:27 are proof positive that the Bible expects us to regard human life as sacred.[5] Akin to both Pope John Paul II and Anderson, David Cairns, another eminent Protestant theologian, sees "the sacredness of man [as] an integral part of the Christian faith" and regards the biblical statement that men and women are made in the divine image as decisive evidence that the sanctity of life view originates with scripture.[6] Yet, unlike Anderson, Cairns does not stop there. He also invokes Genesis 9:5–7 as another fundamental biblical affirmation of human sacredness.[7] In the cited passage, the book of Genesis declares that any person or beast that slays a human being must forfeit his or her own life. Cairns reasons that the Bible would not mandate such a severe penalty and personal forfeiture if its inspired authors did not already perceive innocent human life as worthy of the utmost reverence and respect. Cairns believes, however, that it is in the writings of the prophets with their distinctive emphasis on God's covenant with all human beings that the "universal sacredness of man" becomes most clear.[8]

BIBLICAL ORIGINS CHALLENGED

Generally speaking, Roman Catholic and Protestant claims about the biblical basis for the sanctity of life have carried the day. The public perception seems to be that a sanctity of life stance is thoroughly biblical. But what advocates for the biblical origins of sanctity of life doctrine would have us believe is settled is actually quite controversial. A host of informed and reputable scholars from the Roman Catholic and Protestant mainstream, plus the secular sphere, have expressed doubts about the biblical basis for a sanctity of life perspective.

It should be noted that those who have most effectively called into question the biblical basis for sanctity of life doctrine are profoundly respectful in their own attitude and approach toward Judeo-Christian scripture. In some cases, they are even sympathetic to fellow Christians who have embraced a sanctity of life perspective in order to counteract what may be perceived as a growing moral callousness towards human life. Still, they view as misguided any attempt to claim that sanctity of life is a biblical doctrine or that scripture is clear and resolute in its own condemnation of practices that sanctity of life adherents regard as anathema.

Secular ethicist Leon Kass, who reports that he has undertaken a "modest and so far unsuccessful effort to trace the origin of the sanctity-of-life doctrine in our own Judeo-Christian traditions," observes that neither of the phrases "sanctity of life" or "sacredness of life" appears in the Old or New Testament.[9] Although the term "sanctity" does regularly surface in Old Testament and New Testament scripture, it is instead consistently associated with the idea of sanctification whereby God's people achieve a state of holiness, purity, and separation from all that is profane and sinful, either by their own act or by the grace of the Holy Spirit.[10] In essence, sanctity, as predicated by the Bible, involves a direct relationship with God. It is not a quality that automatically adheres to human life. Nor is it a respect that God confers upon human life in the absence of an affirmed or acknowledged relationship with him.[11]

According to biblical scholars, the Bible is even elusive on the sacredness of life when it comes to the two Old Testament passages most often cited by sanctity of life advocates. Although Judeo-Christian opposition to practices such as euthanasia and infanticide is attributed to biblical teaching, the considered opinion of many scholars and theologians is that neither the sixth commandment from Mt. Sinai nor the statement that God "made man in his own image" was ever intended to express a conviction or mandate about the overall sacredness of human life.[12] Only subsequent theological interpretation and gloss have made them so.

THE IMAGO DEI

No one challenges the obvious fact that the creation of men and women in the "image of God" can be construed as a positive biblical statement about the human condition in the totality of its prospects. Quite sensibly, some biblically oriented sanctity of life advocates have also asserted that the writers of the Old Testament viewed human beings as a psycho-physical unity. Most simply stated, within the Old Testament "man's physical being is not to be excluded from the image concept."[13]

Similarly, the same sanctity of life advocates have also been within bounds to take issue with the notion propagated by Augustine, Luther, and Calvin that the Old Testament views humankind as falling away from a state of perfection into depravity with a consequent effacement of divine image.[14] In fact, as some sanctity of life advocates maintain, the Old Testament for the most part seems to have a more sanguine estimate of the present human circumstances than that.

At the same time, in their study and review of the Old Testament "image of God" concept, sanctity of life advocates are not able to turn up very much in the Old Testament that unequivocally supports a biblical warrant for the sacredness of human life as a principle. Part of the problem may be with the history of the imago Dei doctrine itself. As much as it may excite the imagination of contemporary sanctity of life advocates, the imago Dei concept stands, according to both Gerhard von Rad and Anders Nygren, on the "margins of the Old Testament" and is not in any way a predominant concern or motif for Old Testament writers, especially when viewed against the wider tableau of scripture.[15] In addition, even such a sanctity of life advocate as James M. Childs has had to concede that the Old Testament never intended to offer "a doctrine of the dignity and worth of man by using the image concept to highlight noble qualities possessed by man."[16] Rather than celebrating human life, the Old Testament exalts God. Any doctrinal claim about the sanctity of human life is out of tune with actual Old Testament emphases.

Childs's assessment of the Old Testament on the sanctity of life issue is not directly challenged by any other author. Instead, Cairns, another early sanctity of life supporter, takes the opposite tack of noting that there is nothing in the Old Testament that would contradict a sanctity of life perspective. Making the most out of any lingering ambiguity within the Old Testament canon, he remarks that "where specialists disagree" about the intended implications of Old Testament imago Dei doctrine, "a certain liberty is left us" regarding the sacredness of human life. What Childs does not mention, however, is that liberty always runs the risk of becoming license in this debate.[17]

Old Testament scripture certainly does not confuse or conflate the human image with God's image as the sanctity of life position can imply.[18] Human beings are only a copy of the divine.[19] In addition, rather than exalting men and women in terms of any sacredness, the Old Testament gives account of "God's struggle to overcome [humankind's] rebellion and establish the personal I-Thou relationship intended by man's creation in the image."[20]

Moreover, according to many biblical scholars, both the Old and New Testaments have an "eschatological orientation."[21] Thus, the "intent of the image notion seems clearly to indicate that the pattern and fulfillment of man's being, his true identity as man, is to be sought outside the created order."[22] The New Testament generally reinforces the idea of the image's fulfillment beyond nature in the resurrection.[23] By any reckoning, the sanctity or sacredness of human life here and now does not appear to be within the parameter of the biblical writers' concern. Those who want to claim that the sanctity of life is a biblical doctrine are forced to seek evidence elsewhere, perhaps in the Old Testament prohibition on killing or the New Testament commandment to love our neighbor.

THE SIXTH COMMANDMENT

In many respects the sixth commandment as found in the Old Testament is a natural place to turn in quest for evidence of a sanctity of life outlook among the Bible's authors. After all, the sixth commandment prohibits killing. More closely assessed, however, this commandment which initially seems to say so much about the sanctity of life actually says relatively little. It is not the straightforward and self-explanatory prohibition that has often been presumed.

Richard Brandt has remarked that the "biblical injunction 'Thou shalt not kill' . . . as it stands and without interpretation, may be taken to forbid suicide, killing of animals, perhaps even plants, and hence cannot be taken seriously." However, in his view, once we accept the fact that the commandment is not an autonomous dictum but requires interpretation, we have to decide whether its "prohibition of killing is *absolute* or only prima facie, meaning by '*prima facie*' that the duty not to kill might be outweighed by some other duty (or right) stronger in the circumstances, which could be fulfilled only by killing."[24]

Other scholars agree in part or full. Rejecting the idea that the sixth commandment was meant to be the bold and sweeping statement against all taking of human life—let alone a statement about life's sanctity—that has been claimed, they too perceive the commandment against killing as either an ideal or a rule rife with implicit qualifications about the proper regard we are to have for human life.[25]

Glanville Williams, a legal scholar who wrote one of the first works on the sanctity of life, has remarked that, when considered in its biblical context, the commandment "Thou shalt not kill" actually means "Thou shalt not commit murder."[26] Protestant theologian Karl Barth would largely concur. Although Barth notes that the sixth commandment protects human life from "arbitrary and therefore wicked extinction," he does not see it as a pacifistic prohibition on all killing or a sacralistic embrace of all human life.[27] Any divine countermanding would overrule the sixth commandment and permit killing:

> Hence, even though we read: "Thou shalt not kill," we must still do so when ordered by someone whose command may not be disregarded. Good care must be taken, however, to see to it that the divine command has been issued beyond any possibility of doubt.[28]

From Barth's perspective, those who seek to uphold the sixth commandment properly have the challenge of differentiating between "murder," which is prohibited, and circumstances where there may be a divine order or sanction to kill.

It is noteworthy that in ancient biblical times, murder seems to have been defined quite narrowly and the divine order to kill quite expansively.[29] As Canadian theologian and ethicist Bruce Kaye has said, the "commandment not to kill [in Jewish law] is given in the context of the holy nation and killing God's enemies is quite another matter." The Old Testament account of Samuel, Saul, and the Amalekites "illustrates absolutely clearly that obedience to the commandment of God is of greater value than a particular human life."[30] In fact, in the first book of Samuel, the prophet orders Saul, who is fighting King Agag and his people, to kill in Yahweh's name "man and woman, child and infant, ox and sheep, camel and donkey."[31] The Old Testament is further replete with other accounts of similar slaughter of noncombatant civilians.[32]

Killing also appears to be sanctioned by the Old Testament in instances where military adversaries are not a part of the picture at all. For example, Deuteronomy 21:18–21 legalizes the execution of disobedient sons. Not dissimilarly, 2 Kings 2:23–24 recounts how Elisha's curse upon a crowd of small boys, who jeer at him, is divinely fulfilled when she-bears come out of the woods and tear apart all forty-two of them. Meanwhile, in Judges 11:29–40, Jephthah the Gileadite fulfills a vow to God in exchange for his victory over the Ammonites by putting his innocent and luckless daughter to death. All of these episodes further belie any facile attempt to read a coherent sanctity of life perspective into the Old Testament canon.[33]

NEW TESTAMENT CLAIMS

Although the New Testament emphasis on a love for neighbor certainly radicalizes and widens the concept of murder that is introduced by the Old Testament,[34] there is nothing in the four Gospels to indicate that a sacralization of human life was intended by this change.[35] While New Testament scripture—not unlike the books of the Old

Testament—appreciates, even cherishes, human life, it does not hold it to be of supreme value. In fact, while the New Testament may be more attentive and respectful than the Old Testament with regard to the overall well-being of the individual, it is more ambivalent and ambiguous about the strict significance of physical human life.[36]

Not surprisingly, recent sanctity of life advocates, especially Roman Catholics, have done their best to highlight whatever appreciation the New Testament does express for the human body. In *The Gospel of Life,* for instance, Pope John Paul II notes how Jesus' acts of healing show *"God's great concern even for man's bodily life."*[37] Likewise, referring to John 1:14, where it is proclaimed that "the Word became flesh," Roman Catholic theologian Bernard Häring insists that no other religion or philosophy has given so much consideration to the dignity of man's body.[38] Yet, no matter how appealing such an interpretation of the gospel may be, it is not necessarily faithful or true to the actual New Testament text or to its message as originally intended and long understood.

Protestant theologian James M. Gustafson has characterized Jesus and his gospel as God-focused. "The gospels," Gustafson comments, "powerfully portray Jesus as one who incarnates in his teachings, his manner, and his actions theocentric piety and fidelity."[39] The New Testament message is about the glory of God and of God's reign that is to come, rather than the splendor of human life.

Perhaps the most balanced and succinct recapitulation of the gospel's attitude toward human life is to be found in an article by the Canadian ethicist and theologian Bruce Kaye. In "The Value of Human Life and Ethical Practice in Medicine," Kaye states:

> When we come to the New Testament religion, the picture of God's dealings with humanity broadens. . . . The particular value attaching to human life and to the human being is at once greater than that which attaches to the rest of creation and it also reaches in significance beyond the present life. In other terms, one might say that there is always an eternal dimension to the human condition and that present circumstances are never ultimate but only ever, at the most, penultimate. It is clear in such a context that while human life attracts the greatest possible respect, it never reaches the position of holding a sanctity which is absolute.[40]

Kaye goes on to observe that the Christian affirmation of humanity carries with it a command of sacrifice and service as exemplified by Jesus on the cross, plus his admonition that "No one has greater love than this, to lay down one's life for one's friends."[41] While Kaye could be accused of ironing out too much of the ambiguity in the gospel's perspective on human life, his exposition nevertheless captures the essential message of the gospel well: mortal human life is not sacred. At most, it is of penultimate, rather than ultimate, value.

This ambivalence towards mortal human life continues in the apostle Paul's writings. Paul avoided the radical spirit-body dualism that characterized the Gnostics. He specifically held that "what is done 'in the body' is morally significant."[42] Still, for him, the overall significance of our physical bodies was relativized by Jesus' resurrection and the prospect of our own resurrection after death.[43] In Paul's view our physical body was to serve our goal of reaching God's realm. In this spirit and with this sensibility, he essentially exhorted fellow Christians to offer their bodies as a "living sacrifice" and to carry "in the body the death of Jesus, so that the life of Jesus may also be made visible in our bodies."[44]

Not without reason, process theologian W. Norman Pittenger regards Paul's emphasis on the spiritual—transcending the physical and the bodily—as the apostle's hallmark.[45] Not without justification either, Beverly Harrison has called Paul "sex negative." Given his apocalyptic perspective—a perspective he shared with Jesus—Paul saw little value in either sex or procreation.[46] This attitude, which is reflected in his several epistles, is a far cry from the outlook of sanctity of life advocates today who, besides exalting the physical functions of the human body, have virtually sacralized the sex act in its procreative aspects. (See chapter 6, "Sacralization as Moral Cap and Gender Constraint.")

While we can never know the mind of Jesus, Paul, or any of the subsequent leaders of the early Christian church, examination of the New Testament text does call into doubt any assertion that Christianity as a faith was centrally concerned with fostering an appreciation for the sacredness of physical human life. Indeed, most evidence points to the contrary.

CAPITAL PUNISHMENT, SUICIDE, AND ABORTION

The lack of biblical warrant for the sacredness of life as a general principle is matched by the absence of any biblical endorsement for the sanctity of life when it comes to particular life and death issues. Study of both the Old and New Testaments makes clear that they do not share many of our contemporary sensibilities about the preservation of human life in applied ethical situations. Indeed, the Bible can be remarkable in what it says or does not say at critical moments. Human actions that dismay sanctity of life advocates so profoundly in the late twentieth century hardly seem to have fazed biblical writers.

Taking on the role of apologists, sanctity of life advocates are disposed to make excuses for biblical writers, especially where their silence on any given issue is now glaring or where their judgments now strike us as morally callous. One common assertion is that the biblical writers said little or nothing on certain moral matters because there was no controversy involved: everybody already knew what was morally right or morally wrong and remained faithful to what was right.[47] Another argument is that the moral perspective of the biblical writers, even if sometimes insensitive in dealing with particular issues, nevertheless reflected a nascent, evolutionary sanctity of life perspective overall. Any failure on their part to perceive all the moral responsibilities attendant upon a sanctity of life principle is only natural under the circumstances and should not be held against them. Nor should it be used to discredit the underlying claim that the sanctity of life has always been a biblical concept.[48]

However, all of these arguments, as propounded by sanctity of life advocates, are tenuous as well as historically tendentious. For instance, it strains credulity to suggest that life in the ancient Jewish and early Christian communities was so ideal and civilized that people of faith never gave thought to the kinds of practices that sanctity of life advocates today find so objectionable. The more reasonable assumption is that the ancient Jews and early Christians, however distinctive in their mind-set, lived in a world no more morally perfect or ideal than our own.[49]

Likewise, the argument that the biblical writers spoke from a nascent sanctity of life perspective simply puts a bright face on one recorded act of violence after another. Indeed, the evidence is quite compelling that the biblical writers—stern faith notwithstanding—either sanctioned capital punishment, suicide, and abortion or proved largely indifferent to any taking of human life involved.

The biblical stance on capital punishment is typical. Although today often identified as a sanctity of life issue, capital punishment escapes any direct or total censure in the Bible. In *Church Dogmatics* Karl Barth mentions such biblical passages as Exodus 27:12, Leviticus 20:2, and Joshua 7:25 as evidence of the acceptability of capital punishment in the Old Testament tradition.[50] Moreover, Barth goes on to note that capital punishment remained permissible within the mores of the New Testament, "according to the will of God . . . in connexion with the life of the state."[51]

As summarized by Barth, the implications of the biblical stance on capital punishment are clear: human life is not so hallowed that it must be preserved in all circumstances and at all costs.

Similarly, suicide also garners little or no outrage from biblical writers. Condemnation of suicide is conspicuously absent from scripture. Again, Barth notes that "in the Bible, suicide is nowhere explicitly forbidden."[52] British legal scholar Glanville Williams offers similar comment, noting that even though "the prohibition of suicide is usually referred to the Bible, it is easy to show the unauthenticity of this." The Old Testament, he states, recounts the suicides of Samson, Saul, Abimelech, and Ahithophel without giving any "indication that they were frowned upon." Subsequently, Williams observes, "both Orthodox Jewish and Christian interpreters had to resort to a strained interpretation of the Sixth Commandment in order to stigmatize suicide as a sin."[53]

In sum, there is no express indication that the Bible's authors had any moral objection to suicide. They certainly did not anathematize it as sanctity of life advocates since have.[54] In some circumstances the Bible's authors may have been inclined to regard suicide as morally advisable. As Leon R. Kass remarks about the Jewish biblical tradition that has informed his own life:

> Life as such is not said to be holy (Gadosh) [in the Hebrew Bible], as is, for example, the Sabbath. . . . True, traditional Judaism places great emphasis on preserving human life—even the holy Sabbath may be violated to save a life, implying to some that a human life is more to be revered than the Sabbath—yet the duty to preserve one's life is not unconditional: to cite only one example, a Jew should accept martyrdom rather than commit idolatry, adultery, or murder.[55]

Kass sees the Hebrew Bible's outlook on suicide and martyrdom as actually undercutting any absolutist claim about the sanctity of life.

For some, the biggest surprise of all may be the simultaneous silence of the biblical writers on induced abortion, which has generated such vehement opposition among present-day sanctity of life advocates. While the Old Testament biblical text clearly acknowledges pregnancy and even makes provision for legal redress and compensatory damages where a miscarriage is brought on by a willful and negligent act of another, it is noticeably quiet about the prospect of deliberate abortion initiated by parents. The New Testament continues this silence.[56]

The Bible's silence on abortion of this kind is so complete that neither Pope John Paul II nor abortion foe John T. Noonan Jr. has been able to ignore it.[57] This, however, has not stopped either of them from persisting with alleged biblical arguments against abortion. In their complaint against a utilitarian reductionism of human life, they and other abortion foes have searched for any scrap of scripture to support their own arguments.[58] There is a certain irony here: those most revulsed by a utilitarian outlook in ethics may be guilty of utilitarianism—at least with regard to the way they treat scripture.

This irony is not lost on biblical scholar J. W. Rogerson. Although he is personally pro-life, he worries about the abuse of scripture in the name of a just cause:

> In the case of the debate about abortion, there are no texts that can be simply applied to the matters. The Bible does not directly mention abortion anywhere. However, this does not prevent the misuse of passages that are thought to indicate a pro-life stance in the Bible, and there is a danger that overzealous advocates of the pro-life viewpoint may damage their cause by using the Bible in ways likely to be repugnant to people who are not hard-line fundamentalists.[59]

For instance, Rogerson is not persuaded when sanctity of life advocates, citing Psalm 139:13–16, have argued that the Bible regards the fetus in the mother's womb as a person.[60] From the biblical texts, Rogerson states, it

> is not clear . . . whether the unborn child was thought of as a person. The Old Testament gives several passages in which the growth of the unborn child is described. Unfortunately, for our purposes, these passages are in poetry, and we cannot be sure whether they represent what the biblical writers actually thought was happening inside the womb.[61]

Elsewhere, Rogerson is even bolder in contradicting the popular view of the Bible held by the pro-life Christians. "We cannot be *certain*," he admits, "that the life of the unborn child was regarded as sacrosanct in the Bible."[62] Overall, Rogerson believes that apart from broad themes stressing the love of God and God's concern for the defenseless and weak, biblically based arguments against abortion and for the defense of the sanctity of life are of limited validity.

Rogerson is impatient with any biblical literalism in the anti-abortion, prosanctity of life camp. As he puts it, "I think that the abortion issue is too important to be argued about in terms more suitable to a biblical and theological kindergarten."[63] While Rogerson seems tempted to emulate Pope John Paul II in arguing that scripture is relatively silent on abortion because it was not a commonplace practice in the less populated and more moral world of biblical times, he restrains himself.[64] He is convinced that it is better not to engage in historical speculation here but to acknowledge, more simply and vaguely, that "the Bible presupposes a social and cultural situation totally different from that which obtains today."[65] The implication of this fact, as Rogerson concedes, is that Christians must rely upon the spirit of scripture, rather than its letter, in making any biblically informed arguments about abortion specifically and the sanctity of life generally.[66]

Among those sympathetic to a sanctity of life perspective, Rogerson is not alone in acknowledging the fallaciousness of claims that the Bible stands squarely against abortion and for the sanctity of life. In an essay titled "Can Bioethics Be Evangelical?" Dennis Hollinger similarly argues that an imperious biblicism needs to be set aside because "the scriptures do not give direct scrutiny to any of the pressing matters: abortion, euthanasia, treatment termination, genetic engineering, reproductive technologies, etc." that concern evangelical Christians.[67] Protestant theologian Roy J. Enquist agrees.[68] So do fellow Protestant theologians Paul D. Simmons and Allen Verhey.[69]

Such insights and warnings are not likely to be well received by many sanctity of life advocates of any denominational or nondenominational stripe. Often ill informed about the actual content of the Bible and not conscious of their own penchant for retrojecting their own social expectations into a hallowed, biblical past, they widely perceive the biblical text as an inerrant and unchanging moral code which strongly supports their position.[70] While their arguments cannot be substantiated, sanctity of life will no doubt continue to be touted and proclaimed as a biblical doctrine.

3

The Theological Origins

Despite the absence of any clear biblical mandate to uphold the sanctity of life, one fact remains: the Judeo-Christian tradition has been credited as the actual or proximate source of the sanctity of life principle for Western civilization. As philosopher William K. Frankena observes, "Theologians, especially Protestant and Jewish ones . . . typically claim . . . that the moral doctrine of the sanctity of life emerged historically from the Judeo-Christian religion, and even that it would not have appeared if that religion had not entered the world."[1]

Support for the idea that Christianity was somehow seminal in the original emergence of sanctity of life doctrine is not limited to theologians, however. Secular writers have also ratified the claim. Representative among them are Helga Kuhse, Norman St. John-Stevas, and, most significant of all, William E. H. Lecky, who may be the ground-zero source for the claim that the sanctity of life concept had its origins in Christianity.[2]

THE LEGACY OF WILLIAM E. H. LECKY

Writing extensively as a historian in the latter half of the nineteenth century, William E. H. Lecky touched upon issues and themes that lately have come to concern us anew. It is believed, for instance, that Lecky coined the term "euthanasia."[3] Philosopher William K. Frankena has also speculated that Lecky may have been the first person to invoke the "sanctity of human life" as a phrase.[4] In fact, in *History of European Morals from Augustus to Charlemagne,* Lecky insisted that the whole idea of life's sanctity was the fruit of Christian church doctrine and belief.[5]

Lecky's account of the evolution of the sanctity of life concept under the aegis of the early Christian churches is engrossing. His basic contention, since reiterated by Norman St. John-Stevas and Helga Kuhse, was that early Christianity's own regard for human life represented a genuine departure from a decadent paganism and "formed a new standard higher than any which then existed in the world."[6] Early Christianity, Lecky maintained, enjoined its followers to view the universe as "transfigured by [divine] love," possessing a "religious sanctity."[7] In turn, by inculcating moral excellence and generating a disinterested enthusiasm for virtue, Christianity "raised its disciples to a very high condition of sanctity" in which they consciously saw themselves as immortal souls "united to one another by a special community of redemption"—a "fraternity of men in Christ."[8] Finally, in Lecky's assessment, this vision of a sanctified universe, combined with a commitment to lead sanctified lives together, fostered recognition that the "first and manifest duty of a Christian man was to look upon his fellow-men as sacred beings." Lecky states that "from this notion grew up the eminently Christian idea of the sanctity of all human life," leading to proscriptions against abortion, infanticide, and suicide.[9]

Lecky admitted that the record of Christianity was somewhat spotted in practice.[10] All the same, he believed that the sanctity of life generally prevailed as a principle over the years because the Christian churches at their best never ceased to actively promote it. As Lecky summarized:

> We are at present concerned with the principles that actuated Christian charity, not with the wisdom of [the churches'] organisations. Whatever mistakes may have been made, the entire movement I have traced deeply displays an anxiety not only for the life, but also for the moral well-being, of the castaways of society, such as the most humane nations of antiquity had never reached. This minute and scrupulous care for human life and human virtue in the humblest forms, in the slave, the gladiator, the savage, or the infant, was indeed wholly foreign to the genius of Paganism. It was produced by the Christian doctrine of the inestimable value of each immortal soul. It is the distinguishing and transcendent characteristic of every society into which the spirit of Christianity has passed.[11]

Plainly, Lecky is persuaded that the sanctity of life principle stands as one of Christianity's greatest contributions to the progress of humanity.

As expounded in this fashion by Lecky more than a hundred years ago—and endorsed in our own century by pro– and anti–sanctity of life commentators who may not be aware of Lecky as their actual precursor and mentor—the historical connection between Christianity and a belief in the sacredness of life may strike us as compelling. Yet how true to genuine fact is it? Prior to Lecky's own century, did the Christian churches really enunciate a formal doctrine about the sanctity of life? Over the course of the history of the Christian churches, was the sanctity of human life decisively and coherently affirmed? Before advocates and detractors of the sanctity of life doctrine further involve the Christian churches in an imbroglio that has the potential to divide it, we need clearer insight into the historic theological tradition of the churches.

EARLY THEOLOGICAL SILENCE

In directly examining the historical record of the Christian churches with regard to the subject of the sanctity of life, it is easy to develop a sense of déjà vu: not unlike

Old and New Testament scripture, which never affirms the sanctity of life directly or emphatically, Christian theology, apart from one exception, remained remarkably silent on human sanctity or sacredness until the advent of the nineteenth and twentieth centuries. Although Lecky may claim that the Christian churches were focused upon affirming human sanctity and cultivating virtue or that their practices had the clear effect of doing so, the actual evidence suggests that for the most part the Christian churches were concerned with human salvation and sanctification, whereby men and women would be restored to a right relationship with God that would assure them of an eternal life beyond the temporal world.

At the heart of every theology stands an anthropology or perspective on the condition of the human life that is in need of salvation. Indeed, Christian theology and anthropology often function as analogs of each other. A theology presupposes a particular anthropology. Christian anthropologies that have emerged in tandem with theology have been wide-ranging. Some Christian anthropologies have offered a positive view of the human condition and prospect, celebrating the higher faculties of men and woman—especially the rational intellect, which they may associate with the soul. Others have, in contrast, been much more negative, stressing human cupidity and depravity.

Positive or negative, however, Christian anthropologies were never traditionally disposed to put much stock in the value of physical human life. The appreciation for physical, embodied life that is today part and parcel of sanctity of life doctrine is alien to early Christian anthropologies and any theological statements supporting them.[12] At no juncture was the metaphysical outlook of the early Christian churches a propitious environment for a flourishing sanctity of life perspective.

Biblical commentators have noted the marginality of the imago Dei concept in the Old and New Testaments. But this was not true in the case of early Christian theology, which freely expanded upon scripture. The imago Dei concept actually figured quite prominently in the theological and anthropological outlook of the early Christian church which, essentially, was trying to harmonize the theology of Jerusalem with the metaphysical philosophies of Rome and Athens. Genesis 1:26-27, on which imago Dei doctrine was based, in fact served as a crucial touchstone for almost all anthropological statements made by the Christian churches in the ensuing years. If the Christian churches were inclined to make affirmations about the sanctity of human life, then surely it would have occurred in the context of discussion about imago Dei doctrine. Apart from one rather isolated exception in the late Middle Ages, this did not happen. Instead, until the dawn of modernity, discussion of imago Dei doctrine was largely bereft of any interpretations that would have readily lent themselves to a sanctity of life affirmation. A review of imago Dei doctrine as it evolved bears this out.

EARLY PERMUTATIONS OF IMAGO DEI

Building upon the story of Adam and Eve in the Garden of Eden (Gen. 1–3), early Christian theology posited two ideas. First, human beings are created in God's image and meant to live in harmony with God. Second, a fall from grace as a result of sin had estranged men and women from God. Jesus' role as savior in life, death, and resurrection was to call attention to the fundamental human estrangement from God and to enable men and women to be restored to a full, unimpeded, harmonious relationship with God by the action of grace.[13]

In the Christian churches, a disagreement seemed to recur perennially between those who felt that the human "fall" from an original and perfect relationship with God was total or near-total—making men and women entirely dependent upon God for a fresh start—and those who believed that the human fall from God, while catastrophic, was not necessarily so thoroughgoing or complete. The disagreement was repeatedly played out in terms of imago Dei theories and sanctification doctrine. For those who held that the rupture between God and humankind had been either total or near-total, a natural corollary was a deep conviction that God's image in men and women also approached extinction. Simultaneously, among those who contended that the rupture between God and humankind was less serious, there was a willingness to believe that a vital remnant of God's image persisted in men and women.

This disagreement about the effacement or survival of the divine image in men and women further expressed itself in more specific anthropological ascriptions. Those who regarded the divine image as mostly effaced saw human beings as horribly corrupted, hardly capable of any good act, let alone holiness and sanctification, except through the active spiritual grace of God in Jesus Christ and the admonitory guidance of God's revealed will. In contrast, Christians, who subscribed to belief in a remnant of the divine image in men and women, saw the potential for a positive interplay between God's spirit (as manifested in Christ), the guidance of God's Word, and the natural gifts with which God has endowed everyone. Working together, all three could restore human beings to a holy, sanctified life and the kind of relationship with God that Adam and Eve knew in Eden and that Jesus Christ knew throughout his life.

Ironically, in the first centuries after the founding of Christianity in Jerusalem, imago Dei and sanctification doctrine had started out on the more positive note. Responding to classical culture and even borrowing heavily from it, the early church fathers developed a concept of humanity in the image that actually spoke of the human capacity for deification and divinization.[14] Among the first major expositors of the divinization doctrine were contemporaries Clement of Alexandria (c. 150–215) and Irenaeus of Lyons (c. 140–202). Although their theological orientations were quite different in other respects, both subscribed to an idea that was foundational for divinization doctrine: namely, that human beings were created in the image and likeness of God only to lose this similitude through the Fall.

Admittedly, the distinction between retained image and lost similitude was, as many commentators have since noted, based on a faulty exegesis of Genesis 1:26— "an error occasioned by homage to Aristotle and his own twofold account of human nature."[15] Nevertheless, faulty or not, the point Irenaeus and Clement were trying to make with the buttress of biblical authority was that human beings in Christ had the potential, thanks to the basic retained image, of being restored to a full likeness with God. This likeness was the ability to live in accordance and harmony with all that was rational. After the Fall, the retained image of God disposed human beings to move towards the fulfillment of this rationality. Clement and Irenaeus each believed that it was possible for human beings to attain a perfection in likeness to God greater than anything Adam and Eve had known in Eden before their expulsion.[16]

A similar doctrine of salvation by divinization was embraced by other church leaders and teachers of the early church period, as well as by the generation of theologians who succeeded them. Indeed, divinization doctrine continued to charm church leaders, reaching its quintessence more than a century later in the theology of the three Cappadocians—Basil of Caesarea; his brother, Gregory of Nyssa; and Gregory of Nazianzus.[17] Their assessment and account of the human condition both before and after the Fall, however, was painted in even more dramatic terms.

For example, according to Gregory of Nyssa, humanity before the Fall shared in a goodness "surpassing every power of perception." Fashioned "to the most exact likeness [of God], according to the image of its prototype," humanity had been endowed with "all those attributes of God" which could now only be a matter of "speculation and conjecture."[18] With the Fall, however, Gregory and his fellow Cappadocian theologians saw the image of God in human beings as grievously disfigured. As Jaroslav Pelikan has explained:

> So disfigured had human nature become and so appalling was its misery that the Cappadocians found it necessary, amid all their celebration of the grandeur of the image of God, to speak soberly about nothing less than "the defacing of that image and the destruction of that divine impress . . . which has been formed in us when we were first created."[19]

Pelikan goes on to note that as "a consequence of the fall of man into sin, [the Cappadocians believed that] each of the three principal components of the image of God enumerated earlier—reason, free will, and immortality—now had its demonic counterpart in this 'image of the contrary nature.'"[20] It was in the context of this dark sensibility about human salvation that Gregory of Nyssa wrote: "Man, as a being, is of no account; he is dust, grass, vanity."[21]

In spite of this gloomy account of the human condition, all was not lost, according to the Cappadocians. As a result of the incarnation of Christ, where God became human, a metamorphosis had occurred, enabling those who embraced Christ through baptism to be fulfilled in the likeness to God for which human beings were created. The Cappadocians actually spoke of the results and possibilities held out by metamorphosis as theosis, a participation in the divine nature and fellowship with God.[22]

The divinization doctrine of salvation embraced by the Patristic fathers, especially the Cappadocians, almost suggests that the early Christian church affirmed the sacredness of human life. Lecky largely interpreted matters in this way.[23] Moreover, Lecky's interpretation appears to have the concurrence of at least one contemporary scholar of the Patristic period, Elaine Pagels. Pagels repeatedly credits the teachings of Clement and other Patristic fathers on the divinization of human nature with laying the basis for the recognition by Western culture of the infinite worth of the individual.[24] Yet any claim that the early Christian church saw human life as sacred in the way that some do today is somewhat more complicated than first meets the eye.

First, for all of their talk of a retained image, the early churches did not invoke the rhetoric about the sacredness of human life that is current today in discussing the circumstances of either the baptized or unbaptized. Second, divinization, as contemplated for those baptized, was a teleological process.[25] Although Irenaeus,

Clement, and other Patristic fathers apparently believed that baptized Christians were actually free from sin, it is not clear at what point, if at any, prior to death and resurrection, they would have regarded a human life as truly divine and, perhaps, fully and emphatically sacred.[26] Third, any supposition that the Patristic fathers might have embraced the sanctity of life on a de facto basis is countermanded by their ambivalence about all physical aspects of human life.

All of these circumstances are revealing and suggestive in their own right. But the ambivalence or aversion to physical life expressed by the Patristic fathers stands out most of all. This ambivalence ran deep: it permeated and shaped the Patristic account of imago Dei doctrine. On the one hand, the Patristic fathers declared that men and women possess God's image bodily in their formation.[27] Specifically, Irenaeus and Gregory of Nyssa taught that "not only the soul, but also the body of man shares in the character of the image, being created in the image of God."[28]

On the other hand, in the development of theosis, these same Patristic fathers and their compatriots believed that, in spite of its participation in the imago Dei, the physical human body was only of secondary importance next to the soul or spirit. Even though Patristic thought concerning the relationship between the human body and soul was heavily nuanced and never entirely systematized, the import of pronouncements by the Patristic fathers was relatively clear: physical bodily existence needed to be transcended in the quest for oneness with God.

Scholar Daniel E. Scuiry has made an especially detailed study of the anthropology of Gregory of Nyssa. According to Scuiry, "Gregory maintains that we are made in the image and likeness of God. . . . The body, too, is in the image of God but only by way of participation in the rational soul. As long as reason is the ruling principle, then the total person images God."[29] Stated another way, only as the physical human body is spiritually transmuted can theosis continue unabated.

In a discussion of the Christology and anthropology developed in the Patristic period, Margaret Miles similarly observes that for humans undergoing divinization the body was subsumed by the soul, just as the human was subsumed by the divine. "The eastern patristic fathers," she explains, "emphasized the subsumption of the human by the divine in Christ." She adds that in "this 'union of predominance'. . . the Logos, the stronger component, completely subsumes the weaker, the 'mortal body,' without undergoing alteration."[30] The Patristic fathers' tacit insistence on the predominance of the soul over the body reflected their ongoing wariness about the physical aspects of human life—a wariness shared by the classical pagan culture of the time.

Significantly, the deification which was to be enjoyed as a gift of grace and further cultivated after baptism in Christ involved a freedom from the passion often associated with the human physical body. In the fulfillment of theosis, upon a person's death and resurrection, a body remained but it was a spirit or angelic body without the problem of impurities that were more likely to be part and parcel of mortal bodies. Thus, for the Patristic fathers, death was a not unwelcome event. Pelikan explains:

> For, as Gregory of Nazianzus put it, the death of the Christian was not
> really to be called a "departure" at all but rather a "fulfillment, a loos-

ing of bonds, or a relief from a great burden." Calamitous and destructive though it certainly was, death also had a constructive purpose in the workings of divine providence. In Nyssen's formulation, "It was this: to refashion human nature once more by means of the resurrection into a sound creature, *apathes,* pure, and with no admixture of evil, after this has been eliminated by the dissolution of body and soul." In the death of the body, passion died with it, but when the body was raised, passion remained dead and life was free of it. As a constituent of the *metamorphosis* of humanity, such an *apatheia* was the counterpart to the freedom of the will as a constituent of the image of God, and was in fact the means through which the will could regain its freedom after sin.[31]

The goal of apatheia in this moral life, as well as the angelic life to come, appears to have included a distancing or removal from all sexuality.[32] Though the Patristic fathers did believe that sexuality belonged to the image of God originally, it was not in their view intended to be a part of resurrected life where men and women were fully restored to the image.[33]

Far, then, from regarding human embodied life as sacred, Patristic theology and anthropology were guarded and circumspect in their valuation of mortal life. Little continuity can be identified between the Patristic fathers' professed beliefs about mortal human life and a more modern theological conviction about the sacredness of human life.

Some pro-life advocates have felt obliged to acknowledge the basic incompatibilities between Patristic thought and the kind of sanctity of life perspective they want to uphold. For example, Protestant theologian David Cairns has noted that the Patristic sacralization of human life, however outwardly appealing, is thoroughly unbiblical and presupposes a lingering human merit after the Fall that should be offensive to bona fide Protestants.[34] James M. Childs Jr., another Protestant writer, observes that the Patristic fathers never did view human life in terms of a psycho-physical unity that would be necessary to affirm biological human life as sacred. Consequently, Childs regards Patristic thought as a setback for a proper appreciation of human life as sacred and inviolable.[35] What Cairns and Childs make clear is that an effort to claim historical antecedents in Patristic thought for contemporary sanctity of life doctrine is destined to fail or, alternatively, to short-shrift the truth.

AUGUSTINE

If an affirmation of the sanctity of embodied human life is less than apparent among the Patristic writers, it becomes even more obscure and uncertain with the next major theological development of Western Christianity, represented by the thought of Augustine of Hippo (354–430 C.E.). Specifically, the new theology and anthropology elucidated by St. Augustine prove paradoxical, especially if viewed in light of their implications for any sanctity of life claim.

In the course of his career as theologian, Augustine refashioned imago Dei doctrine in a way that sharply distinguishes him from the earlier Patristic tradition. He completely rejected, for instance, the idea that a human being "embodies a scintilla of the divine essence, the mere possession of which constitutes a prima-facie claim to divinity."[36] Also eliminated in Augustine's mature theology was the Patristic writers' twofold interpretation of the image, which continued to have appeal to some, most notably Thomas Aquinas, even after Augustine had long departed.[37] In place of this twofold interpretation of the image, Augustine posited a single, continuous image.[38]

For Augustine, that human beings are created in the image of God meant quite positively that we are in an "ontological relationship to God."[39] The ability of human beings "to know and love God" through their "rational soul" was "both the evidence of this [ontological] relationship and the result of this relationship."[40] A "perverse desire" to be like God, however, had prompted human beings to revolt against their creature-condition or createdness, putting them ineradicably at odds with God.[41] Their likeness to God was correspondingly marred and diminished.[42] Still, salvation in Christ, Augustine said, remained possible because the image of God persisted even in the hearts of unbelievers.[43] In turn, the image of God could be strengthened and "preserved" anew in those human beings who opted for a restored relationship with God through Jesus Christ.[44]

As historian Charles N. Cochrane notes, Augustine presented this salvation-preservation process as one of "sublimation." The same human creature who initially revolted against its own createdness suddenly "discovers a new centre of fixation," specifically God, as revealed in Jesus Christ.[45] Although he had a healthy respect for human life, Augustine's focus thus always remained upon the attraction of God. Augustine personally believed that only in a resurrection at the end of mortal life would the image of God be entirely renewed.[46]

At a time when incarnational theology within the Christian churches was in thorough disarray, Augustine was able to offer a helpful conceptualization of the proper interface between the human and the divine in Christ and between the physical and the spiritual within human beings. Augustine's distinctive approach—a high accomplishment—was to speak of the human and the divine in Christ, plus the body and the soul in human beings, in terms of two natures coexisting in inseparable combination as a persona, discarding the traditional Patristic concern with the predominance of the one over the other. Moreover, Augustine regarded the unity of the human and the divine, as well as that of the body and the soul, in a positive light: neither the divine in Christ nor the soul in human beings was defiled or contaminated by a contact with the human body that amounted to mingling, even mixing.[47] As Augustine scholar Margaret Miles has remarked:

> The enriched sense of *mixtura* in the later Augustine is highly significant; no longer reflecting the classical uneasiness with "mixture," Augustine is free to image the conjunction of God and human in Christ as the highest *activity*; the unity of Christ is no longer imaged statically as a "watering down" of the human nature by the God nature, but as a *summit*, an extreme of achievement and value, a "mixture" in which human nature is immeasurably enriched. The assumption of human nature by the divine Word means that human nature is infinitely valuable. Incarnation is then truly the basis for the

redemption of the *whole* human being, not just the "highest part." It is no longer only the Godlike and beautiful in human beings that is salvaged out of the clutter and inertia of the body, but the whole experience of human being.[48]

Borrowing from neo-Platonist tradition, Augustine is the first to employ the idea of hypostatic union in Christian theology.[49] He also treats human beings as a psycho-physical unity.

Although Augustine does not appear to include the body in the imago Dei, he certainly had far fewer reservations than his Patristic predecessors about the human body.[50] He seems to have developed a more positive outlook on the human body over the years. In contrast to an earlier point in his life where he referred to the human body as a "cage" or "snare," Augustine began to metaphorically speak of the body as a "spouse" to the soul.[51] For Augustine the fact that God became incarnate in a human body stood as powerful evidence that nothing is inherently wrong with the human body.

Such statements notwithstanding, Augustine can hardly be said to endorse the sanctity of life as a concept. While Augustine's view of the soul-body relationship in human beings and his basic respect for the body might endear him to partisans for the sacredness of embodied human life, other dimensions of his outlook make it doubtful that he would have found their particular rhetoric congenial to his own temperament and anthropological ideas.

First, though he had a healthy respect for human life, Augustine remained focused on the sovereignty of God rather than the sacredness of men and women. His profound wariness of human hubris and conceit further made him eager to set aside, once and for all, the old notion of a divine spark in the human breast, as preached by the Stoics and revived by the Patristic fathers. Consequently, his own rhetoric avoided all references to human divinity or sacredness.

Second, despite his more elevated estimate of the human body, original for his time, Augustine had a much less sanguine perception of the human soul, which he regarded as the activating principle for the body and the real source of sin.[52] That is, Augustine's more positive view of the human body was checkmated by his palpable sense of the acute human sinfulness of the human soul. This led him to contend that the image of God in human beings could only be completely renewed in the resurrection at the end of our mortal lives.[53]

Third, in one more significant departure from the Patristic fathers, who perceived the end of mortal life as a liberation, Augustine regarded death as a deserved punishment for the sinfulness of the human soul. As a deserved punishment, death was to be accepted and not unduly thwarted.[54]

Not without reason, scholars who are inclined to cherish Patristic divinization doctrine as a source for Western culture's evolving respect for human worth are bound to regard Augustine and his anthropology as a "spoiler."[55] All the same, unless one is, in the name of the sanctity of life, completely wedded to the ideas of human divinization and moral perfectibility, it is hard not to appreciate Augustine. His thinking does not lend itself well to any kind of sanctity of life perspective. Yet Augustine's fresh perceptions of the human body, his complex understanding of sin, and his renewed emphasis on the sovereignty of God offered the Christian churches an alternative to the outlook and ideals of classical culture. They also laid important groundwork for subsequent Protestant theology.[56]

MARTIN LUTHER

Although Augustine's theological and anthropological insights were not at first widely appropriated by the Christian churches, their impact was increasingly felt in the ensuing years. During the fifth-century controversies over Pelagianism and semi-Pelagianism, which raised profound questions about the existence and depth of original sin, those Christians claiming to be orthodox not only rejected the Patristic idea of moral perfectibility. They also accepted Augustine's view of human sin as a dire consequence of the fall of Adam and Eve.[57] Subsequently, Augustine's more positive understanding of the body—as distinguished from the soul—began to take firm hold.[58] By the sixteenth-century Protestant Reformation, even Augustine's distinctive account of the relational nature of the imago Dei found strong support and following.[59] None of these developments were congenial to a sanctity of life perspective. If anything, the growing embrace of Augustinian ideas, especially by Protestants, led to the opposite result.

During the first years of the Reformation, the overlap between Protestant theology and its Roman Catholic antecedents was perhaps the greatest. In his sermons, Martin Luther (1483–1546), who was banned from the Roman Catholic Church as a heretic, spoke in terms of a twofold imago Dei doctrine, positing a public and private image roughly analogous to the imago and similitudo of Patristic theology and medieval Scholasticism. Subsequently, however, Luther began to preach that the image was an original righteousness lost completely in the Fall.[60] According to Luther's revised assessment, all that was left from the image and its original righteousness was the faintest "relic," which left humankind with a sense or inkling of God's intention for us. This intention could only be fulfilled by heartfelt faith in Jesus Christ.[61]

Given his stance on the relic of God's image within human beings, Luther willingly granted that a person's "life and body" are the "greatest treasure" that he or she has on earth.[62] In view of humankind's eternal destiny, however, he was not inclined to view mortal life as possessed of anything approaching infinite value. Nor was Luther disposed to speak of mortal life in terms of something sacred.[63] Luther's revision of imago Dei doctrine was clearly motivated by his desire to put further distance between Reformation theology and its Patristic and Scholastic antecedents. In denying any continuing prominence to the image, Luther was seeking once and for all to eliminate any possible basis for salvation apart from Christ.

Other leaders of the Reformation largely concurred with Luther's new approach to the image and its attendant implications for the value of mortal life. As Roy J. Enquist notes, Melanchthon (1497–1560) also "urged a non-scholastic, operational understanding of the imago," believing that it had conferred an original wisdom and righteousness enabling human beings to know, fear, and trust God. While there was still some dispute as to whether any imago remained for human beings after the Fall, the Formula of Concord, which in 1577 outlined the basic doctrines of the Lutheran churches, held that "original sin is the complete lack or absence of the image of God according to which man was originally created in truth, holiness and righteousness."[64] In short, a total or near-total loss of the divine image was decisively affirmed, underscoring the perniciousness of the human fall, the thoroughness of human depravity, and the impossibility of human salvation apart from a renewed relationship with God through Jesus Christ.[65] There was no talk about the sanctity of human life.

Granted, the pronouncements of Luther, Melanchthon, and their coterie were not necessarily the exclusive word from the perspective of Protestantism on the status of the imago Dei in human beings after the Fall. In at least one notable instance, which will be discussed below, relic talk did resurface as a part of Reformation theology. This also led to rather uncharacteristic Protestant statements about the sacredness of human life which seemed to have greater affinity to the humanistic Renaissance than the theocentric Reformation. In the larger sweep of the Reformation, however, such rhetoric proved entirely fleeting and evanescent, underscoring the fact that it was indeed fundamentally alien to a Protestant Christian perspective and was, either at that time or shortly thereafter, tacitly recognized as such.

JOHN CALVIN'S ANOMALOUS STANCE

Swiss theologian John Calvin (1509–1564) was the seminal figure in a renewed, even if temporary, Reformation emphasis on the survival of a relic or remnant of the imago Dei. Though often remembered as a contemporary of Martin Luther, Calvin was twenty-five years younger and thus of another generation altogether. Calvin's theology and anthropology perhaps reflected this fact: both were innovative and markedly different from what some of the other reformers espoused, particularly when it came to imago Dei doctrine.

In a departure from Luther's perspective and what Helmut Thielicke has called the "Protestant thesis" on the imago Dei, Calvin could wax enthusiastic about the surviving relic or remnant of the image of God in men and women. While still emphatically Protestant in his denial of human moral perfectibility and the salvific merit of any imago Dei relic, Calvin quite forcefully contended that the continuing existence of such a relic stood as a souvenir of humankind's original holiness before the Fall and as a token of God's ultimate intention to redeem men and women through Jesus Christ. In another fresh twist, Calvin also insisted that God's intention for humankind, signified by a continuing remnant of the imago Dei, lent an extrinsic dignity and worth to human life that other human beings were wrong to wantonly violate. According to Calvin, to violate innocent human life was to violate God.

Calvin was quite explicit and direct in arguing that the abiding presence of the imago Dei should function as a moral constraint and foster a respect for human life. As he declared in his commentary on Galatians 5:13–14: "Above all, the image of God ought to be the bond of a holy union among us. Therefore, here there can be no question of friend or enemy: for, no evil in man can destroy his nature."[66] Here Calvin was asserting that the remnant of the imago Dei was so integral to human nature and being that it could never be lost. This image, as held in common, required that all men and women should have respect for each other.

Calvin picked up on exactly the same theme in his *Institutes of the Christian Religion*. Emphasizing the relevance for Christian conduct of the continued presence of the relic in all men and women, Calvin stated:

> The Lord commands us to do "good unto all men" [Heb. 13:16] universally, a great part of whom, estimated according to their own merits, are very undeserving; but here Scripture assists us with an excellent rule, when it inculcates, that we must not regard the intrinsic merit of men, but must consider the image of God in them, to which we owe all possible honour and love; but that this image is most carefully to be observed in them "who are of the household of faith" [Gal. 6:10], inasmuch as it is renewed and restored by the Spirit of Christ.[67]

Essentially, Calvin chose to impute to the Old Testament's prohibition against killing and the New Testament's positive exhortation about love for neighbor his own ideas concerning the imago Dei in remnant form and the notion of human life as possessed of extrinsic or alien worth.

Calvin, who could rhapsodize about the greatness of what God had created in human beings, ultimately proved so vehement about the significance of the relic or remnant in humankind that he, borrowing language from the ancient Stoics, called upon men and women to regard the bond between themselves as sacred. Thus, in his *Institutes of the Christian Religion*, Calvin stated: "Wherefore, unless we would violate the image of God, we ought to hold the personal safety of our neighbour inviolably sacred; and unless we would divest ourselves of humanity, we ought to cherish him as our own flesh."[68]

Almost identical remarks appeared in Calvin's own *Instruction in Faith* of 1537, as well as the *Catechism of the Church of Geneva* published among his treatises. Specifically, Calvin's *Instruction in Faith* stated that "we must hold our neighbor as holy and sacred, in such a way that he may not be violated without violating also the image of God in him."[69] Meanwhile, discussing the second table of the Decalogue, plus Jesus' own command that we should love our neighbor as ourselves, the Geneva Catechism insists upon the existence of "a tie, sacred and inviolable," gathering the "whole human race at once," which "cannot be loosed by depravity." The Catechism added that "God's order stands inviolable, and establishes this connection between us."[70]

Such affirmations of a sacred and inviolable tie between human beings as children of God certainly are impressive, seeming to lend support to the argument that the sacredness of life is an essential Christian doctrine. However, a more thoroughgoing review of Calvin's works indicates that those who might look to the Swiss theologian as an unimpeachable prophet of human sanctity may need to look for another.

At numerous points, Calvin actually undercuts his own pronouncements about the significance of the imago Dei in human beings and the sacred bond it purportedly creates. Contradictions emerge in Calvin's thought that cannot be bridged. Indeed, the sanctity of life doctrine, which fails to cohere to earlier Christian tradition, proves incoherent in quite another sense when Calvin consciously and conspicuously tries to incorporate it into his own thought. Basically, Calvin gives not one but three different accounts of the imago Dei, which besides being mutually exclusive, or nearly so, are not at all equal in their compatibility with the idea that human life is sacred.

Possibly reflecting some vestige of his earlier enthrallment with Stoicism, which stands out rather clearly in one of his first works, Calvin chose in various discussions of the imago Dei to emphasize the positive content of the remnant which had survived the Fall from the Garden of Eden.[71] Employing language highly reminiscent of Stoicism, Calvin in more than one instance described the remnant of the imago Dei in men and women as an inextinguishable divine spark. In his sermon on the Fourth Gospel, Calvin remarked:

> But even if men, following Satan's suggestion, have extinguished the light of God, it is nevertheless true that the devil has not been able, by his astuteness, to prevent the light of God from shining still in the midst of the shadows. . . . So one still always sees some light that God has left there, some spark from his lamp. . . . So [for example] there is some seed of religion in men, they have some remnant of their first creation; one sees still even in the most wicked and reprobate that there is some impression of the image of God.[72]

Elsewhere in his writings Calvin also offered an outright paean to the human intellectual abilities which he believed had survived the Fall as a part of the relic or remnant of the divine image:

> The manifold agility of the soul, which enables it to take a survey of heaven and earth; to join the past and the present; to retain the memory of things heard long ago; to conceive of whatever it chooses by the help of imagination; its ingenuity also in the invention of such admirable arts,—are certain proofs of the divinity in man. Besides, in sleep, it not only turns and moves itself round, but conceives many useful ideas, reasons on various subjects, and even divines future events. What shall we say, but that the vestiges of immortality impressed upon man are absolutely indelible?[73]

In Calvin's view, at least as registered here, every gift of the human soul and mind was an obvious residue of the divine image and, as such, worthy of celebration.

Still, no sooner did Calvin express such sentiments than he embarked on another tack altogether—his second approach to the divine image. Abandoning any humanist sentiment, Calvin could and did proceed to argue that Christians should not ascribe undue significance to any surviving remnant of the imago Dei. In fact, Calvin went to great lengths to cast the surviving remnant of the imago Dei in the most derogatory light. While the remnant yet survived in men and women, it did so, Calvin averred, in a pathetically crimped and inverted state.[74] Nowhere is this second tack or attitude on Calvin's part more conspicuous than in his *Sermons from Job:*

Since we are as corrupted in Adam as we are, it is certain that we ought to be doubly ashamed. And why? We were created after the Image of God. And what manner of Image is it now? It is disfigured; we are so perverted that the mark which God had put into us to be glorified thereby is turned to His shame; and all the gracious gifts that were bestowed upon us are so many witnesses to render us guilty before God, because we defile them; and as long as we continue in our nature, we only abuse the benefits that we have received, and apply them to all evil. So you see our confusion always increases by all the gifts which God has communicated to us.[75]

Essentially, Calvin's argument is that our natural gifts and talents, which point to a remnant of the imago Dei, disguise the true dreadfulness of our spiritual condition, leaving us unduly arrogant and self-righteous. In the aftermath of the Fall, the image of God in us has become such a "frightful deformity" that, in truth, we can do absolutely nothing right. Ultimately, the only good thing that the relic, as manifested in us through our natural gifts, can possibly enable us to do is to recognize our total sinfulness and culpability before God.

While this second tack on the imago Dei and its remnant already offered a sharp and definite contrast to Calvin's first claims about its positive survival, the Swiss theologian did not necessarily let matters rest there. Carrying the theme of human perversity even further in some of his same works, Calvin appeared to elaborate a third position on the state of the imago Dei in men and women—one which, at least tacitly, embraced the "Protestant thesis" that the imago Dei had been altogether forfeited at the time of the Fall and was now nonexistent. In his sermon on Deuteronomy 24:19, Calvin spoke most emphatically: "It is true that our Lord created us after His own image and likeness, but that was wholly defaced and wiped out in us by the sin of Adam: we are accursed, we are by nature shut out from all hope of life."[76] The import of Calvin's third position was simply this: while the imago Dei had a past among human beings and could, by the grace of God in Jesus Christ, have a future too, it possesses no present—no immediate significance, efficacy, or even, perhaps, existence.

Calvin's apologists have sought to harmonize his disparate remarks on the state of the imago Dei in men and women. Though acknowledging some "unsettling rhetorical shifts" in his statements—sometimes in the same sermon or treatise—they have argued that Calvin is not really as inconsistent as he sounds.[77] Indeed, they are inclined to treat Calvin's first two positions on the status of the relic as merely paradoxical and to chalk up his third stance to rhetorical excess.[78] Nevertheless, some of these same apologists have ultimately conceded that there is a definite and unmistakable incoherence to Calvin's pronouncements about the imago Dei and the sacredness of life, especially when his doctrines of total human perversity and divine predestination are also taken into account.

Although profoundly sympathetic to Calvin, both David Cairns and Thomas F. Torrance have, for example, forthrightly acknowledged the Swiss theologian's palpable deficiencies. Cairns, who is a strong personal advocate of the sanctity of life and thus not one to criticize Calvin rashly, pointedly observes that Calvin "is sometimes led into inconsistency, and interprets man's perversity in such a sense that the dignity and sacredness of human nature appear to have perished with the Fall."[79] Torrance is even more specific in his identification of Calvin's latent and disabling contradictions:

> It is difficult to see how there can be any ultimate reconciliation between Calvin's doctrine of total perversity and his doctrine of a remnant of the imago dei, though the very fact that he can give them both in the same breath seems to indicate that he had no difficulty in reconciling them. That there is an ultimate inconsistency seems demanded by Calvin's denial that there is any seed of election or any germ of righteousness in fallen man. In other words, both the doctrine of election as Calvin holds it and the doctrine of justification by faith alone [as maintained by Luther] seem to imply that there is no remnant of the imago dei.[80]

As both Cairns and Torrance underscore, a belief in total human depravity would logically appear to preclude the presence of any remnant of the imago Dei—and vice versa. Moreover, if there is no imago Dei present in men and women there would seem to be no basis for asserting the kind of sacred and inviolable bond between human beings upon which Calvin insists.

Cairns and Torrance see Calvin's predestination doctrine as freighted with problems for his argument that human life deserves to be treated as sacred. If, as Calvin contends, men and women are destined to either salvation or damnation before they are even born—with an elect group alone fated to know and enjoy the full restoration of the imago Dei in their persons—any remnant of the imago Dei which may universally persist among men and women is not likely to be a particularly meaningful basis for moral solidarity and mutual respect. Indeed, God's peremptory judgment in this case, dividing humankind into the saved and the damned, would seem to radically depreciate the significance of any lingering remnant of the imago Dei held in common by all men and women.[81]

In a further twist it should be noted that for all the theological novelty which Calvin introduced to Christianity by arguing on behalf of the extrinsic sacredness of human life, he did not fundamentally diverge from conventional Christian wisdom and piety when it came to outlining the right attitude that Christians should maintain towards their own mortal life. Never forgetting the eternal destiny of the human soul, he too relativized the value of mortal life and its continuation. For instance, even though Calvin proposed that we should have an "affectionate regard" for our bodies, he elsewhere asserted that "we ought to divest ourselves of all terrestrial affection, and aspire thither [to heaven] with all our soul."[82] At still another juncture, Calvin was even more explicit about the limited significance of mortal life against the wider tableau of our relationship with God and our servanthood within God's realm.

In exegetical remarks on John 12:25, where Jesus declares, "Those who love their life shall lose it, and those who hate their life in this world will keep it for eternal life," Calvin stated:

Since [Jesus] opposes the love of life to the hatred of it, we should understand what it is to love and hate life. Anyone who desires the present life so much that he will not let go of it except by force is said to love life. Anyone who despises life so much as to be willing with courage to go to his death is said to hate life. Life should not be hated as such, because it is regarded rightly as among God's chief blessings. Still, believers should be willing to lay it down when it keeps them from Christ, just as a man in a hurry to go somewhere will throw a troublesome and unwieldy burden off his shoulder. In short, it is not in itself wrong to love this life, provided we walk its course with our eyes upon our ultimate end. We love life rightly when we remain in it according to God's intention for us, and are ready to leave it according to his will: in a word, when as it were we carry it in our hands and offer it to God as a sacrifice. Anyone who is unduly attached to this world loses his life; that is, he hurls it to everlasting ruin. . . . Whoever is attached to this world deprives himself of heavenly life, to which we cannot be heirs unless we live as strangers and sojourners in this world. Hence it is that anyone who is too anxious for his security in this world is an alien to the Kingdom of God, or the true life. . . . Anyone who does not turn his eyes to heaven has not learned how to take care of this life.[83]

Plainly, Calvin argues for a nongrasping attitude towards mortal life. Although he teaches that mortal life ought to be regarded as a blessing, he does not contend that it should be preserved at all costs. Instead, Calvin suggests that human life should be functionally viewed as both the medium and the means by which we move towards our end in God. However someone might want to construe Calvin's sanctity of life talk elsewhere, his message here is that the faithful must always be prepared to relinquish mortal life for God's sake and according to God's sovereign bidding.

Coupled with the already cited contradictions, such conventional piety on Calvin's part raises the question whether his pronouncements on the sacredness of life were integral to his theology. One possibility looms: Calvin's sacredness of life posture may have always been theologically extraneous and rather secondary for him. In appropriating such a posture from the Stoic tradition in transmuted form, Calvin may simply have been seeking to fend off the arguments of Erasmus and others who saw in the negative and fatalistic anthropologies of Protestantism a disincentive to virtue.[84] That is, by issuing a dicta about the sacredness of life (based upon a respect for God's original and future intentions for humankind and the corresponding idea that all men and women share in the imago Dei's remnant), Calvin may have been doing nothing more than putting everyone on notice that his parallel doctrines of divine predestination and total human depravity were not to be taken as a license for murder and mayhem in human relationships.

The generations who immediately followed the great reformer have come into some criticism from Calvin's modern-day apologists for interpreting and appropriating his theology too lopsidedly. They have been accused of ignoring Calvin's sometimes positive account of natural human gifts, as well as his contention that human life should be treated as sacred.[85] Yet given the contradictions in Calvin's thought—which have led one commentator to speak of Calvin as "against himself"—can his followers be entirely faulted?[86] Perhaps Calvin's successors recognized his sacredness-of-life rhetoric as having a rather profound attraction and indebtedness to Renaissance humanism which they, coming a little later, did not share. Battling against Pelagianism, they might well have regarded the whole idea of the sacredness of life as counterproductive to their immediate efforts to uphold Calvin's more central teachings on human perversity and predestination.[87]

In any event, the subsequent catechisms, which emerged in whole or in part from the Calvinist churches, are totally bereft of any statements about the sanctity of life. This is specifically true for the Heidelberg Catechism of 1563.[88] Yet the same can be said for a stream of other, less well-known catechisms that emerged over the subsequent three centuries.[89]

Such silence with regard to the sanctity of life in the aftermath of John Calvin's own career as theologian and Reformation leader is more than curious: it is in its own right compelling. The complete dearth of references to the sanctity or sacredness of life in the creeds and catechisms of Christianity after Calvin, in spite of his personal endorsement and support for the idea, testifies as to just how anomalous the sacredness of life concept remained for orthodox Christian belief. Change came only with the nineteenth and twentieth centuries, when the Protestant and Roman Catholic churches found themselves face-to-face with a reemerging humanism that in its very momentum seemed destined to overrun and displace them unless they were willing to bend and adapt their own principles and values.

4

Early Christian Practices

Protestant and Roman Catholic sanctity of life advocates have been unwilling to concede that sanctity of life is an anomalous doctrine for the Christian churches. They have, however, had to deal directly or indirectly with an issue arising from that fact, namely, the lack of consistent church statements upholding the sanctity of life, both before and after John Calvin. Their response has been to argue that even if any consistent, specific, and formal pronouncements about the sanctity of life are lacking, the Christian churches were in practice always implicitly committed to a high valuation of mortal life.

Roman Catholic theologian José Comblin has been among those eager to make a distinction between theory and praxis for the Christian churches. While he has acknowledged the historical diffidence of official church doctrine on issues that many now view through the lens of a sanctity of life principle, he nevertheless contends that the "authentic Christian conception of person must be sought in a practice to which Christians have never managed to give theoretical expression."[1] Though somewhat less forthright on the matter, John T. Noonan has seconded this view.[2] It also appears to have become a backup position for Pope John Paul II.[3]

Given what is known about the interplay of religion and culture in the Western world, who can doubt that the Christian churches helped here or there in practical ways to shape positive Western attitudes toward human life overall? Yet the question remains whether the two-thousand-year practice of the Christian churches ever clearly and resolutely affirmed the sacredness of life as sanctity of life advocates today insist.

Protestant theologian James M. Gustafson has observed that every theology involves a selective retrieval of elements from a great store of biblical and traditional claims.[4] Any proof that the Christian churches were committed to the sanctity of life as a uniquely Christian moral paradigm hinges upon a highly selective and biased reading of the historical record. In fact, a sanctity of life paradigm cannot be substantiated in any detail.

Take, for instance, the current stance of sanctity of life advocates toward abortion, euthanasia, and assisted suicide: an almost rabid animus against each—without regard to particular circumstances—is virtually regarded as a litmus test of a true sanctity of life conviction. As can be historically established, however, the Christian churches did not necessarily inveigh against such practices. On the contrary, the early Christian attitude toward mortal life was in action and deed quite complex and variegated, and not nearly as humane as it has been made out to be.

THE ROOTS OF CHRISTIAN OPPOSITION TO ABORTION

Today, no single issue dominates the sanctity of life controversy as much as abortion. Yet, ironically, it is an examination of this issue from a historical perspective that most markedly reveals the complexity and diffidence of the Christian churches' stance on respect for life. Review of an extensive literature discloses that any traditional opposition to abortion was motivated by a variety of moral attitudes and soteriological concerns that add up into something quite different from a sanctity of life affirmation.[5] The same literature makes it clear that the Christian churches did not regard the value of "innocent" fetal life as absolute.[6] Instead, church leaders were more sensitive to the moral and biological complexities involved in the gestation of new human life than we might today expect. In the end, the history of the Christian churches' attitude toward the human fetus and abortion gives no indication of even a nascent commitment to the sanctity of life.

Many modern-day sanctity of life advocates have cited the condemnation of abortion by early Christian documents, among them the *Didache or The Teachings of the Twelve Apostles* and the *Septuagint*. These significant documents do set forth prescribed and proscribed practices for at least some quarters of the Christian community. Yet the admonitions of the *Didache* or the *Septuagint* do not necessarily reflect any universal moral standard or practice on the part of the early Christian churches. Moreover, as a diverse array of Christian scholars admit, at the heart of both documents' condemnation of abortion was an almost obsessive fear that a termination of pregnancy could or would be employed to conceal illicit relationships and sexual impropriety.[7]

Overall, the asceticism of the early Christian community made it averse to sexual intercourse for the sake of pleasure. Copulation was to be reserved for procreative purposes only.[8] Under the circumstances, the constant possibility of pregnancy in intercourse was regarded by the Christian churches as fortunate for the spiritual life of men and women: it provided a natural brake to impure passion and fornication within marriage and to the temptation of adultery outside it.[9] This same aversion to nonprocreative sex prompted the churches' prohibitions on sterilization, contraception, and infanticide as well as abortion. Similarly, the exposure and abandonment of children was at an early point condemned because it too suggested that the parents involved had not been committed to the possibility of offspring but had engaged in sex for pleasurable, nonprocreative purposes.

Coming out of the ascetically minded culture of his native Alexandria, Clement (150–215), for instance, was as much anti-fornication as anti-abortion, if not more.[10] Likewise, Tertullian (160–240), who was elsewhere at pains to defend

Christians against Roman accusations that they sacrificed human life, similarly attacked the practice of abortion because he saw it as a means of concealing illicit sex.[11] Still later, another church father, Jerome (347–419), complained of "widows who [by means of abortion and sterilization] try to protect their consciences by throwing a cloak of deceit over their violations of chastity." Jerome actually went so far as to accuse women of murder where they took actions to render themselves sterile.[12] In this case and others, talk of homicide and murder appears to be used to stress the grievous sinfulness of nonprocreative sex.

On the basis of Augustine's belief that a fetus was ensouled from the moment of conception, both John Connery and John T. Noonan have asserted that this eminent church father was adamantly opposed to abortion.[13] Meticulously reviewing Augustine's writings, however, another scholar, Daniel Dombrowski, reports otherwise. Rather than being an anti-abortion crusader per se, or advocating the sanctity of life, Augustine was bent, like his predecessors, on curtailing the expression of sexual concupiscence and lust. As Dombrowski states:

> Augustine's position on sex is quite forcefully put in his work "On Marriage and Concupiscence" (*De Nupiis et Concupiscentia*, I, 17). Married persons who have intercourse only *(sola)* for the wish to beget children do not sin, whereas those who mix pleasure with sex, even if it is sex with one's spouse, commit sin. A remarkable view. It must be granted that this sin is venial (i.e. *venia* or pardonable), but the mere fact that it is a sin at all should alert us to how negative Augustine's view of sex is. Even worse than intending pleasure in sex is to try to prevent pregnancy, say through an evil appliance. . . . For Augustine those who use such contraceptive devices retain no vestige of true matrimony, which is synonymous with, not accidentally connected to, propagation. These people sometimes *(aliquando)* go so far as to have abortions in their lustful cruelty *(libidinosa crudelitas)*. Since Augustine also accuses those who have merely used contraceptive devices of being cruel, we can be sure that it is not cruelty to a human being inside the womb that he is worried about. . . . Lust itself (or even the *desire* for sexual pleasure) is cruel whether or not a fetus is aborted. . . . Both here and elsewhere in "On Marriage and Concupiscence" Augustine indicates that sex is a necessary evil, necessary, that is, for having children.[14]

Resoundingly evident in Augustine's work is a general aversion to sex typical of the early Christian period.[15] Subsequent church fathers who recorded their opposition to abortion, including Thomas Aquinas, were similarly trying to check the enjoyment of a spiritually defiling sexuality.[16]

Of course, over time, the Roman Catholic Church began to mellow somewhat in its outlook. While nonprocreative sex—and anything that might facilitate it—continued to receive loud condemnation, church leaders began to extol human fertility and procreation. Saying yes to one's own natural fertility was increasingly construed as a devotional act. This veneration of fertility in the Roman Catholic

Church, which should not be confused with a sanctity of life affirmation, reached its apotheosis in 1854 when Pope Pius IX proclaimed the doctrine of the immaculate conception.[17]

The seriousness of the veneration accorded to an unimpeded fertility in the twentieth century is substantiated in statements made by the Roman pontiff Pius XI. In his 1930 encyclical, *Casti Connubii,* for instance, he writes:

> Since, therefore, the conjugal act is destined primarily by nature for the begetting of children, those who in exercising it deliberately frustrate its natural power and purpose sin against nature and commit a deed which is shameful and intrinsically vicious. Small wonder, therefore, if Holy Writ bears witness that the Divine Majesty regards with greatest detestation this horrible crime and at times has punished it with death.[18]

However stern, the pope's message is clear: God has no respect for the lives of those who obstruct human fertility. According to the pope, God in the past has actually put such people to death. Amazingly, there is absolutely no awareness in this papal statement of a possible contradiction between extolling human generativity on the one hand and, on the other, threatening death and damnation to those who do not join in its veneration.

THE SALVATION OF FETAL SOULS

Before a veneration of human fecundity overtook some of the Christian churches, laying the basis for the modern-day opposition to abortion, it seems clear that the salvation of souls continued to be the preeminent Christian concern. This concern for salvation was reflected not only in the Christian churches' negative attitude toward pleasurable, nonprocreative sex for adults, which it viewed as spiritually defiling. It also shaped the Christian churches' ambivalent perspective on the significance of fetal life and the welfare of infants and children.

In discussing the theology and ethics of Thomas Aquinas, James M. Gustafson has noted how the salvation of souls took center stage in all church doctrine, teaching, and practice. The Christian churches traditionally believed, Gustafson observes, that the "salvation of a single person, 'grace in one,' is greater than the good of the entire universe."[19] Gustafson further adds that "the concept of the ensouled body, which gives it supreme value, has in Catholic ethics had a decisive significance for certain moral choices."[20] Under the circumstances the Christian churches were prompted to evaluate every human act in terms of its impact upon the moral and spiritual well-being of the human soul. This proved no less true where the life of fetuses, infants, and children were involved.

Sanctity of life advocates today may suggest that the Christian churches had an abiding concern for the preservation of nascent and young life. Yet that is not the full story. In the moral schema of the Christian churches the condition of the immortal soul of a fetus, infant, or child was infinitely more important than any defense of its physical and mortal life.[21] Accordingly, the Christian churches were actually willing to sacrifice whatever mortal life an ill or sickly fetus might yet have if there was a possibility it could be successfully delivered for purposes of a baptism, thereby gaining a better assurance of a heavenly salvation when death came. For example, it was deemed morally permissible and even morally salutatory by the church fathers to baptize a baby under ice water in an emergency situation "even though it may shorten the life of the child."[22] The concern for fetal soul-life even led the Christian churches to take upon occasion a pro-abortion stance. To be specific, the Christian churches actually supported induced abortion in cases where the mother's physical health was not immediately in danger but a problematical pregnancy raised questions whether the fetus, awaiting natural, full-term birth, would actually survive until then. Here again, the purpose of such induced abortions was to ensure a baptism that might otherwise be precluded.[23]

By the time of the Middle Ages, the concern about baptizing defective fetuses became so obsessive and extreme—at least in theory—that some moral theologians felt it necessary to speak up for the prerogatives of mothers, who directly or indirectly were being called upon to sacrifice their own mortal lives for the sake of their fetus's soul. Accordingly, it was affirmed that a mother could say no to such an induced abortion if the surgical procedure threatened her life at a time when, because of unrepented sin, her own soul was in a state of mortal jeopardy.[24]

CHRISTIAN FETAL GESTATIONAL THEORIES

If there is any lingering doubt about the Christian churches' overarching focus on the salvation of human souls, rather than on the sanctity of all human biological life, it is dispelled by an awareness of the profound and insistent distinction made between ensouled and unensouled fetal life throughout much of the churches' history. While two scholars, John Connery and John T. Noonan Jr., have alleged that the church fathers more or less consistently regarded human fetal life as sacred from conception,[25] this is thoroughly refuted by the fact that these same church fathers, whose own theories associated ensoulment with a later stage in the gestational process, displayed relatively little concern for unensouled fetal life. It was only with the dawn of the modern era that the Christian churches, influenced by secular developments, began to embrace a different attitude toward all fetal life that dismissed some of the once-acknowledged complexities of the gestational process.

The Greek philosopher Aristotle has been credited as the source of the distinction between the ensouled and unensouled fetus.[26] In line with Aristotle's teaching, the prevailing conviction for much of the history of the Christian churches was that ensoulment and spiritual animation of the fetus occurred after conception, rather than simultaneous with it.[27] Such a distinguished father of the early Christian churches as Clement of Alexander held that the fetus did not belong to the human species until after forty days.[28] Later, Augustine viewed forty-six days as the animation or ensoulment time.[29] As Noonan admits, by the fourth century, the distinction between a formed and an unformed fetus loomed large in the perceptions of the Christian community.[30] If the pregnancy was not the result of illicit sexual practices, within or outside marriage, abortion was morally permissible when the fetus was unensouled and less than forty days old.[31] In fact, where pre-ensouled fetal life was

involved without complicating moral factors on the parents' part, there was sometimes reluctance among ecclesiastical authorities to speak of the termination of a
pregnancy as an abortion.[32]

The Middle Ages saw a continuation of the ensouled-unensouled distinction and
a tolerance for abortion under certain ideal circumstances. In their writings, the great
clerics Henry of Ghent and Saint Anselm distinguished between the conception of the
seed and the conception of the soul.[33] Though Thomas Aquinas never gave much attention to abortion, he similarly distinguished between an ensouled fetus and a merely
fertilized egg.[34]

If there is any doubt about the extent to which the Christian churches relativized
the status of the unensouled fetus, one need only consider the different penances and
punishments that came to be meted out, plus the particular justification given for each,
in instances of abortion for an animated or unanimated fetus. As early as 60–100 C.E.
the *Didache* had ranked abortion as a principal sin.[35] All the same, contraception and
abortion were treated at any stage as homicides for purposes of spiritual penance, rather
than punishment before the law.[36] Up until the fourteenth century, abortion of an
unformed fetus was construed as an "anticipated" or "interpretive" homicide, not a
genuine homicide at all.[37] Between the fourteenth and eighteenth centuries and even
later, abortion of an unformed fetus was exempted from condemnation altogether.[38]
Though in earlier years penance was the same for any act of abortion before ensoulment, abortion was penitentially viewed as a sin against marriage, not against the fetus.[39]

In 848, the Council of Worms "prescribed that a woman who aborted a fetus before
term was to be considered a homicide . . . [possibly] the first explicit classification of
abortion as homicide by a council in the Western Church."[40] But the pronouncement
was nothing new. The distinction between an animated or unanimated fetus in determining the presence of actual homicide was a constant. Pope Alexander III officially
declared that no homicide was involved where the fetus was unformed.[41] Pope
Innocent III reaffirmed the same policy in a decision whether a monk responsible for
causing an abortion in a woman he impregnated was guilty of homicide.[42] Thomas
Aquinas concurred in this distinction between the formed and unformed fetus.[43]

In 1588 Pope Sixtus V took the surprising measure of attaching an order of
excommunication to all acts of abortion and sterilization. As Connery notes,
"Absolution from the penalty was also reserved to the supreme pontiff, except when
the one who had incurred it was in danger of death."[44] The new and unexpected rule,
however, proved too extreme. Consequently, in 1591 a new pope, Gregory XIV,
restricted the ban to instances of abortion involving an ensouled fetus.[45] Moreover,
the absolution necessary to revoke excommunication in all the remaining cases was
granted to local bishops and their authorized delegates. For the next three centuries
excommunication was reserved for the abortion of a formed fetus.[46]

For reasons that need to be further examined in a wider social and cultural context, the attitude and policy of the Roman Catholic Church took its present shape during the latter half of the nineteenth century. Restrictions on abortion, which persist
today, were first promulgated at that time.

As early as 1679, the hierarchy of the Roman Catholic Church came under criticism for the laxness of its stand on abortion.[47] At about the same time, the idea of
immediate animation or ensoulment was coming into wider vogue among theolo-

gians based upon early science that is now conceded to have been faulty.[48] But actual change was slow in the Roman Catholic Church's official position. Indeed, commentators have observed that both the Roman Catholic and Protestant churches were surprisingly quiet during the mid-nineteenth century amid a successful campaign by physicians in both Europe and America to prohibit abortion before the law.[49]

In 1869 Pope Pius IX did successfully remove the 1591 restriction against excommunication for abortion involving a fetus that from a developmental perspective would be regarded as unensouled.[50] Nevertheless, it was only on May 31, 1884, that the Roman Catholic Church declared that fetal craniotomy, which had evidently been used to save the lives of mothers faced with obstetric crises, could not be taught as morally acceptable. An outright ban on medical abortion for nonviable fetuses was not instituted until July 24, 1895.[51]

Even with this ban, the Roman Catholic Church never went so far as to formally adopt immediate animation theory as an official doctrine of the church.[52] Moreover, as even its defenders agree, the absolute prohibition of abortion within the Roman Catholic Church was more a triumph of ecclesial politics than an expression of genuine moral consensus. As Noonan writes with remarkable candidness:

> Like other developed Christian teaching on slavery, on the rights of labor, on war, [the ultimate prohibition on abortion by the Catholic Church] embodied a sensitivity to certain values affirmed in the Gospel but not made effective in Roman, medieval, or post-Reformation culture. In the formation of teaching, the pastoral interest of the papacy played a strong part; and it was the central authority of the Church, far more prestigious in moral matters in the period 1880–1950 than ever before in its history, which dominated the development. The moral theologians and canonists bent to the papal leadership which, while reflecting the view of moral theologians, incorporated a broader sense of situation and likely trends and dangers. In 1588 Sixtus V, the most energetic of popes [who sought to institute a penalty of excommunication for all acts of abortion], could do nothing to change the views of the dominant moralists; beginning with the papacy of Leo XIII [in 1878] the moralists, in this area of thought, followed the papal lead.[53]

The historical record indicates that the Roman Catholic Church faced tremendous difficulties in reaching the point where it could with confidence profess a conviction about the inviolability of fetal life from conception. In the end, only an authoritarian papacy had the political clout to enforce conformity.[54]

Still not clear in Roman Catholic dogma of the period is any commitment to the idea of human sacredness that looms so large in present-day Catholic theology. Following the 1895 ban on medical abortion, it would be another fifty to eighty years before the Roman Catholic Church's critique of abortion, sterilization, and contraception would take on the sanctity of life rhetoric we hear today. In other words, it took another half century or more for the Roman Catholic Church to update and transmute its ambivalence about sexuality, its sacralization of nature's generativity, and its overarching concern with the condition of the human soul—often at the expense of preserving life—into a more novel and complex affirmation of the sanctity of life as a principle.[55]

Significantly, even as the Roman Catholic Church finally did move toward restrictions on abortion and, much later, to affirmation of the sanctity of life, their Protestant brethren did not readily follow suit. Any Protestant reservations about abortion remained a pale echo of what their Roman Catholic counterparts were beginning to express. Protestants proved astonishingly tolerant toward the abortion of unformed fetuses at least until a secular medical campaign against abortion during the nineteenth century decisively altered the entire moral climate of the United States and Europe.[56]

In more cases than not, Protestant churches in this century have continued to shy away from an immediate animation theory of fetal life—or any contemporary theoretical equivalents. If some Protestant denominations have since embraced the idea of the sacredness of human life in a biological sense, they have often been reluctant partners in corresponding efforts to reestablish strict laws on abortion and other issues associated with the sanctity of life stance.

The disparity between Roman Catholics and Protestants on abortion and the wider sanctity of life principle has prompted the feminist theologian Beverly Harrison to remark that "we need to be honest about the depth of difference that exists within religious groups."[57]

INFANTICIDE, CHILD EXPOSURE, AND ABANDONMENT

As the history of Christian attitudes toward abortion suggests, the Christian churches' support for the sanctity or sacredness of life is not as evident as has often been claimed. The absence of any single-minded commitment to the sanctity of life, however, becomes obvious when the Christian churches' stance on infanticide and child exposure or abandonment is considered.

Sanctity of life supporters have sought to portray the pagan culture that preceded and coexisted with Christianity as notoriously callous toward infant life. G. Bonner has claimed that Christianity brought infanticide to a halt,[58] and Pope John Paul II has joined him in such a claim.[59] Yet nothing could be further from the truth.

First of all, pagan Rome was not as cruel toward newborn life as it has been made out to be. Second, the Christian community as a whole was not as protective of infant children as commonly supposed.[60] In fact, it can be fairly argued that a soul-focused Christianity contributed to a worsening of social conditions for infants and children and even became complicit in institutional infanticide.

Generally not appreciated in discussions concerning infanticide and child abandonment is the vast difference between the two acts in the late antique period of the Roman Empire when Christianity was emerging.[61] While abandonment to a lonely crag to die may be the popular image of child exposure, it was not necessarily the historical reality—at least not at the start of the late antique period.[62] As the late historian John Boswell has recounted, well-developed custom, even rule, governed the entire exposure practice. Most pagan parents who exposed and abandoned children did not have infanticide in mind. Making use of designated locales for exposure and abandonment, they counted on the adoption of their biological offspring by strangers.[63]

Those in the ascendant Christian community who went on record condemning child abandonment and exposure often exaggerated the malevolence of parents involved. Moreover, their own concern did not necessarily lie with the material welfare of the children affected. Instead, these Christian leaders, who were actually fewer in number than frequently suggested, were morally outraged by what child exposure and abandonment, not unlike abortion, implied—namely, that parents had given vent to sexual lust without procreative intent. Whatever empathy church leaders did express for the children who were subject to exposure was also largely fed by sex-related concerns. Christianity's more ascetically minded leaders, such as Athenagoras, Justin Martyr, Clement of Alexandria, and Tertullian, feared that exposed or abandoned children might be adopted by those interested in eventually employing them in the prostitution trade—a truly soul-damning prospect.[64]

No matter how haunting such a prospect remained for some, no clear and lasting ban on child exposure and abandonment emerged from the larger Christian community.[65] In fact, contrary to what sanctity of life advocates have claimed, Christians generally adopted the old Roman custom of child exposure and abandonment and quickly made it their own. Boswell has reported that during the first three centuries of the Christian era the abandonment rates for children actually grew from twenty percent to forty percent.[66] This simple fact prompted Boswell to ask:

> Did Christians abandon children? No mystery remains here: they did. Even if one discounted injunctions against abandonment as evidence of its occurrence, prohibitions of other activities such as promiscuity and recourse to prostitutes are predicated on the consequences of Christian parents having exposed children, and by the fourth century, theology, Christian law, and conciliar canons all provide abundant testimony that abandonment was widespread among Christians, apparently as familiar as it had been among pagan Romans. [Christianity's emerging] ethical tradition not only accommodated but in some ways institutionalized forms of abandonment.[67]

In short, the Christian churches, which came to adopt an "entirely realistic attitude toward child abandonment," became directly involved in facilitating and administering the exposure and abandonment process.[68]

Given the fact that abandonment, as originally practiced, went hand in hand with adoption rather than infanticide, ecclesial involvement cannot in itself be entirely faulted. Subsequently, however, the Christian churches, which had enormous prestige and authority, presided over a genuine decline in the protections long afforded to abandoned children under pagan law.[69] Boswell has reported that "under Christian influence abandonment [became] largely irrevocable by the end of the fifth century." Moreover, "despite imperial efforts to restore freedom to large numbers of children sold by their parents into slavery, at the local level parents were not allowed by the church to reclaim [them] after ten days, under threat of severe penalty, and finders could rear foundlings however they wished—even as slaves."[70] As Boswell reveals here, there was little or no tender regard for children in a society where the Christian churches continued to be the predominant moral and spiritual influence.

Later, responding to a growing public concern with family blood lineage in the late medieval period, which made the adoption of children less appealing, the Christian churches moved to assist in the creation of municipal foundling homes.[71] Yet these institutions quickly became notorious dens of death for infants and children: abandonment to them became tantamount to infanticide. As Boswell has summarized the grim statistics:

> In the later fourteenth century 20 percent of the infants died within a month of their arrival at San Gallo [foundling home], and another 30 percent within a year. Only 32 percent lived to age five. At La Scala in the next century 25 percent died within a month, and another 40 percent within a year; only 13 percent reached their sixth year. The statistics were less horrifying at the Innocenti when it opened, but within a century an abandoning parent was "consigning his child to death."[72]

The mortality rates of children under the care of the foundling homes, which were poorly staffed and maintained, did not stir those in a position to know about them, including religious authorities, from their moral complacency and indifference.[73] Clearly, no principle of sanctity of life was operative here.

According to another historian and anthropologist, Laila Williamson, there were no meaningful attempts to reduce the death rate of infants and children in such institutions until the latter half of the nineteenth century.[74] Even then, the initiative for reform came not from the leaders of the Christian churches but from citizens shaped by philosophical influences apart from Christianity.

KILLING AND CAPITAL PUNISHMENT

If the conduct of Christians was not entirely exemplary when it came to respect for young life, it was no more admirable when it came to respect for anyone else. William E. H. Lecky has claimed that Christian belief in the inestimable value of the soul prompted Christians to view fellow human beings in a new and more respectful and appreciative light: he cites a pacifistic tendency among them.[75] Perhaps illustrative of Lecky's claim, Peter Brown recounts how the labors of Christian monks in hospital food supply centers and burial associations did help convey the Christian message in tangible ways to humble people. But Brown also notes that in Upper Egypt the same Christian monks, who so charitably "organized an ambulance service, carrying and nursing the wounded during a barbarian invasion," had previously waged a campaign of terror against pagans.[76] In a similar outbreak of Christian violence, there is record of monks lynching a noble woman.[77]

Marvin Kohl has suggested that the Christian churches, historically speaking, were not opposed to killing per se, only unjust killing or the killing of the innocent.[78] Unfortunately, in this case too, the definition of innocent life, deserving respect and protection, was narrow from the outset and remained so.

A Christian militancy, going against the grain of respect for human life, was certainly much in evidence in dealing with lawbreakers and sinners. The great Scholastic theologian Thomas Aquinas declared that homicide was justification for capital punishment.[79] Over nearly two thousand years of the Christian churches' history, human execution for the sake of the "common good" was sanctioned quite liberally. Like the pagans terrorized and lynched by Christian monks in Upper Egypt, heretics were deemed appropriate candidates for capital punishment or outright massacre. By the peculiar moral logic that prevailed among Christians, it was seen as spiritually advantageous to the heretic to end his or her life with all possible alacrity. As one historian, William Clebsch, has explained the Christian mentality of that period, "To cut short the earthly life of a soul thus in league with the devil might increase its chances in purgatory" for eventual salvation.[80] Glanville Williams was not exaggerating when he observed that over the course of history the Christian churches "sometimes forgot all decency and humanity to the living."[81] An "increasing frequency and intensification of capital punishment" actually went "hand in hand with the expansion of Christianity."[82] The frightening punishments imposed by an ostensibly Christian society through everyday use of "the sword, the gallows, the wheel and the stake" further belied any absolute or near-absolute respect for life.[83]

In their own time the Protestant reformers brought many changes to the Christian churches. But they did not measurably reform Christian attitudes toward killing.[84] Quite the obverse. Martin Luther, who at one point suffered persecution at the hands of fellow church members, was no less severe than his Roman Catholic brethren on the subject of putting heretics and other alleged wrongdoers to death.[85] John Calvin, another major reformer, was not too reticent about capital punishment either, as his support for the burning of Michael Servetus as a heretic in Geneva testifies.[86]

Although it today stands as an embarrassment to many, the Christian churches continued to support public execution at least up until the twentieth century. Protestant theologian Karl Barth has remarked that the continued incidence of capital punishment "under the very eyes and with the secret or public connivance of all Christian churches is one of the many phenomena which must be taken into account when we ask why the Gospel has been quietly discredited in the modern world."[87] Barth was frank enough to note that the initiative to restrict and abolish capital punishment ultimately came from secular sources, rather than from the Roman Catholic or Protestant churches or any identified Christian activists. He did not even hesitate to acknowledge that the movement against capital punishment was actually contested tooth and nail by professed Christians, including many in his native Switzerland.[88] Nevertheless, Barth proved no more willing than anyone else to look deeply within Christianity to explain the Christian churches' not-so-loving sensibility on the capital punishment issue. Instead, Barth blamed the churches' spotted record on "weakness" or a "secularisation," beginning in the age of Constantine.[89] Completely ignored by Barth, as well as others, however, was the possibility that Christianity's support for capital punishment had roots in its own fundamentally otherworldly orientation which, encouraging a more ambivalent valuation of mortal life, simply did not share all the sensitivities espoused by the non-Christian, this-worldly culture that was increasingly enveloping its own community of believers.

SUICIDE

It is surely a great historical paradox that the Christian churches, which are becoming identified in the public mind as upholders of the sanctity of life, received their original claim to fame in the public imagination of earlier times by the way they encouraged and sustained their own members in acts of suffering, self-denial, and holy dying. In fact, mortal death was more than a shadow looming over the lives of early Christians. It was an omnipresent reality which Christianity encouraged its disciples to regard almost as a friend.

Not unlike some Jews before them, many of the earliest Christians had a truly apocalyptic perspective—the world was going to come to a prompt end. Faced with the kingdom's delay, plus persecution here and now, the generations that immediately followed had a martyr's mind-set. Heaven was just on the other side of their earthly persecution and pain.

In his volume *The Christians As the Romans Saw Them,* Robert L. Wilken observes that the early Christians garnered both notoriety and awe from the pagan community because of their fearless contempt for death.[90] Glanville Williams also captures the tenor of the early Christian era when he states that there "is no condemnation of suicide in the New Testament, and little to be found among the early Christians, who were, indeed, morbidly obsessed with death." As Williams adds: "Those were the days when, instead of learning how to live, men studied how to die."[91] Williams relates that believers committed "suicide by provoking infidels to martyr [them], or by austerities so severe that they undermined the constitution, but in the last resort [they] might do away with [themselves] directly."[92] Certainly, prominent church leaders gave their outright sanction and blessing to suicide. Eusebius, Jerome, and Chrysostom, for instance, all speak favorably in their writings on behalf of suicide by women to protect their virginity and chastity.[93]

In the first years, the Christian churches may have opposed the taking of one's own life in some cases. Yet the objection to suicide even here would always have lain not with the act itself but with intention behind the act. More specifically, Christians were called not only to "live in the Lord" but also "to die in the Lord." Consequently, only those who appeared to commit suicide for selfish, unfounded reasons would have been objects of censure. Later, those who, committing suicide, did not die for God were more firmly anathematized.[94] Nevertheless, what is striking is that the condemnation of suicide did not come quickly to the churches and only then in response to genuine excesses. Over the two millennia of Christian history, suicide provokes relatively little thoroughgoing theological discussion in the Christian churches, apart from remarks by a few church fathers, until the advent of the sanctity of life movement in the nineteenth and twentieth centuries.[95]

Augustine spoke up against suicide. So did Thomas Aquinas at a subsequent juncture. Apparently, their complete and total condemnation eventually carried the day and shapes many Christian perceptions of suicide even to the present.[96] But their loud protestations were not a profession about the sanctity of life as Lecky once averred.[97] Nor could they obscure the older and profound gospel tradition which, always percolating within the Christian churches, calls Christians to keep the meaning of mortal life in perspective and to be willing to sacrifice one's life for God's purposes and according to God's command.

Augustine's own comments on suicide were forceful and direct. As he stated in the *City of God:*

> The commandment is "Thou shalt not kill man," therefore neither another nor yourself, for he who kills himself still kills nothing else than man. . . . It is not without significance that in no passage of the holy canonical books can there be found either divine precept or permission to take away our life, whether for the sake of entering on the enjoyment of immortality, or for shunning, or ridding ourselves of any evil whatever.[98]

Augustine's main object in an age of both waning apocalyptic faith and dwindling persecution was to preclude suicide as an acceptable option for those who simply wanted to avoid any prolongation of their earthly exposure to salvation-imperiling sin.[99] As paraphrased by one historical commentator, Augustine feared that "if suicide were permissible to avoid sin, then suicide would become the logical recourse for those who were fresh from baptism."[100]

Worth noting, however, is that Augustine did not call for any punishment against attempted and unsuccessful suicidal acts. Nor did he morally and spiritually discredit every possible act of suicide. Even if Augustine was skeptical about the excesses of suicide in his own time, he allowed that suicide might still be appropriate in some cases, even commanded by God. In instances where God's command might be claimed, Augustine's advice to a would-be suicide was quite simple—"only let him be very sure that the divine command has been signified."[101] Here it is quite apparent that Augustine was simply trying to moderate a zeal for death, rather than affirm a more encompassing principle of the sanctity of human life.

Aquinas proved even more stern than Augustine on the morality of suicide. He insisted, for instance, that suicide was in itself a mortal sin, always wrong with no self-justifying exceptions.[102] Ostensibly, Aquinas's ultimate objection to suicide was that, in a catch-22, it precluded the possibility of repenting of one's final sin, specifically, the taking of what belonged to God.

Still, even in Aquinas's desire to prohibit suicide, there was no attendant rhetoric about the sacredness of life. The condition and fate of a person's soul in the hereafter, rather than the mere preservation of human life in the here and now, remained Aquinas's utmost concern. Moreover, some of Aquinas's stronger arguments against suicide were largely indebted to secular and non-Christian sources.[103] For instance, Aquinas's claim that self-destruction is contrary to natural law and his insistence that society has a right to forbid the taking of one's own life are at least partially Stoic recrudescences, which have little to do with the gospel. Equally problematical is Aquinas's argument that we are God's "property" and that God alone can appoint the time for our life and death.[104]

First of all, the notion that humans are God's property steps well beyond the traditional Christian sensibility that we are God's own children: it reduces human beings to divine chattel. Second, over and against an earlier Christian tradition on suicide, Aquinas's argument seems disposed to promote a passive resignation to the vagaries of biological nature. In making the claim that we are God's property, Aquinas at least intimates that our sheer biological endurance as human beings is always a matter of divine judgment and will. Tragically, given the anguish and suffering that await many as they approach their deathbeds, this perspective sets God up as potentially "cruel and capricious [rather] than admit [that God] may not be totally in control of every [life and death] event" and circumstance.[105] In addition, this perspective also contradicts the emphasis on prayerful moral discernment as to what God may be willing for us both through and beyond our mortal nature that has generally been a long-standing hallmark of the Christian community.[106]

Ironically, Aquinas in his arguments against suicide speaks of the duty of charity which human beings have with regard to themselves.[107] Yet Aquinas, whose writings were often notable for their pastoral awareness, is not necessarily consistent here. He seems disinclined to extend any charity and forgiveness to a person who commits suicide. Nor he is willing to presume that God will.

What Aquinas fails to acknowledge is what the Bible makes so abundantly clear. Namely, none of us as Christians are in a position to harshly and definitively judge someone who has committed suicide. After all, as in the biblical cases of Saul, Ahithophel, Judas and, perhaps, Samson, it remains within God's province to "command" or call someone to take his or her own life, even if such an act by God is morally incomprehensible to us.[108] Moreover, in those instances where human initiative, rather than divine command, may be actually responsible for a suicide, who can doubt that spiritual conflict and sheer human anguish are at least among the precipitating factors? Whatever our moral judgment on suicide may be, these circumstances deserve pastoral sensitivity.[109] Aquinas's own attachment to classical arguments against suicide appears to have thwarted his capacity for Christian sympathy and forgiveness.

FAITH AND ACCEPTANCE OF DEATH

Whether or not the rational arguments of St. Augustine and St. Thomas Aquinas were persuasive in their own times, public attitudes toward suicide definitely did undergo change. As the legal historian Glanville Williams has noted, some Christian communities increasingly began to stigmatize the corpses of suicides.[110] Significantly, the French historian Albert Bayet has argued that the practice of dishonoring the corpse in such cases was actually "an irruption into the church of the pre-Christian popular horror of suicide . . . a pagan intrusion upon the simple philosophy of the Gospels."[111] Yet the public revulsion against suicide was not necessarily based upon ancient pagan precedent: instead, it seems to have been fed by more localized superstitions and irrational impulses on the European continent and elsewhere.

Horror of suicide as it emerged in the Middle Ages did not, however, mean a total eclipse of an earlier faith-filled Christian outlook on death. Even as public sanctions against suicide became more prevalent, the old Christian idea of life relinquished as an act of faithful martyrdom persisted and continued to inform the act of dying for most Christians. Perhaps because medical options were limited, life was not yet seen as something to be preserved at all costs. Death was still accepted with a certain equanimity.[112]

In his historical survey of Western attitudes toward death, Philippe Ariès has contended that the way of death practiced among early- to mid-twentieth-century Soviet peasants—at least as described by Russian novelist Alexander Solzhenitsyn—is much akin to the calm and simplicity with which ordinary people faced death in the Middle Ages. In Solzhenitsyn's novel *Cancer Ward,* protagonist Yefrem Podduyez, as cited by Ariès, specifically recollects:

> how the old folk used to die back home on the Kama—Russians, Tartars, Votyaks, or whatever they were. They didn't puff themselves up or fight against it and brag that they weren't going to die—they took death calmly. They didn't stall squaring things away, they prepared themselves quietly and in good time. . . . And they departed easily, as if they were just moving into a new house.[113]

Ariès finds Podduyez's description most apt. "People," Ariès comments in response, "had been dying like that for centuries or millennia," in other words, going all the way back to the Christian Middle Ages and even earlier.[114]

Funeral customs of the Middle Ages and beyond further underscore the fact that the significance of mortal life paled before the prospect of being united with God. As Ariès has directly observed:

> As yet unborn was the modern idea that the dead person should be installed in a sort of house unto himself, a house of which he was the perpetual owner or at least the long-term tenant, a house in which he would be at home and from which he could not be evicted. In the Middle Ages and even as late as the sixteenth and seventeenth centuries the exact destination of one's bones was of little concern so long as they remained near the saints, or in the church, near the altar of the Virgin or of the Holy Sacrament. Thus the body was entrusted to the Church. It made little difference what the Church saw fit to do with these bodies so long as they remained within its holy precincts.[115]

For the Christians of the time, the sense of God as the alpha and omega of human existence was still profoundly felt. Both the desire and confidence with which Christians anticipated the prospect of union with God—in this case, temporarily represented by the holy yet anonymous burial within the precincts of the church—was great.

ORDINARY AND EXTRAORDINARY MEANS OF CONSERVING LIFE

The kind of nuanced attitude toward life which Philippe Ariès has described continued to find respectable expression in Christian theology even as the turmoil of the Reformation and the Counter Reformation got under way. In the view of the churches' leaders and thinkers, human life did not have to be preserved at all costs. Instead, the expectation was that Christians would more simply and faithfully seek to conserve life.

Although not always explicit, this distinction between life preservation and life conservation found expression in Roman Catholic perspectives on medical treatment as either morally obligatory or optional. The church fathers held that only ordinary means to maintain life were morally obligatory. Any available extraordinary means were deemed "heroic" and morally optional.

This Roman Catholic distinction between ordinary versus extraordinary means was especially well elaborated by the theologian Vitoria in the mid-1500s. In *Relectiones Theologiae*, Vitoria declared that "man is not held to employ all the possible means of conserving his life, but the means which are per se intended for that purpose."[116]

For instance, Vitoria suggested that if "consternation in the appetitive power" made eating a certain torture for a sick man or woman, he or she did not mortally sin in refusing food. This in Vitoria's eyes was especially true when there was little or no hope of benefit, i.e., longer-term survival.[117] Likewise, "abstinence" from proffered drugs was not a mortal sin for a sick person either if there was no "moral certitude" that it would restore health. The lack of certainty about a treatment's efficacy rendered it an extraordinary and morally unnecessary recourse.[118] Men and women, Vitoria opined, were not required to expend all of their material resources to briefly extend their lives:

> I believe that the individual is not held to give his whole inheritance to preserve his life. . . . From this also it is inferred that when one is sick without hope of life, granted that a certain precious drug could produce life for some hours or even days, he would not be held to buy it but it is sufficient to use common remedies and he is considered as though dead.[119]

Vitoria explicitly rejects the kind of "no expense spared" mentality that has become so pervasive among twentieth-century sanctity of life advocates. Vitoria even went so far as to say that even if particular "delicate" foods could virtually guarantee someone another twenty years of life, he or she would not be morally obligated to purchase or consume them. Common foods, which Vitoria regarded as "natural" or "reasonable," were all that were morally mandated if a patient could eat.[120] Two Roman Catholic theologians, Bishop Daniel A. Cronin and Father Albert Moraczewski, have cited this and other precedents to argue that artificial hydration and nutrition should not be deemed morally requisite for the terminally ill.[121]

The church fathers who followed Vitoria further distinguished between ordinary and extraordinary means in decisions as to whether medical treatment should be morally obligatory. In all their discussions there was a keen sense of proportion in terms of the good to be realized over and against the human and material cost to accomplish it. At the beginning of the seventeenth century, for instance, Gregory Sayrus argued that "mutilation" or amputation of limbs could not be morally forced upon an individual unless it was for the common good. Sayrus wrote:

> Since by the natural law each one is bound to employ for the conservation of his body those licit means which he can conveniently under-

take, the individual undoubtedly would sin who, when there is not
question of great pain, would permit himself to die when he could
take care of the health of his body. To this, however, that he suffer the
very intense pain of the amputation of a member or of an incision into
his body, neither a prelate can oblige his subject, nor a father his
son.—The reason is both because the sick individual is not held to
conserve the life of his body with such great pain and torture and
because superiors can not prescribe all things licit and honest but
those only which are moderate.[122]

The prospect of great pain and torment, which awaited all who underwent amputation prior to the advent of modern anesthetics, shaped Sayrus's conviction that
amputational surgeries should be held morally optional and extraordinary as a means
to preserve life. Sayrus's emphasis upon the conservation of the body through licit
means "conveniently" undertaken was echoed by a dozen other Roman Catholic
moralists.[123]

Over the next two centuries, there emerged a whole list of morally legitimate reasons for forgoing either nutrition or medical care. Women protecting their personal
privacy and chastity were morally excused from undertaking medical examination
or treatment even if faced with life-threatening disease. Medical care under such circumstances was deemed to be extraordinary.[124] Similarly, an inordinate fear, no matter how subjective and irrational, of a particular medical treatment or its consequences
was also held to be a sufficient basis for declaring the treatment to be an extraordinary means that could be refused without incurring a grave sin.[125]

In keeping with the traditional Christian emphasis upon the eternal destiny
of men and women and the spiritual impropriety of an undue attachment to mortal life, sixteenth-, seventeenth-, and eighteenth-century Roman Catholic moralists noted that "it is one thing not to prolong life and it is another to shorten
life."[126] As C. La Croix explained, "The prolongation of life implies a singular
assiduity to which we are not held, whereas the non-abbreviation or the conservation of life implies only a common diligence to which we are obliged."[127]
Even the nineteenth-century Roman Catholic moralist C. Billuart stated plainly:
"God does not command that we be solicitous of a longer life."[128] Yet it was
Cardinal DeLugo, a citizen of the late seventeenth century, who expounded the
rich spiritual nuances of the Roman Catholic perspective most clearly and
emphatically:

[A human being] is not held to the extraordinary and difficult
means. . . . The "bonum" of his life is not of such great moment,
however, that its conservation must be effected with extraordinary
diligence: it is one thing not to neglect and rashly throw it away, to
which a man is bound: it is another however, to seek after it and
retain it by exquisite means as it is escaping away from him, to
which he is not held; neither is he on that account considered
morally to will or seek his death.[129]

DeLugo's statement continued to be representative of Roman Catholic moral sentiment until the dawn of the modern era.

While the stances of Roman Catholic moralists from the sixteenth through the nineteenth centuries clearly preclude any acts of voluntary or involuntary euthanasia, they do allow or regard as morally licit indirect involuntary euthanasia. Meanwhile, they are completely silent about the sanctity of life.

THE PRACTICE OF "HOLY DYING"

Paradoxically, even as they affirm the sanctity of life, the Christian churches continue to cling to the rhetoric of an earlier age when a nongrasping attitude toward mortal life prevailed. In this respect, Pope John Paul II is typical: he invokes the language of this earlier era at the same time that he defends the opposite idea that mortal life must always be upheld, protected, and preserved. For instance, in his encyclical *The Gospel of Life* the pope states that "what is more important [than bodily life] is remaining faithful to the word of the Lord even at the risk of one's [own] life." In other words, the pope is suggesting that a believer may be asked to give up his or her life for a still greater good.[130] Yet almost immediately thereafter the pope appears to construe martyrdom as an extreme and exceptional act.[131] Absent from the pope's sensibility and outlook is a sense of Christian martyrdom as a kind of ongoing and ultimate faith witness in which—in the words of the apostle Paul—we "are always being given up to death for Jesus' sake, so that the life of Jesus may be made visible in our mortal flesh."[132]

The pope is not alone in his use of paradoxical and ambiguous rhetoric. Overall, the modern Christian churches profess admiration for the martyrs of old who were ready to sacrifice life and limb. But for our own day they have kept the ante for martyrdom remarkably high: the "greater good" that would make the personal sacrifice of our lives morally permissible has come to be narrowly conceived or defined. Not many causes are deemed worthy enough to override the importance of individual self-preservation. What seems to be especially absent among sanctity of life Christians is any positive vision of martyrdom and death, which used to be a prominent aspect of the Christian ethic.[133]

Timothy F. Sedgwick recalls with appreciation a time in which our predecessors in Christian faith engaged in "holy dying," rejecting the kind of biological vitalism which has gained such currency in the twentieth century. Sedgwick personally believes that a "holy dying" perspective still holds great possibilities and promise for Christians today:

> For the patient nurtured in the Christian tradition, death provides the opportunity to confront his or her own finitude and in its light the dependencies that mark life itself. . . . Dying remains a privileged occasion in which the gift of life may be embraced for what it is and not in the more narrow and finally inadequate terms of one's own self and its particular enhancement. Such transformation of the will in the reconciliation of the self only happens through specific practices that speak concretely of death and of the vanity in life

while holding up a broader meaning which encompasses dying as well as living.[134]

Sedgwick believes that we can only make the greatest affirmation about life—specifically, that it is a gift from God—when we refuse to cling to it self-centeredly.

A comparable appreciation for an earlier Christian understanding of life, death, and martyrdom pervades the theological outlook of Protestant theologian John H. Yoder:

> Christians have held that the death of a Christian believer, as a result of his behaving in a Christian way at the hands of the agents of evil, can become through no merit of his or her own a special witness and a monument of the power of God. . . . Why not accept suffering? Jesus did.[135]

Of course, Jesus not only accepted suffering. He accepted death too.

Yoder's perspective is fully embraced by fellow Protestant theologian Stanley Hauerwas. Like Yoder, Hauerwas rejects the notion that mortal life is sacred or that it is helpful to make such a claim. Throughout his work Hauerwas vigorously insists that suffering and death can be meaningful if we truly ground ourselves in our Christian faith.[136] In his view, what our circumstances require are a heartfelt, faith-filled conviction that in dying, as much as in living, we can serve God.[137]

A similar perspective is shared by at least some Roman Catholic thinkers and theologians. Perhaps representative of them is John Paris of the College of the Holy Cross. His observations have been neatly summarized by Jeff Lyon in a chapter-essay entitled "Sanctity of Life vs. Quality of Life: The Ethics of Neonatal Care":

> If one truly believes there is a hereafter, says the Reverend Paris, then the death of a child, or of anyone else for that matter, is not an evil but a part of the natural order of things. "Life is not only a gift and a task," he says; "it is also a journey. We are on a journey from God back to God and death is a part of that journey. Death is not the victor, it is the transition state, not a final state. . . . Thus it is eternal life and not life itself which is the ultimate." He continues: "If you doubt that this is an age of nonbelief, ask yourself what is the response of all those believing Christians who enter hospitals when the death process begins. When was the last time you heard anyone say: 'This patient had a wonderful life; he fought the good fight. . . . Now it is time for him to go to his Maker.' . . . For the individual whose journey has indeed come to its conclusion, for example, the individual with end-stage liver disease whose heart stops, we do not say: 'At last he is at peace.' Instead we shout: 'Code Blue.' That is the problem."[138]

Face to face with efforts to evade death at all costs, Paris and Lyon are left to ponder the contradiction and hypocrisy involved, at least for Christians. Indeed, as the echo of every "Code Blue" recedes, some unsettling questions linger. How did the original Christian acceptance of suffering and death become so totally lost or displaced? Moreover, if an aversion to death has pagan origins and contradicts early Christian sensibilities, to what extent is the affirmation of the sanctity of life in our Christian churches today actually a statement about their co-option by secular and pagan thinking, with a consequent diminution of our own historic faith? These are crucial matters that deserve our most thoughtful attention.

5

The Non-Christian Origins

Whether they personally embrace the sanctity of life concept or take issue with it, most observers have repeatedly credited its origins to Christianity, albeit as an heir of Judaism with its own concern for human life. In fact, the widespread modern-day belief in the sanctity of life has been hailed by Christian and secular commentators alike as one of the distinctive accomplishments of Christian civilization. For instance, K. Danner Clouser contends that the sanctity of life concept "surfaces throughout our Judeo-Christian traditions."[1] Likewise, William K. Frankena asserts that "most historians of Western morals agree with [historian William] Lecky that the rise of Judaism, and even more of Christianity, had a great deal to do with the growth of the 'sense of the sanctity of human life'—that there was either little or no recognition of the sanctity of life in ancient pagan culture, and that any such recognition was either generated or greatly increased by the advent of the Judaic and Christian religions, through their doctrines of creation, the nature of God, ethics, the immortality of the soul, and the hereafter."[2] Even more recently, Helga Kuhse, who rejects the sanctity of life concept altogether, argues that "the sanctity-of-life view" became part of Western civilization's "unquestioned moral tradition" during "the long period when Christian beliefs moulded European thought."[3]

A review of scripture, however, suggests that the sanctity of life, while purportedly affirmed by various biblical prohibitions and admonitions, is not in any genuine sense articulated there. Similarly, as the extensive tradition of the Christian churches is examined up to the seventeenth century, it becomes obvious that sanctity of life does not emerge in any coherent and consistent fashion from its historical sweep either. Thus, it becomes imperative to look beyond Christianity for the sources of sanctity of life as a doctrine. Scrutiny of Western civilization suggests that sanctity of life doctrine actually emerged from a paganism antecedent to Christianity and later enjoyed a subsequent revival thanks to the European Renaissance and the eighteenth-century Enlightenment. Rather than giving birth to sanctity of life doctrine, Christianity largely resisted it—at least, that is, until an ascendant humanism overtook its own theological and anthropological outlook.

PAGAN CUSTOM AND THE HIPPOCRATIC OATH

At first glance, any Western pagan sources for the sanctity of life are difficult to identify. The sanctity of life does not appear to have had much currency as an idea in truly ancient times. As Ludwig Edelstein has noted:

> Ancient jurisdiction did not discriminate against suicide; it did not attach any disgrace to it, provided that there was sufficient reason for such an act. And self-murder as a relief from illness was regarded as justifiable. . . . In some states it was an institution duly legalized by the authorities. Nor did Greek or Roman law protect the unborn child. If, in certain cities, abortion was prosecuted it was because the father's right to his offspring had been violated by the mother's action. Ancient religion did not proscribe suicide. It did not know of any eternal punishment for those who voluntarily ended their lives. Likewise it remained indifferent to foeticide. . . . Law and religion then left the physician free to do whatever seemed best to him. . . . Platonists, Cynics, and Stoics . . . held suicide permissible for the diseased. Some . . . even extolled such an act as the greatest triumph of men over fate. Aristotle . . . and Epicurus [stood personally opposed to suicide but this] did not involve moral censure. If men decided to take their lives, they were within their rights. . . . The Aristotelian and Epicurean schools condoned suicide. Later on the Aristotelians . . . under the onslaught of Stoic attack . . . withdrew their disapproval of self-murder. . . . Indeed among all Greek thinkers the Pythagoreans alone outlawed suicide and did so without qualification. . . . The same can be asserted of the rule forbidding abortion. . . . Most of the Greek philosophers even commended abortion. For Plato, foeticide is one of the regular institutions of the ideal state. . . . Aristotle reckons abortion the best procedure to keep the population within the limits which he considers essential for a well-ordered community.[4]

Under the complex, highly pluralistic circumstances of the ancient world, physicians treating men, women, and children were relatively free to do what seemed best in their personal judgment.[5]

Admittedly, the Hippocratic oath, which has survived from early antiquity, does speak in terms that have been interpreted as affirming the sacredness or inviolability of human life.[6] Specifically, the Hippocratic physician is admonished not to give "a deadly drug even if asked for it."[7] Nevertheless, the idea that physicians must prolong life does not seem required on the basis of these words alone. This suggests that the duty of the physician to prolong life is "apparently a much more modern notion."[8] In addition, there are serious questions extant as to how widely physicians of the ancient world even accepted and embraced the Hippocratic oath.[9]

Significantly, the only ancient pagans known to have outlawed suicide among themselves without qualification were the devotees of Pythagoras, rather than Hippocrates. Yet even the Pythagoreans did not have an outlook on physiological life consonant with a sanctity of life perspective. Their belief in the transmigration of souls and their view of the body as a tomb from which the soul must escape precluded any sacralization of human life in the temporal realm.[10] Still, within the ancient Greek philosophical community one group did demonstrate an overall sensitivity to the sanctity of life, namely the Stoics.

STOIC SOURCES

Although they started as a small philosophical school and remained so, the Stoics in their time, both before and simultaneous with Christianity, gained a wide influence and following among the ruling classes of Greece and Rome.[11] The Stoics held suicide permissible for the diseased and attacked the Aristotelians for their disapproval of self-murder.[12] In spite of this, Stoic thought in other ways was clearly disposed to look at human life in terms of sacredness, ultimately laying the basis for a modern sanctity of life doctrine to emerge in Western society.

A short but impressive list of scholars have acknowledged an intimate tie between Stoicism and the sanctity of life notion. David Cairns, a strong advocate for contemporary sanctity of life doctrine, has declared without equivocation that "Stoicism has been in all ages a main root of thought about the dignity of man."[13] Historian Kingsley Martin has expressed a concurring view.[14] Similarly, in *Basic Christian Ethics,* Protestant theologian and ethicist Paul Ramsey stated:

> The ancient Stoics spoke of a "divine spark" within man, by which man shares in the "eternal fire" pervading all Nature. This viewpoint, strongly revived during the eighteenth-century Enlightenment, decisively influenced modern rationalism and modern secular democratic thought. The idea that there is a spark of the divine in every man (the Stoic notion) gave rise to our modern conceptions of the inherent natural sacredness of human personality as much as or more than did Christianity. Just so, most current formulations of the universal brotherhood of mankind have to be traced home to the cosmopolitan outlook of Stoicism.[15]

As a system of metaphysical belief that can be termed "monistic materialism," Stoicism is somewhat complex.[16] According to historian Frederick Copleston, Stoicism viewed God as an "active fire . . . immanent in the universe." In a dynamic process, this fire was the "primal source" for all matter and the state or condition to which all matter eventually returned.[17]

For the Stoics, reason was a quintessential expression or manifestation of God, the active fire. In turn, as creatures able to engage in rational thought and discourse, humans were deemed to possess a "divine spark" and to most closely approximate the total being of God. All human beings had a choice—to live in harmony with reason, giving expression to the law of God in nature, or to act in rebellion against it.

Devotees of Stoicism were encouraged to live in accordance with nature by cultivating rational virtue in their lives.[18]

The Stoics believed in the complete benevolence of God, which prompted them to view the material universe in the most positive possible light. God, it was held, had arranged "everything for the good of man."[19] Moreover, because every individual possessed the "divine spark" and had personal access to God, as discernible in the law and order of nature, Stoics also believed in the *autarkeia*, or autonomy, of virtuous human beings. In principle, the universality of the divine spark meant that all human beings were equal without regard to their present caste, class, or achievement.[20] Given their belief in human autonomy, the Stoics saw each person as entitled to make decisions about his or her own life and death, including suicide.[21] Nevertheless, with their view of a benevolent God and cosmos, they encouraged a love of self and others.[22]

As Christianity triumphed in the waning days of the Roman Empire, Stoicism went into general eclipse. But its teachings, particularly those concerning the sacredness of life, percolated anew in elements of Cappadocian divinization doctrine and found further expression in the natural law ethics of Thomas Aquinas. Still later, in the Renaissance, ancient Stoic ideas about the sacredness of embodied human life once again powerfully resurfaced, offering an immediate cultural counterpoint to the Christian churches' Platonic or neo-Platonic otherworldliness.[23]

From the Renaissance on, Stoicism and its sacralizing notions were never entirely submerged again. They ideologically informed and fed a secular civil society that now flourished alongside preexisting, theocentrically oriented institutions. In time, Stoic teachings on the value of embodied human life actually began to gain an upper hand, stealthily displacing a more traditional Christian outlook.[24]

In retrospect, the reemergence and reascendancy of Stoic thinking on the value of human life are apparent in some of the greatest hallmarks of the Renaissance period. Palpably reflecting Stoic influence, for example, the Renaissance philosopher Marsilio Ficino boldly declared that human beings were "the centre of nature, the middle of the universe, the chain of the world."[25] Subsequently, this same profound humanism with its sacralizing Stoic overtones found clear and definite expression in high Renaissance art: Renaissance artists accepted the challenge of rendering the human figure and its flesh in a manner as much celebratory as realistic.[26] Just as directly and explicitly, however, a revived Stoic-like secular sensibility concerning the sanctity or sacredness of life can be witnessed during the Renaissance period in evolving public perceptions regarding death which overturned long-standing Christian custom and facilitated a further veneration of mortal life.

VENERATION OF THE DEAD

In *Western Attitudes toward Death from the Middle Ages to the Present,* French scholar Philippe Ariès has noted the quiet acceptance of death that universally prevailed from early Christian times to the Middle Ages in Western Europe.[27] Burial was often anonymous within the precincts of the local church: there was great confidence in the Christian promise of the resurrection.

With the advent of the Middle Ages, however, there came major change, if not outright "historical mutation."[28] Ariès has observed that "beginning with the eleventh century a formerly unknown relationship developed between the death of each individual and his awareness of being an individual."[29] Put more simply, there emerged an unprecedented concern among men and women about their own death. This new concern increasingly registered itself through a reversal of funeral custom, specifically a movement away from the completely anonymous interment of bodily remains.

In the thirteenth century, for instance, the use of tomb inscriptions, which had disappeared eight or nine hundred years before with the waning of the Roman Empire and the ascendancy of the Christian era, made a reappearance[30] in the reindividualizing of tombs and sepulchers. By the eighteenth century, the repudiation of the tradition of anonymous Christian burial where a "dead person was given over to the Church, which took care of him until the Resurrection Day" was nearly complete.[31] In fact, the Christian churches found themselves subject to intense criticism because of their casual attitude toward keeping the dead. As Ariès has explained:

> [For the eighteenth century mind] the flooring of the churches and the ground of the cemeteries, which were saturated with cadavers, and the exhibition of bones in the charnel houses all constituted a permanent violation of the dignity of the dead. The Church was reproached for having done everything for the soul and nothing for the body, of taking money for masses and showing no concern for the tombs. The example of the Ancients, their piety toward the dead as shown by the remnants of their tombs as at Pompeii and by the eloquence of their funeral inscriptions, was called to mind. The dead should no longer poison the living [by the unsanitary disposal of their bodies], and the living should form a veritable lay cult to show their veneration of the dead. Their tombs therefore began to serve as a sign of their presence after death, a presence which did not necessarily derive from the concept of immortality central to religions of salvation such as Christianity. It derived instead from the survivors' unwillingness to accept the departure of their loved one. People held on to the remains.[32]

Elaborate arrangements for the keeping of the dead became a moral imperative.

The protest against the undignified disposal of human bodily remains by the Christian churches corresponded to other changing attitudes towards death. In the fifteenth century, for example, death suddenly came to be portrayed in funeral iconography and art as a putrefying corpse.[33] By the sixteenth and seventeenth centuries, Western society began to directly perceive death as a tragic rupture.[34] During the nineteenth century, this new sense of rupture lent itself to an almost "hysterical mourning" at the bedsides of the dying and at funeral services for them afterwards. Such emotional response had little, if any, precedent in the Christian tradition.[35] Hope of heaven and an eternal life appeared to provide less consolation for the bereaved than before.

In the renewed veneration of the dead, which echoed an earlier pagan era, and the hysterical mourning over loved ones, which suggested a lack of confidence in the resurrection, Ariès saw all the signs of an outright de-Christianization of Western society.[36] Moreover, Ariès noted one more phenomenon signaling "the overthrow of the Christian scheme of life"—namely, an enthusiasm and love for mortal life at odds with the traditionally qualified stance of Christianity towards everything temporal.[37]

Although in retrospect it is amazing, the Christian churches, Roman Catholic and Protestant alike, did not notice or comprehend what was actually taking place. In spite of the fact that the "exalted and emotive" cult of the dead had a "positivist," rather than Christian, origin, the churches—with Roman Catholicism leading the way—"rallied to it and assimilated it so perfectly that they thought it was indigenous to their religion."[38] Likewise, assimilating Western society's newly refound enthusiasm for mortal life, the Christian churches increasingly gave themselves over to the incipient worship of life. In time, the Christian churches began to believe that this sacralizing worship of life was completely "indigenous" to Christianity too.

ENLIGHTENMENT'S CULTUS OF LIFE

Just as Philippe Ariès has traced the emergence of a new secular cult of the dead over several centuries, following the Middle Ages, we can trace the evolution of a cultus of life, which specifically manifested itself in a belief in the sacredness of life. This new cultus became especially pronounced by the eighteenth and nineteenth centuries.

In the final phases of the Middle Ages Western Europe entered an intellectually fecund period, later known as the Renaissance. During this time the empirical sciences gained tremendous momentum, offering fresh ways to look at the physical or material world. In addition, the development of navigational technology encouraged unprecedented overseas exploration and trade. Thus, literally and figuratively, whole new horizons were rapidly developing for Western Europeans, radically altering their outlook on life and promoting a more comfortable this-worldly focus.[39]

In the midst of this new confidence a reaction set in. Its first phase was the Protestant Reformation, led by Martin Luther;[40] its second, the Roman Catholic Counter Reformation, inaugurated by the Council of Trent.[41] Although with their less than sanguine anthropologies both the Protestant Reformation and the Roman Catholic Counter Reformation can be seen as efforts to contain, if not curtail, the very humanism that the Renaissance had precipitated, they certainly did not succeed in returning any *genii* to the bottle.[42] Both the secularism and the humanism, which had received such a boost from the late Middle Ages and the Renaissance, managed to maintain themselves in various forms throughout the sixteenth and seventeenth centuries. Clearly, by the seventeenth century, secularism and humanism were again ascendant. Simultaneously, Western culture was fast approaching a genuine watershed in which traditional Christian teachings relativizing the value of mortal life would be supplanted by a burgeoning veneration of life. Indeed, with the end of the seventeenth century and the start of the eighteenth, "the libertine spirit [preoccupied with freedom, reason, and empiricism] was strengthened and a doctrine of normative providential order was gradually withdrawn."[43]

In many respects the Western European Enlightenment was a fresh manifestation of ancient Stoic ideas—or at least variations on them. At the heart of the Enlightenment was a conviction that human beings could universally commune with God through the exercise of their own human reason and the discernment of natural laws that God, as creator, had instituted. Like the ancient Stoics, the men and women of the Enlightenment regarded the individual human being, gifted with reason, as a "microcosm of the universe."[44] Trusting the same human capacity for reason, they placed more and more emphasis on subjective experience alone.[45] The individual was released from any ultimate accountability to an "outer authority."[46] Historian Carl Becker summarized the Enlightenment faith as follows:

> The essential articles of the religion of the Enlightenment may be stated thus: (1) man is not natively depraved; (2) the end of life is life itself, the good life on earth instead of the beatific life after death; (3) man is capable, guided solely by the light of reason and experience, of perfecting the good life on earth; and (4) the first and essential condition of the good life on earth is the freeing of men's minds from the bonds of ignorance and superstition, and of their bodies from the arbitrary oppression of the constituted social authorities.[47]

Echoing the Stoics, the Enlightenment thinkers viewed the human being as touched by divinity, not beset by depravity. If this was not apparent in the immediate claims of the *philosophes*, it quickly became so as the Enlightenment ideals were played out during the French Revolution.

A decree was issued by French revolutionary leaders in May 1794 establishing a new religion. The language of the decree was telling:

> The French people recognize the existence of the Supreme Being and the immortality of the soul. —It recognizes that the worship worthy of the Supreme Being is in the practice of the duties of man. —It places in the front rank of these duties to detest bad faith and tyranny, to punish tyrants and traitors, to aid the unfortunate, to respect the weak, to defend the oppressed, to do onto others all possible good and to be injust to no one. —There shall be instituted fetes in order to remind man of the Divinity and of the dignity of his being.[48]

In less radical form, a similar emphasis on the divinity of human beings came to be expressed in the liberal Protestant Christianity of roughly the same and subsequent period, most notably in both European and American Unitarianism and, later, Transcendentalism.[49]

Ironically, the very Enlightenment culture that was adamant about eliminating old strictures and taboos in religious and secular life was busy setting up some of its own. One historical commentator has claimed that the difference between medieval and modern cultures has been the sacralizing tendencies of the first and the impetus towards desacralization to be found in the latter. But a more careful scrutiny of the *philosophes* in terms of their practices and ideals calls this conventional wisdom into question. The focus of their sacralization was merely different. For the philosophes the sacred was simply located in whatever affirmed human dignity and divinity.

As reflected in the decree initiating the religion of humanity in revolutionary France, the physical conditions of life were now also considered all-important. Unless the "unfortunate" were aided, their progress to perfectibility, dignity, and divinity would also be impeded.[50] Rights talk became the way to create and secure the holy space that human beings needed to realize the divine within themselves and to bring their lives into harmony with it. The Enlightenment philosopher John Locke, whose work *An Essay Concerning Human Understanding* has been called "the psychological gospel of the eighteenth century," took great pains to emphasize that the human rights to "life, liberty and the pursuit of happiness" were inherent in nature, not dependent upon any conferral from a political state.[51] Significantly, for Locke the right to life was so elemental in attaining all the other goods in life that no one could relinquish it or give it up.

Unlike the ancient Stoics and some present-day liberals, who have exalted human autonomy and all its prerogatives in the face of any contravening authority, Locke was an outspoken opponent of suicide. Political science theorist Carole Pateman has summarized Locke's stance:

> Individuals are God's property and must not destroy themselves. The law of nature "willeth the Peace and Preservation of all Mankind" and tells individuals what they ought to do to protect and preserve each other. The law [of nature] is concerned with individuals collectively, not singularly, and it states that "being all equal and independent, no one ought to harm another in his Life, Health, Liberty, or Possessions." The law of nature thus establishes the basic rules of mutual aid and forbearance that are fundamental to social life.[52]

Here we have a prohibition on suicide genuinely grounded in a larger concern for the sacredness of human life. While reminiscent of Thomas Aquinas's arguments against suicide, Locke's prohibition is entirely free from any pretense that it is grounded in Christian thought or practice.

IMMANUEL KANT

If John Locke's writings provided a "gospel" for the Enlightenment, as Carl Becker suggests, the writings of Immanuel Kant a century or more later served as the "epistles" that secured the Enlightenment faith once and for all. Significantly, Kant's philosophy did much to consolidate Enlightenment convictions about the ultimate worth and sacredness of human life. Kant's work, like the writings of his distinguished Enlightenment counterparts, picked up on various Stoic themes and sensibilities, including those pertaining to human sacredness.

At the heart of Kant's moral philosophy were two foundational principles, which he termed respectively the "categorical imperative" and the "practical imperative." Kant's categorical imperative declared: "Act only on that maxim through which

you can at the same time will that it should become a universal law." Kant's categorical imperative was intended to dissuade men and women from personal actions
that they would abhor if others did them or that, if widely pursued, would produce deleterious consequences for all. Meanwhile, Kant's practical imperative stated:
"So act as to treat humanity, whether in your own person or in that of any other,
always at the same time as an end, and never merely as a means." This second
imperative anathematized any reduction of human persons into mere things or
objects.[53]

Although Kant's philosophy eschewed any Stoic notion of the divine spark in
the human breast, his metaphysical arguments, affirming human life as always an
end and never a mere means, reached virtually the same conclusion. Kant essentially sacralizes the human individual, as popular commentaries in standard reference works make clear.[54]

Kant's inclination to make man the measure of all things was made explicit in
some of his writings. At one point, Kant stated:

> If things in the world, which are dependent in their existence, need a
> supreme cause acting towards ends, then man is the final end of cre-
> ation; for without him the chain of graduated ends would not be per-
> fectly grounded, and only in man (but in him only as subject to
> morality) is there unconditional legislation with respect to ends. This
> alone makes him capable of being a final end, to which all nature is
> teleologically subordinated.[55]

Unlike the ancient Stoics, Kant does not see an ultimate, thoroughgoing harmony
between human beings and the rest of nature. Nevertheless, Kant believes that human
beings are meant to be the "lord of nature" and more.[56]

Certain perennial Stoic themes surfaced as leitmotifs in Kant's writing. Operating
in a larger synergy with each other, they seem to lead Kant inexorably to the most
emphatic affirmation of the sanctity of human life. Kant regarded "true religion,"
for example, as reverencing God by obeying the moral laws.[57] Under the circumstances, God and these moral laws, which we have a duty to discern, respect, and
obey, are virtually equated. Yet the greatest moral law for Kant is the practical imperative to treat men and women always as an end, never merely as a means. Thus,
through this kind of interconnected logic, Kant's reverence for human life was
constantly reinforced.

Morally, Kant asserted, we have a duty to respect others because they, like ourselves, embody an autonomous will too. In other words, respect for persons can never
be contingent on their "achievement and other qualities that evoke admiration."[58]

Breaking with his own Pietistic Protestant upbringing, Kant completely rejected the
notion of the total depravity of nature.[59] Part and parcel of this rejection for Kant was
a Stoic-like conviction that God was always calling men and women to perfection.
Though at an early point in his career as teacher and philosopher Kant seems to have
viewed human perfection as a matter of inevitable destiny, his outlook subsequently
changed. As James M. Gustafson has trenchantly observed, "destiny becomes a duty"
in the later Kant.[60] For example, in *Religion within the Limits of Reason Alone*, Kant

wrote, "Now it is our universal duty as men to *elevate* ourselves to this ideal of moral perfection, that is, to this archetype of the moral disposition in all its purity—and for this the ideal itself, which reason presents to us for our zealous emulation, can give us power."[61] In short, Kant argues that men and women have a responsibility to actively strive for moral perfection.[62]

Nominally, Kant appears to have identified himself as a Christian. He professed hopes that his own philosophy would contribute to the revamping of Christianity on a more rational basis.[63] Nevertheless, the greater part of Kant's work always remained philosophical rather than theological and secular rather than religious. In a sense, his very distance from traditional Christianity gave Kant a freedom to address issues about the value and worth of human life which the Christian churches until then had kept veiled in a certain ambivalence and ambiguity.

In accord with the ancient Stoics and earlier Enlightenment philosophers, Kant subscribed to the radical autonomy of the individual.[64] But in his view even this autonomy remained accountable to both his categorical and practical imperatives. Kant's respect for the sacredness of human life was so great and so elemental that he was opposed to any exercise of autonomy that led to suicide. Indeed, Kant was adamant on this point:

> Man cannot deprive himself of his personality so long as one speaks of duties, thus so long as one lives. . . . To destroy the subject of morality in his own person is tantamount to obliterating from the world, as far as he can, the very existence of morality itself; but morality is, nevertheless, an end in itself. Accordingly, to dispose of oneself as a mere means to some end of one's own liking is to degrade the humanity in one's person *(homo noumenon),* which, after all, was entrusted to man *(homo phaenomen)* to preserve.[65]

Most plainly put, Kant believes that an act of suicide is a betrayal of the sacred humanity in us all.

While Kant's work mentioned "classic circumstances in which suicide has been justified . . . e.g., martyrdom for a good cause, avoidance of harm to others, avoidance of the onset of madness due to disease and the like," he did not, says James M. Gustafson, "give clear answers" as to his own response to any of these situations.[66] The thrust of Kant's categorical and practical imperatives would appear to preclude any of these rationales. It is hard to imagine how Kant, who viewed God as benevolent, could embrace the traditional Christian idea that God might command us to martyr our lives through an act of suicide for a "higher good." As Gustafson so ably summarizes: "An act on which very few of our contemporaries dare to make a moral judgement is for Kant clearly morally wrong."[67] Kant's philosophy holds that, whatever our desires may be, we have a moral duty to preserve our own life.[68]

Recently Kant has been criticized for not being sufficiently broad and encompassing in his affirmation of human sacredness.[69] Such criticism notwithstanding, no one seriously challenges or doubts the fact that the "Kantian mode of thinking has provided much of the basis for contemporary moral philosophy's account of the peculiar worth and importance of persons"—indeed, their sacredness.[70] Kant's philosophy continues to have a wide-ranging and dynamic impact on modern thinking, whether philosophical or theological.[71] Significantly, theologian and ethicist Kenneth Vaux does not mince words about Kant or his impact: Kant's philosophy, he contends, has largely ignited the present-day controversy and crisis over abortion and the right to life.[72]

AUTONOMOUS CULTURE

Immanuel Kant, one of the last great figures of the Western European Enlightenment, died at the start of the nineteenth century in his quaint and peaceful hometown of Königsberg in East Prussia.[73] Over the next century or more many of the elements of Kant's particular philosophy, which had much in common with other Enlightenment thinking, ended up enshrined at the very heart of a liberal culture in both Europe and America.

Both Europe and America remained ostensibly Christian. Yet, thanks to a residual wariness about religion in public life, perhaps due in part to past religious conflicts over alleged heresies and infidelities, there was a new openness to the possibility of a civil society constituted on a relatively autonomous, secular basis. Enlightenment philosopher John Locke was quite helpful in this regard. Although Locke was very much a Protestant Christian in many of his sensibilities, as recent research has affirmed, his essays and treatises encouraged a balance of power in government, plus a separation of church and state.[74] It did not take long for the culture of those societies, influenced by Locke and other Enlightenment philosophers, to begin marching to the sound of a different drummer in noticeable and decisive ways. The result was a de-Christianization of Western society.[75] Paradoxically, however, the telltale signs of de-Christianization—namely, a growing celebration of humanity and human rights, very much in keeping with Enlightenment ideals—were never quite recognized for what they were.[76]

As the new order emerged, it was sometimes alleged that the fresh sensitivity to the conditions and circumstances of humanity, in place of a more traditional focus upon otherworldly, soteriological questions, was merely a return to the more simple and original gospel of Jesus.[77] Certainly this is the idea implicit in the work of liberal historians and apologists such as William E. H. Lecky, who imputed to the historical Christian community the same concern for the sanctity of life that was increasingly preoccupying nineteenth-century thinkers shaped by the Enlightenment.[78] Yet, in all probability, it was the tolerance of humanistically disposed thinkers and their attendant reluctance to engage in rancorous metaphysical debate with potential critics that left the de-Christianizing elements of their stance mostly unscrutinized and unchallenged.[79] These liberals were confident that their "new faith" would carry the day. It did.

UNITARIAN-TRANSCENDENTALIST CONTRIBUTIONS

Of all those who contributed to the Enlightenment conquest of both Christianity and civil society, perhaps the most interesting and influential, at least on American shores, were the Unitarians.[80] By profession a Christian sect, the American Unitarians had come into existence in 1819 after schismatically breaking away from Trinitarian Congregationalism.[81] The early leader of the Unitarians was William Ellery Channing, an irenic, Harvard-educated Boston divine, who occupied one of the premier pulpits of early-nineteenth-century America.

Admirably schooled and respectably credentialed in the heritage of the Christian churches, Channing still spoke in the generous cadences and lofty rhetoric of an earlier ecclesiastical age. Nevertheless, the substance of his preaching revealed him to be very much a child of the Enlightenment with a fondness for pre-Christian Stoic ideals.[82] Indeed, in Channing's sermons we see a ready confluence of Christian references and Stoic ideals—all affirming that human life is sacred or has the potential to be. A sermon delivered by Channing in Baltimore, Maryland, announcing the emergence of a Unitarian Christian movement, created a sensation: it became the most widely circulated and read document in America and purportedly kept that record for a decade.[83]

In both the Baltimore sermon, published as "Unitarian Christianity," and a second address, entitled "Likeness to God," Channing rejected the traditional Christian notion of human depravity, particularly as expressed in an extreme form by Calvinism.[84] In its stead, Channing revived ancient Stoic themes that affirmed both the possibility and importance of realizing human sacredness, albeit in the guise of affirming a truer Christianity. For instance, in "Likeness to God," while claiming consistency with his New Testament lection, Channing stated early on that "true religion consists in proposing, as our great end, a growing likeness to the Supreme Being" in which we become "more and more partakers of the Divinity" and the "bright image of God."[85] Channing added:

> I exhort you to no extravagance. I reverence human nature too much to do it violence. I see too much divinity in its ordinary operations, to urge on it a forced and vehement virtue. To grow in the likeness of God, we need not cease to be men. This likeness does not consist in extraordinary or miraculous gifts, in supernatural additions to the soul, or in any thing foreign to our original constitution; but in our essential faculties, unfolded by vigorous and conscientious exertion in the ordinary circumstances assigned by God. To resemble our Creator, we need not fly from society, and entrance ourselves in lonely contemplation and prayer.[86]

In his carefully chosen words, Channing was advocating a very worldly Christian humanism, influenced more by the ideals of the Enlightenment than by any traditional Christian teachings.[87] Here and elsewhere, he used his authority as an ostensibly Christian leader to confer a blessing on what has come to be called the "modernist synthesis," in which the secularization and sacralization of human life went hand in hand.[88]

As it turned out, within a short time, some of Channing's fellow Unitarians were disposed to make even more dramatic and thoroughgoing departures from traditional Christianity, affirming in its place a new spirituality and a decidedly non-Christian humanism which, clearly rooted in neo-Stoic themes and ideals, was intent on even further sacralizing mortal life. The clarion call for the "latest form of infidelity"—as it was even then described—was Ralph Waldo Emerson's "Divinity School Address," delivered before the graduating class of the Harvard Divinity School on July 15, 1838.[89]

Emerson, who exhorted the class to "cast behind you all conformity, and acquaint men at first hand with Deity," used the occasion of the sermon or lecture to celebrate the benevolence and harmony of nature and the capacity of human reason to intuit the unchanging physical and moral laws of the universe, plus the prospect of an indwelling divinity or sacredness within every human being.[90] "The sublime is excited in me," he explained, "by the great stoical doctrine, Obey thyself."[91] Emerson viewed the cultivation of personal virtue as the highest human task. To the extent that we achieve the virtuous life, we become, he intimated, another Christ—at one with the divine. The virtuous human soul possesses or is possessed by sacredness.[92]

Significantly, Emerson, who had become associated with a Transcendentalist circle among a younger generation of Unitarians, abandoned the Christian ministry at about the time of his landmark address in order to take up a career as an essayist and public lecturer with a special concern for the development of moral culture.[93] Even now, what is striking is the sheer number of Emerson's friends, cohorts, and acquaintances from a decidedly humanistic Unitarianism and Transcendentalism who, bringing a passionate moral sensibility to secular culture, became engaged in active social change. The Unitarian ranks alone produced such secular saints as Horace Mann, Dorothea Dix, and Samuel Gridley Howe, all ardent reformers who contributed enormously to the establishment of the modern professions of education and social work.[94] Meanwhile, on the more strictly Transcendentalist or post-Transcendentalist side, individuals such as Margaret Fuller and Theodore Parker were instrumental in furthering the cause of women's rights and abolitionism respectively.[95]

At every turn these reformers, inspired not a little by Channing and Emerson, committed to the extension of individual human freedom and the triumph of what was deemed reasonable and humane, over and against institutions perceived as oppressive. They were also dedicated to the alleviation of physical or material squalor, which they viewed as a blight upon individual moral and spiritual development.[96] Fair to say, the reformers' goal was the elevation of humankind to new moral and material conditions where proper homage would be paid to human sanctity or sacredness.

While the human-centered attitude and outlook of the Unitarians and Transcendentalists led them to distance themselves from a strictly Christian profession of faith, their idealism clearly influenced others who were more inclined to remain within the Christian fold. Consciously or unconsciously, the Christian Personalism movement within late-nineteenth- and early-twentieth-century American Protestantism—a movement that affirmed the sacredness of human personality—can be fairly regarded as a wholesale effort to graft the ideals of these earlier Unitarians and Transcendentalists onto the main body of Christianity.[97]

PRISON REFORM AND CAPITAL PUNISHMENT

In the midst of American religious and social ferment leading to a more widespread sacralization of human life in public affairs, very similar liberal reform movements were simultaneously under way on the European continent. Indeed, throughout the nineteenth century a concern for the natural "rights of man," and human improvement generally, remained the *Zeitgeist* for Europeans. As in America, the fruits of this spirit included the termination of the slave trade, the development of social pension or welfare programs, and efforts at prison reform.

The liberal French aristocrat Alexis de Tocqueville, author of *Democracy in America,* specifically made his visit to the United States during the 1830s to study the progressive American experiment with prison reform.[98] Tocqueville hoped to bring about the establishment of a more humane prison system in his native France that would focus on the moral rehabilitation of criminals rather than merely punishment.[99] The idea of criminal rehabilitation was simply a variation on the fundamental and positive conviction among liberals that human beings possessed a sacred soul and were perfectible.[100]

Ultimately, the high value that Enlightenment liberals and humanists in Europe accorded to less than innocent mortal life and the prospect of rehabilitation took them to yet another moral frontier—namely, a crusade to abolish capital punishment. The crusade was controversial and not especially well received among Christians, to say the least. As Karl Barth notes, the "impetus towards a basic challenging of capital punishment did not come from Christians," or even from such major Enlightenment figures as Locke, Rousseau, or Kant, "who all conceded its necessity, but from the enlightened Italian Cesare Beccaria (1764), whose protest led to rapidly mounting pressure for its restriction and then to a widening demand for its complete abolition as a Liberal postulate."[101] Barth asks:

> What can we say when we consider that among German Protestant theologians of the 19th century not only the stolid Vilmar but even the sensitive R. Rothe and the otherwise radical D. F. Strauss were so definitely in favour of [capital punishment's] widespread retention? Is it not remarkable that where its abolition has been carried [out] it has always been in face of a more or less powerful Christian opposition, as, for example, in Switzerland, where it had to meet the resistance of the Catholic Conservative Party, which so intransigently refuses to agree to any legalisation of abortion? Is there any genuine reason for this?[102]

As Barth attests, European Christians consistently opposed the abolition of capital punishment. It came to an end in some European countries only because secular humanists eventually prevailed against the Christian opposition. If this victory over lethal punishments lodged the sanctity of life a little more firmly at the center of Western civilized life, it was no thanks to the Christian churches, which dragged their feet all the way.

IMPACT OF THE NEW PROFESSIONS

Amid the reforms being promulgated by liberals during the nineteenth century, numerous "helping professions" began to emerge to provide leadership for further change in both Europe and America. Each of these new professions readily absorbed the Enlightenment concern with reason, human improvement or per-fectibility, and a scientifically disposed naturalism. The medical profession, which has been extolled by some in our present day as a lingering center of virtue and described by others as a bastion of Enlightenment thought, was perhaps foremost in its devotion to basic Enlightenment and neo-Stoic ideals.[103] More than any other modern profession, medicine became—in the spirit of liberal humanism—an agent for the affirmation of the sacredness of life.

The most cursory review of nineteenth-century literature suggests the hold that the modern medical profession gained on the public imagination of the time. While their fictional lives are cautionary tales, Doctors Victor Frankenstein and Charles Bovary are expressions of the new enthrallment.[104] Throughout the nineteenth century, the medical profession set about to confirm its sacred role as a new priest-hood for the burgeoning secular humanist age.

Social historian James C. Mohr and sociologist Kristin Luker have documented the rise to prominence of the American medical profession and the manner in which its enhanced status was directly tied to its widening campaign against abor-tion and in favor of what we today call "the right to life."[105] Mohr and Luker note that, contrary to popular impression today, abortion was relatively common and wide-spread in early-nineteenth-century America, often induced with the assistance of mid-wives. Though possibly inflated, estimates at the time suggested that one in four or perhaps even one in three of all pregnancies ended in abortion.[106] Making his own assessment, Mohr endorses a more modest ratio of "one abortion for every five or six live births by the 1850s and 1860s."[107] Whatever the exact percentage, physi-cians in the mid-nineteenth century began to actively work to end public tolerance for abortion. As Luker observes:

> The membership of the American Medical Association (AMA), found-ed in 1847 to upgrade and protect the interests of the profession, was deeply divided on many issues. But by 1859 it was able to pass a res-olution condemning induced abortion and urging state legislatures to pass laws forbidding it; in 1860, Henry Miller, the president-elect of the association, devoted much of his presidential address to attacking abortion; and in 1864 the AMA established a prize to be awarded to the best anti-abortion book written for the lay public. Slowly physi-cians responded to the AMA's call and began to lobby in state legisla-tures for laws forbidding abortion.[108]

Throughout the nineteenth century, physicians continued to be the moral power-house behind all anti-abortion legislation. As Mohr affirms: "The nation's regular doctors, probably more so than any identifiable group in the late nineteenth cen-tury, including the clergy, defended the value of human life per se as an absolute."[109]

Both Mohr and Luker have examined the stated motives of nineteenth-century physicians, who were quite open and voluble on the subject. On the basis of the his-torical record, Luker remarks:

> Why should nineteenth-century physicians have become so involved with the question of abortion? The physicians themselves gave two

related explanations for their activities, and these explanations have been taken at face value ever since. First, they argued, they were compelled to address the abortion question because American women were committing a moral crime based on ignorance about the proper value of embryonic life. According to these physicians, women sought abortions because the doctrine of quickening led them to believe that the embryo was not alive, and therefore aborting it was perfectly proper. Second, they argued, they were obliged to act in order to save women from their own ignorance because only physicians were in possession of new scientific evidence which demonstrated beyond a shadow of a doubt that the embryo was a child from conception onward.[110]

Assessing the physicians' professed motives, Luker agrees that there was an explosion of empirical gynecological knowledge during the nineteenth century that might have disposed the medical profession to regard embryonic life with greater regard. Nevertheless, she, like Mohr, is struck by the way in which the American medical profession presented abortion as a moral issue. In its campaign against abortion, the medical profession not only vilified traditional midwives, who were now classed with quacks, but also usurped the moral authority of the Christian churches and other American religious institutions.[111] Mohr has suggested that the physicians' underlying intention was to strengthen their own profession and enhance their social status and influence.[112]

While in the late twentieth century an anti-abortion stance stands as the linchpin in most declarations concerning the sanctity of life, nineteenth-century Christian churches, whether Protestant or Roman Catholic, were not ready participants in the anti-abortion campaign being waged by physicians. The most avid secular abortion opponents of the nineteenth century complained bitterly about the persistent silence of clergy on the subject of abortion.[113] Objects of their rancor included female "professors of religion" who were said to favor the availability of abortion.[114] Mohr and Luker report other evidence suggesting that nineteenth-century parish clergy were largely supportive of women who aborted unwanted fetuses.[115] In fact, it was only as the nineteenth century approached its close and statutory bans on abortion were already in place that the Christian churches, swept along by a change in public opinion, finally joined the secular priesthood of physicians in any true condemnation of abortion.

Interestingly enough, the physicians involved in the anti-abortion campaign took what might be called a very "liberal" stance towards women who sought out or supported abortion. Rather than condemn them as evil, the physicians chose to treat them as ignorant—a position not out of keeping with Stoic doctrine, which assumes sin to be a privation of knowledge.[116] In this vein, a medical school professor from Michigan "accused and absolved" women in the same breath, first stating that the "crime" of abortion is "wholly inconsistent with the purity of woman's nature, and revolting to her moral sentiments" and then adding that it "is generally the act of those who know not what they do."[117] Under the circumstances, the function and role of the physicians was to educate women about the true laws of nature and enable them thereby to be restored to moral purity.

In retrospect it is easy to be cynical about the dynamics within the medical profession and wider secular society that fed the eventual outlawing of abortion, except for therapeutic purposes. To be fair, however, we need to acknowledge that the medical profession, enveloped by the Enlightenment, ended up sincerely convinced of the rightness of its cause and campaign. As the historian Carl Degler comments:

> Seen against the broad canvas of humanitarian thought and practice in Western society from the seventeenth to the twentieth century, the expansion of the definition of life to include the whole career of the fetus rather than only the months after quickening is quite consistent. It is in line with a number of movements to reduce cruelty and to expand the concept of sanctity of life.[118]

Ultimately, with the successful abolition of legal, nontherapeutic abortion in America, as well as in Europe, the wider notion of the sanctity of life was on its way to becoming ever more firmly ensconced in popular Western thought.[119]

ALBERT SCHWEITZER

As the nineteenth century closed and the twentieth century got under way, liberalism and humanism approached their high tide. Few persons exemplified the spirit of that high tide better than Albert Schweitzer. Largely thanks to Schweitzer and the attention his personal philosophy and career received, the sanctity of life became a popular axiom and household phrase of the modern age.

Schweitzer gained his initial renown in the pre–First World War period as a church historian. Yet, in what must be considered one of the more amazing career moves of the twentieth century, Schweitzer relinquished his clerical collar and scholar's robe for a doctor's stethoscope. Eschewing the vaunted sanctuaries and elegant salons of Europe, he became a physician at a mission hospital in the wilds of French Equatorial Africa.

There was much behind this move. In the time leading up to it, Schweitzer had been brooding deeply about the state and fate of Western civilization. On the eve of the First World War, he was already convinced that Western society was facing a spiritual crisis, a crisis that Christianity did not have the means to avert or overcome. The actual outbreak of the war, which seemed unprecedented in the scale of its technological violence, simply confirmed Schweitzer in the belief that Western civilization was in need of total spiritual renewal.[120] Schweitzer's "reverence for life" philosophy, transcending any traditional Christianity, was an outgrowth of his broodings.

By now regarding Christianity as a spent force, Schweitzer called for a new life-affirming attitude that would seek to "preserve life, promote life, help life to achieve its highest destiny."[121] He also invited respect for nonhuman life forms:

> To the truly ethical man, all life is sacred, including forms of life that from the human point of view may seem to be lower than ours. He makes distinctions only from case to case, and under pressure of

necessity, when he is forced to decide which life he will sacrifice in order to preserve other lives. In thus deciding from case to case, he is aware that he is proceeding subjectively and arbitrarily, and that he is accountable for the lives thus sacrificed.[122]

Identifying himself with pre-Christian Stoicism, as well as with humanism and liberal notions of progress and perfectibility, Schweitzer described the challenge of embracing the sacredness of life in terms of becoming "more finely and deeply human."[123]

Given the wide publicity which Schweitzer and his new philosophy garnered, the Christian communities in Europe and America had countless opportunities to brand Schweitzer as the apostate which he, in fact, was. Yet, perhaps because liberal ideas about the sanctity of life had substantially permeated their own thinking, they did not have the heart to do so. Even those most theologically astute and committed within the Christian communities largely treated Schweitzer as a beloved infidel.[124] While Schweitzer's "reverence for life" philosophy sometimes took him to absurd limits, he continued to be celebrated as a paragon of Western civilization's most refined moral sensibilities.

At the time that he introduced it, Schweitzer's ethical mysticism may have seemed quite daring: his concern for animal and plant life was certainly novel for the West. Overall, however, Schweitzer's philosophy was not especially original. While an element of ethical mysticism, particularly its respect for nonhuman life forms, was borrowed from Eastern religious traditions, it was in the main a direct extension of liberal thinking, merely expanding or extrapolating upon liberalism's conception of the sanctity or sacredness of life.

All in all, though he was operating in a global theater, Schweitzer's spiritual odyssey closely paralleled the experience of such earlier American liberals as Channing and Emerson. Like them, Schweitzer started out as an ostensibly orthodox Christian thinker and scholar. Like them too, however, he subsequently abandoned any formal or traditional Christianity in order to become a secular or secularly disposed apostle on behalf of the sanctity of life.

In Schweitzer a major cultural trend thus persisted. The growing movement within liberal culture away from any formal allegiance to Christianity and towards so-called secularization was inexorably leading it towards an ever more thoroughgoing sacralization of life.

ANTIDOTE FOR MORAL CRISIS IN LIBERAL SOCIETY

Akin to ancient Stoic doctrine, liberalism from its eighteenth-century inception has been imbued with a belief in both human perfectibility and progress. These twin beliefs persist today among liberals. Consequently, any destructive elements that surface as human destiny takes shape are invariably seen as unnatural. If serious enough, they are commonly described as political, moral, or social crises.

As in the example of Albert Schweitzer, the response of liberals to such real or imagined crises has been to propose new organizations and concepts to replace old institutions and customs that are deemed to be inadequate. The perennial belief and hope among liberals is that with sufficient prescience and commitment the imperfect element in human existence can be finally conquered and tamed.[125]

A continuing concern with human perfectibility and progress—and the structure and organization necessary to achieve them—was certainly evident as the twentieth century continued. Just as these preoccupations provided the impetus for Schweitzer's "reverence for life" philosophy earlier in the century, they prompted another fresh swell of support for the sanctity of life concept in the decades following the Second World War. Indeed, over the course of the twentieth century the sanctity of life emerged as the holy grail for a liberal culture always on the verge of disillusionment with itself and in need of an antidote for its many disappointments and discontents.

In the United States, for instance, a post–Second World War peace was marred by international Cold War politics and the nation's own involvement in unpopular military conflicts in Korea and then Vietnam. Perhaps borrowing from a Humphrey Bogart film, the popular rubric of the times was that "life was cheap" abroad—in other words, not valued— especially in places such as Asia. Yet, by the time of the Vietnam War, increasingly radicalized liberals began to see their own country as the culprit in the devaluation of human life and protested accordingly.

In the aftermath of the My Lai massacre and the repeated carpet bombings of Hanoi, the disenchantment and outrage amongst those most avowedly liberal became especially intense. Some of the prominent fictional literature of the time took on an apocalyptic tone.[126] A similar end-of-the-world sensibility dominated political discussion and generated nihilism among younger people. The refrain of the Vietnam era was not unlike that which rose up in Schweitzer and others in response to the terrible carnage of the First World War: *The future of humankind was at grave risk. Christianity and other expressions of traditional religious belief were compromised and discredited by their participation in the old order and inadequate to address the real moral crisis at hand. Consequently, departing from traditional religion, secular society needed to vigorously commit itself to the sanctity of life in order to restore sanity and hope and thereby overcome the human callousness towards life that had become so prevalent.*

As evidenced by the sheer proliferation of articles on the subject, secular interest in the sanctity of life reached a crescendo in the mid-1960s and persisted for the next decade or more. Interest leveled off or declined only when more traditional and highly conservative religious communities, usually Christian, began appropriating for their own use similar ideas and language. Thereafter, discomfited secularists either pulled back or simply became quieter in their own sanctity of life pronouncements. At the height of its vogue, however, secular talk about the sanctity of life had wide intellectual appeal and cachet. The only real question for many liberal, secular intellectuals was how flexible—or how rigid and absolute—a sanctity of life standard should be.

RESISTANCE TO UTILITARIANISM AND THE TECHNOLOGICAL IMPERATIVE

Unlike much of the liberal mainstream, which remained enamored with the prospect of technological progress, those radicalized liberals and humanists drawn to an avowed sanctity of life perspective in the post–World War II era were profoundly worried about what technology had already wrought and what it was making possible. The apocalyptic fears most commonly expressed, however, were not singularly or even predominantly focused on the possibility of atomic holocaust. Instead, they were directed against a more encompassing utilitarian attitude towards human life, which science and technology were credited with fostering.[127] These critics of a utilitarian ethic and the instrumental reason underlying it felt that the survival of humankind was imperiled at all levels.

In an introduction to a collection of essays that emerged from a symposium on the sanctity of life that took place at Reed College in the mid-1960s, Daniel Labby poignantly detailed the *Sitz im Leben* or context for the discussion that took place:

> There is little difficulty recalling the details of the birth of this first symposium in the Sanctity of Life series. The planning committee had wrestled for some weeks with a wide variety of universal social problems, but when the idea of "The Sanctity of Life" was first presented, its appeal was sensed unanimously: At the moment an unpopular war was threatening to escalate insanely, and the use of nuclear power in war was a world-wide anxiety. The problems of racism and rioting were again aflame, the wounds of the thalidomide tragedy were still unhealed, and contraception and abortion were troublesome moral dilemmas. There could be no more opportune topic for a conference than one that would explore the ethics and options controlling the powers of life and death. Is life more, or less valuable today, than at any moment in the recorded history of man? Could one identify the forces in society that determine how valuable one man holds the life of another? Do adequate guidelines exist in law, theology, or in the liberal arts? Are the biomedical sciences, dedicated to preserving health and prolonging life, taking undue liberties in the guise of improving man's condition?[128]

The gravest forebodings about undue liberties being taken with human life were expressed again and again at the Reed College symposium.

Conferee Edward Shils was especially eloquent on the dangers to human life. Citing the example of Nazi Germany and the American bombings of Hiroshima and Nagasaki, where human rationality produced unprecedented destruction, Shils noted "that many sensitive persons have now come to feel that we live unsteadily and unceasingly suspended over an abyss of unlimited murderousness."[129] He then went on to ask how "the human race . . . with all its deficiencies, [is] to be protected from the murderous and manipulative wickedness of some of its members and from the passionate curiosity and the scientific and technological genius of others."[130] Answering his own question, Shils argued that only a general adherence to a sanctity of life doctrine would keep science from becoming ensnared by sadistic and inhumane impulses.[131]

Labby's and Shil's sense of acute cultural and social crises was reiterated by other commentators from the same period and in the decade that followed. Only a couple of years after the Reed College symposium, the budding philosopher and ethicist Daniel Callahan published an extended essay, also called "The Sanctity of Life."[132] In his own remarks about the growing threat to human well-being in modern society, Callahan was reluctant to criticize any particular group or lend himself to conspiracy thinking. Instead, he saw more innocent problems at work. Callahan noted that "the proliferation of state supported hospitals and research facilities very often means that people come together only in relatively impersonal, professional relationships." Consequently, he added, "the layman, whether as client or patient or experiment subject, is wholly at the mercy of a professional or an institution." Under the circumstances the "possibilities of abuse" were "considerable, perhaps less because of any deliberate attempt to misuse professional or institutional power than due to the indifference and insensitivity which impersonal, fleeting relationships often carry with them, particularly when large masses of people are handled or treated."[133] In Callahan's view the sheer size and impersonality of the institutions providing health care and pursuing human research—the result of modern-day concerns with rational efficiency and economies of scale—presented serious hazards that bore watching lest human beings be unwittingly reduced to objects and things.

Depersonalization and dehumanization in a rational, efficient, technologically driven society were also on the mind of Julian R. Pleasants, who responded to Callahan in a brief companion essay. Contemplating the prospect of a full-blown human disaster just around the corner, he warned:

> Unless mankind can reach some consensus about the sanctity of human life, not only within groups of humans, but between groups . . . it may commit the ultimate biological sin for any species, self-extermination. . . . *Brave New World* is closer than we think, and the responsibility should very properly awe us. . . . What scientific advancement has suddenly brought home to white America is the possibility of doing things to each other, within our group, that we have been doing indirectly and even unconsciously to those outside our group, deciding who shall live and who shall die and who shall half-live, manipulating people by the way we manipulate the tremendous resources of land, energy, and talent which we have managed to keep at our disposal. We stand at a kind of moral crossroads.[134]

Though Pleasants agreed that the impersonality of modern technological society was undermining a respect for human life, he did not see it as an entirely new problem. What was different, according to Pleasants, was that the pernicious effects of advanced technology were beginning to impact upon the elites who, thanks to wealth and position, had previously been shielded from such depersonalization and dehumanization.

At nearly the same time that Callahan and his cohorts were complaining about the dehumanization wrought directly or indirectly by technology and warning about a "moral crossroads," another philosopher, Hans Jonas, was independently making a similar point about the precariousness of a technological future. The "slow-working accidents of nature," he ruefully remarked, "are to be replaced by the fast-working accidents of man's hasty and biased decisions, not exposed to the long test of the ages." "Never," Jonas added, "was so much power coupled with so little guidance for its use."[135]

Concurring with Jonas, another scientist and ethicist, Leon Kass, expressed frustration at the frightening lack of rational discourse among scientists about the ends and purposes of their work. Any lingering scientific commitment to righteousness or justice or truth, he asserted, rested "upon the receding wisdom of an earlier age."[136] Clearly, in his estimation, new wisdom was needed.

NEED FOR A SECULAR ETHICS IN DEFENSE OF HUMAN LIFE

As alarmed as these commentators were about the moral abyss they saw opening up before their eyes, not one of them looked seriously to organized Western religion as a source of guidance. In fact, Christianity was seen to be part of the problem.

Edward Shils was especially blunt in his remarks at the Reed College symposium. In opening his presentation, he stated: "The cognitive content of Christian doctrine, and above all the grandiose Christian symbolization of man's origin and destiny, have now lost much of their appeal."[137] He further issued a less than subtle slap at Christianity when he averred that "Germany, not particularly dechristianized as compared with the other countries of the modern world, participated in the deliberate murder of numerous millions of persons of alien ethnic stocks."[138]

A similar condescension toward Christianity, if not outright contempt, affected other thinkers of the period. Most prominent in this regard was Daniel Callahan, who made it clear that Christianity was not up to the moral task that the times required.

Callahan's complaint against Christianity was multifold. Christianity in his view had not systematically addressed the problem posed by technological power.[139] It encouraged moral passivity where human responsibility and action were needed.[140] Consequently, "professed believers often act as badly as professed non-believers."[141] In addition, Christians were a minority on the planet. Hence Christianity could not "readily provide a consensual norm to which all men can have recourse."[142] At the crux of Callahan's objections to any central role for Christianity, however, was his passionate conviction that in the face of modern technological development, fraught with both peril and promise, human beings needed to make use of their own gifts of reason and experience, rather than blindly follow heteronomous principles from the past.

Callahan argued that "all moral rules are human artifacts" and that "the fiction of divinely imposed rules does justice neither to the moral rules nor to God."[143]

Callahan went on to reveal that the idea of a transcendent God, historically central to Christianity, had already ceased to have any role in his own thought, especially when it came to working out the awesome moral dilemmas confronting humankind. In a provocative statement, Callahan wrote:

> It is an utter abdication of human responsibility to passively place on God's shoulders the care and protection of human life. Human experience together with a contemplation of human freedom and divine providence show that God does not directly enter into the processes of nature and human life, at least not in the sense of immediately inter-

vening in the biological processes of life and death. . . . Man is responsible for everything to do with man, including control over life and
death. This is the last step that much Christian theology has been slow
to take, but it is now imperative. Contraception, abortion, euthanasia,
medical experimentation, and the prolongation of human life are all
problems which fall *totally* within the sphere of human rules and
human judgements. To place the solution of these problems "in the
hands of God" is to misjudge God's role and to misuse human reason
and freedom. . . . The theology behind the excuse that man can't "play
God" is a defective theology.[144]

In the decade that followed Callahan's treatise, other secular thinkers ratified his arguments for total human autonomy in decisions concerning the biological processes
of life and death. They too treated traditional Christian theology in such situations
as virtually irrelevant.

Typical was Edward Keyserlingk, author of a study written expressly for the Law
Reform Commission of Canada, entitled *Sanctity of Life or Quality of Life in the
Context of Ethics, Medicine, and Law.*[145] Keyserlingk stated that "since both [con-
temporary] theology and human experience suggest that God does not in fact
directly intervene in the biological processes of life or make life and death decisions,
humans would be abdicating responsibility to passively leave the care, protection
and control of life to God."[146] Like Callahan, Keyserlingk appeared unaware of the
diverse ways in which contemporary Christian theology has addressed divine transcendence and immanence—and their relation to human autonomy—without completely divorcing God from the natural world or even human decision-making.[147]

PROTORELIGIOUS NATURAL METAPHYSIC

Given their view of civilization and its discontents, including the real or imagined
deficiencies of Christianity, most secular humanists felt obliged to articulate a rationally autonomous sanctity of life principle in the defense of human life. For some,
however, this challenge was not as daunting as it first looked: nature, they believed,
was literally and figuratively on their side.

Bucking popular prejudice, Edward Shils, for instance, argued that the sanctity
of life as a living principle had never been dependent upon Christian theology or
any other code of belief. Instead, it was a sensibility that came naturally to men and
women. Indeed, if Christianity had historically taken a stand against the violation
of human life, it was, according to Shils, led to do so only from a natural revulsion that preceded all dogma:

It seems to me that the apprehension about the intervention of medical, psychological, and electronic technology [in the lives of men and
women, which has arisen for us in recent times,] has an even deeper
source in human existence than is to be found in the cultural traditions
resting on Christian theology. The source of the revulsion or apprehension [towards any trespass against life] is deeper than the culture
of Christianity and its doctrine of the soul. Indeed, it might be said

that the Christian doctrine was enabled to maintain its long prosperity and to become so effective because it was able to conform for so many centuries to a deeper, protoreligious "natural metaphysic."[148]

For Shils this protoreligious "natural metaphysic" was quite simple: it amounted to an innate awareness on the part of all men and women that life is sacred. As Shils subsequently explained in even more detail:

> The chief feature of the protoreligious "natural metaphysic" is the affirmation that life is sacred. It is believed to be sacred not because it is a manifestation of a transcendent creator from whom life comes: It is believed to be sacred because it is life. The idea of sacredness is generated by the primordial experience of being alive, of experiencing the elemental sensation of vitality and the elemental fear of its extinction. Man stands in awe before his own vitality, the vitality of his lineage and of his species. The sense of awe is the attribution and therefore the acknowledgment of sanctity.[149]

From Shils's perspective no supernatural revelation, mediated by organized religion, is ever needed to know that life is sacred. Quite on our own, even though we may at times deny it, human beings intuitively grasp this.[150]

Shils's protoreligious natural metaphysic struck a chord with many other secular sanctity of life advocates. Articles from the same and later periods brim with direct or indirect endorsements. Abraham Kaplan declared that "for us to cope with the problems of the sanctity of life it is not necessary . . . to settle any questions of the relation between religious doctrine and moral practice." To the contrary, he stated, "I believe that we can all agree on the basic principle . . . that life is sanctified because for us, the living, it is the locus of all value." Kaplan added: "If life is not sacred, nothing else could be."[151] Significantly, Kaplan's view of human life as the "locus of all value" was not only in keeping with Shils but also with the teachings of the sage of Königsberg, Immanuel Kant.

Comparable sentiments about a natural metaphysic underlying the sanctity of life were echoed by others, including Bernard Nathanson, who remarked that the sanctity of life "is not a theological but a secular concept, which should be perfectly acceptable to my fellow atheists."[152] In an article entitled "Death with Dignity and Sanctity of Life," Leon Kass similarly claimed that biblical texts merely point to more fundamental humanist truth when the subject turns to the sanctity of life.[153] As Kass explained, "whatever [sacredness is, various parties, religious and nonreligious, agree that it] inheres in life itself, and that life, *by its very being*, calls forth an appropriate human response, whether of veneration or restraint."[154] Although he was not entirely committal about his own views, William K. Frankena also seemed disposed to the notion of sanctity of life as a "natural metaphysic."[155]

EDUCATING AND NEGOTIATING FOR RESPECT

However popular in some quarters, the notion of a natural metaphysic was far from universally upheld. Among the secularists Daniel Callahan displayed the most ambivalence about claims that a natural metaphysic underlay the sanctity of life. Although at moments he seemed tempted to believe in such a natural metaphysic and was largely sympathetic towards those who did, he could not close his eyes to evidence that suggested something quite contrary.

At one point, Callahan observed that "on the basis of this principle, moral rules have been framed, human rights claimed and defended, and cultural, political, and social priorities established."[156] Still, Callahan noted, any "natural" commitment to sanctity of life did not seem to run very deep:

> All societies and all nations, so far as I know, pay lip service to the need to respect life; yet that just doesn't seem to stop the killing, the wars, and all the immoralities which violate human dignity. What is lacking seems to be a thoroughly deep-seated rational and emotional repugnance in the face of a temptation to violate life. National, private, and scientific "interests" have a way of washing principles away or enabling us to rationalize their meaning in a way favorable to our [personal] interests.[157]

If such ambivalence about the sanctity of life as a natural metaphysic distinguished him from his cohorts, Callahan's residual optimism about the human condition nevertheless narrowed the gap which might have separated him from them. Callahan was personally convinced that the sanctity of life deserved to be upheld on the basis of an intercommunal consensus. "To be sure," he admitted, the sanctity of life "principle is vague in its wording, erratically affirmed in practice, and open to innumerable differences in interpretation." All the same, the sanctity of life concept possessed a "deep cultural resonance" for the religious and the nonreligious alike, giving it a "continuing utility, at least as a point of departure."[158]

For Callahan both education and negotiation were key in rallying all sides to the rational consensus necessary to uphold and sustain the sanctity of life.[159] Tolerant and pragmatic, Callahan was not averse to cooperating with those who believed that sanctity of life was heteronomously ordained by God. He honestly believed that through discussion common ground could be found with nearly anyone.[160]

Although himself a true believer in the sanctity of life, Callahan retained sufficient objectivity and insight to appreciate the possible incongruity of trying to establish on a consensual basis what he wanted to see respected as an absolute taboo—or something akin to that. Yet he quite ably justified this incongruity as a mere paradox:

> By and large, for the sake of achieving a moral consensus, our rules [about sanctity of life] should be as clear as possible. This is particularly important when one person puts his body or life in the hands of another—clarity and commonly binding consensus help provide the basis for trust and security. Our rules should also be capable of change if circumstances or changing moral evaluations point toward the need for change. At the same time, I think it imperative to avoid any theory of rules which would preclude human beings from establishing absolute, unbreakable rules, at least absolute for a time and under cer-

tain specified social conditions. "Absolute taboos, with their underlying mystique about life," Joseph Fletcher has written, "make a farce
of human freedom. All such taboos cut the ground out from under
morality because nothing we do lies in the moral order if it is not
humanly chosen." One can see what Professor Fletcher is driving at
here, but some qualifications are in order. All "taboos," for one thing,
need not spring from a "mystique about life." They could be the result
of very rational decisions.[161]

Under the rubric of a general sanctity of life principle, Callahan appears to contemplate
a series of specific interrelated taboos, which would include, for instance, a ban on
genocide.[162] Essentially, Callahan seems to be expressing an oxymoronic hope for
the best of all worlds—an absolute yet flexible commitment against the violation
of human life that will engender wide and deep loyalty. Despite Joseph Fletcher's
cited distaste for absolute rules, Callahan personally viewed the prospect of taboos
against the violation of human life as "very wise," provided they represented in each
case a "human choice" that was "reasonable, sensitive and imaginative."[163]

MORAL ABSOLUTISM

As it turned out, secular ethicists for the sanctity of life who put their trust in a natural metaphysic or who had hopes of winning a consensus for their cause had some
winning over to do within their own ranks. On some very critical issues, going well
beyond the immediate debate over whether the sanctity of life was a natural metaphysic or a strictly consensual artifact, not even secular advocates of sanctity of life
could forge ready or abiding agreement.

For instance, if the sanctity of life principle is absolute or at least firm, how absolute
is absolute or how firm is firm? Also problematical for any agreement among secular sanctity of life advocates was the unresolved question of what aspect or dimension of human existence should be held sacred or inviolable. In other words, was
the preservation of human bodily life the supreme value that should be affirmed?
Or, alternatively, was it the human being in his or her psychosocial capacities that
mattered most? Furthermore, which was more important or sacred in a conflict-of-
values situation—the life of a human individual, the well-being of a community, or
the long-term survival of the entire human species?

Secular humanist Baruch Brody was among those who took what can be called
an absolute sanctity of life or "right to life" position, especially on abortion.
Stressing the responsibilities we have for each other, Brody argued that there are very
limited conditions under which we can morally take the life of another human
being.[164] Asserting his own conviction that there might be occasions when a political majority should be prevented from following its own conscience and exercising its guaranteed rights,[165] Brody identified abortion as one of these "occasions."

Acknowledging his differences with other secular humanists, including Daniel
Callahan, Glanville Williams, and Roger Werthheimer, Brody endorsed an "essen-
tialist" perspective for determining the status of embryonic life.[166] Furthermore, arguing for the importance of correlative criteria for the start and end of life, Brody

proposed that the fetus with a basically functioning brain at two to twelve weeks after conception had the "essential" features to be deemed a human being with all the attendant sacred status and right to life.[167]

These assertions proved to be the prelude to an adamant condemnation of abortion, even in instances where a continuing pregnancy was life-threatening for the mother.[168] In his own defense of the absolute inviolability of life, Brody suggested that feminist libertarianism, a certain confusion on the part of medical doctors, and the dual problem of global overpopulation and malnutrition were the driving forces behind the act of murderous abortion. Assuming a prophetic tone, Brody warned that the tolerance of abortion—a breach in the general respect for human life—would come to haunt us in untold ways.[169]

PRIMA FACIE ETHIC

While his fellow advocates for a secular sanctity of life principle may have been sympathetic to certain elements in Baruch Brody's right to life perspective, they did not seem inclined to agree with Brody across the board, especially with regard to abortion and the moral rigidity and absolutism that went along with his response. In his presentation at Reed College, for instance, Edward Shils affirmed that individual human life was sacred. But he excluded the human fetus from sanctity.[170] Ethicist Sissela Bok, who can hardly be called a feminist libertarian, also appeared to take a position at odds with Brody. In her judgment, the fetus in the early stages of gestation is simply not a human person.[171]

Contemporaneously, Leon Kass, another secular sanctity of life advocate, criticized an inflated rights rhetoric. Though his immediate objective was to counter claims about a "right to die," his argument inevitably brushed against Brody's claim about an absolute right to life:

> No one bothers very much about where these putative rights come from or what makes them right, and simple reflection will show that many of them are incoherent. . . . Is not this intransigent language of rights and duties unsuitable for finding the best course of action, in these terribly ambiguous and weighty matters? We must try to become more thoughtful about the terms we use and the questions we pose.[172]

Setting aside rights talk for himself, Kass proceeded to elucidate a qualified sanctity of life stance that would allow individuals to make decisions within certain moral limits about their continued life. Specifically, Kass acknowledged a distinction between killing and letting die based upon particular intentions and deeds, causes and results, goals and outcomes.[173] Though he opposed active euthanasia, Kass favored and supported the morality of a decision to let die. Death with dignity for Kass, however, was never a matter of ending a life made unseemly by illness or disability. Instead, true to a Stoic sensibility, Kass viewed "death with dignity, in its most important sense, [as] a dignified attitude and virtuous conduct in the face of death."[174]

Other secular humanists also took issue with an absolute sanctity of life standard. Writing for the Law Reform Commission of Canada, Edward Keyserlingk earnestly argued that public policy and the law should continue to affirm the absolute value, equality, and sanctity of human life. Nevertheless, he proceeded to reject biological vitalism, whereby the continuation of biological life is treated as an end in itself.[175] He also confessed difficulties with any absolute adherence to "Kant's thesis that persons are ends in themselves, not means."[176] Death, Keyserlingk asserted, should not always be resisted: preserving life can actually dishonor the sanctity of life.[177] For Keyserlingk the sanctity of life principle correctly functioned to impose the burden of proof in life and death situations on those who would opt for a cessation of medical treatment and life support.[178]

Keyserlingk denied any conflict between "sanctity of life" and "quality of life" positions. Still, Keyserlingk was not ambiguous about his own stance: as he saw it, the sanctity of human life referred to the absolute value of human personhood. Where a personal life is no longer possible, he insisted, human bodily life does not need to be preserved.[179]

Specifically, Keyserlingk quoted H. Tristram Engelhardt, who has contended that "there is no unambiguous sense of being simply 'pro-life'—one must decide what sort of life one wishes to defend."[180] Keyserlingk admitted that a considerable elasticity was present in his own idea of sacred personhood. Yet this elasticity did not seem to disturb him.[181] Later, Keyserlingk went on to propose elements that he felt should be included in any overall sanctity of life principle defending and supporting the well-being of the human person—namely, measures to enhance human species survival, freedom from external hindrance to propagation, and no unjust taking of individual human life.[182]

Articulating a similarly qualified approach to the sanctity of life, philosopher William K. Frankena was nevertheless more precise in describing areas of agreement and disagreement in the debate about life's sacredness. Almost immediately, Frankena distinguished between a comprehensive and a noncomprehensive respect for life,[183] subsequently indicating his own support for the latter.

According to Frankena's schema, human bodily life is to be respected because it is the seat of consciousness.[184] The sanctity of life principle is important because it establishes the presumption that it is wrong to end human life.[185] At the same time, it is only a prima facie wrong which can be rebutted by conflicting claims arising from a given situation.[186] Applying his distinction between a prima facie wrong and an absolute wrong to abortion, Frankena wrote:

> While I am not sure that or when a fetus is a human being or a person, I myself find it hard to deny that, since it is a nascent human being and person, it is prima facie wrong intentionally to destroy it or let it die. I doubt, however, that this is true simply because the fetus is alive. But it seems clear to me that it is, at most, only prima facie and not absolutely wrong, though I do not believe that its prima facie wrongness is as easily outweighed or overridden as many recent defenders of abortion do.[187]

For Frankena, human life is intrinsically sacred because, unlike other forms of life, we are endowed by nature with rational consciousness. The absence of such consciousness in a specific instance would call into question human sacredness. As Frankena consequently stated:

> This means, as I see it, that bodily life, even in the case of a human being, does not have sanctity *as such*, but only qua [sic] being a seat for the realization of something more. In this sense, respect for human life—for what I called quantity of bodily life—turns out to be based on concern about the quality of such life after all. It also follows, of course, that our respect for human bodily life is or should be indirect or derivative, rather than direct or basic. . . . It is not necessarily wrong morally, perhaps not even prima facie wrong, to end or let end the life of a person who has become hopelessly comatose, at least if it is done under certain conditions.[188]

Frankena takes specific issue here with a comprehensive sanctity of life position that would prevent us from saying no to any human life.[189] As Frankena pointedly summed up: "In short, I see no sanctity in mere life, in life that is not at least capable of conscious aversion, desire, enjoyment, fear, relief, pain, satisfaction, or suffering—and rather little in life that is capable of these but incapable of thought, purpose, hope, regret, and the like."[190]

For all his concern about elaborating an absolute sanctity of life principle and specific taboos to support it, Daniel Callahan also proved to be a subscriber to a qualified or noncomprehensive ethic. Generally speaking, he suggested, individual human life is sacred but there are situations where it might be secondary to a still higher good. Callahan explained:

> As suggested, the claim of the individual's "right to life" as the pre-eminent rule seems well-founded. Yet it is clearly conceivable that this right, and the attendant rules protecting it, could come into question if the survival of a whole people or nation were in danger from over-population, a scarcity of medical facilities, or in time of war.[191]

As Callahan viewed matters, the right to life of the individual could be superseded by the needs of the community in extreme or especially compelling situations. For him there was no contradiction here: in certain dire circumstances the latter serves the sanctity of life as much, if not more, than the former.

At the same time there is other evidence that Callahan's ultimate stance on the sanctity of life was even less rigid and far more qualified than his allowance for a rebuttable "right to life" might alone suggest. Citing the philosophical influences of Henry Aiken, Callahan proposed that sanctity of life principle should be "procedural, rather than substantive in aim." In other words, the whole sanctity of life principle should be kept very general, creating space and opportunity for subjective judgment. As Callahan expounded further:

The point about the phrase "the sanctity of life" is that it is trying to say the most that can be said about the value of life. It signifies a whole cluster of final meanings, each of which is related to and dependent upon the other to give it sense and significance. In a very real way, then, the principle of the sanctity of life is indeterminate and vague, but not meaningless for all that. It says life is to be affirmed, cherished, and respected, and as a principle, it can be defined in terms of a large range of words which themselves have meaning, yet without this process of definition overdefining the principle (which would make it too determinate to be useful as an ethical principle). When used in its primary function of judging lower level rules, the principle is employed to interrogate the rules: do the rules foster the respect due human life? Do the rules lead people to protect human life? Do the rules exemplify the awe we ought to feel in the presence of human life? If the answer is "no," then we would be justified in rejecting, modifying or changing the rules.[192]

Here Callahan outlines a process for the deployment of the sanctity of life principle that relies on both rational and intuitive discernment.

At first Callahan's approach seems eminently attractive. The flexibility built into a sanctity of life ethic that is procedural rather than substantive is appealing in that it avoids a dogmatic deontological ethics. But closer scrutiny raises doubts whether Callahan's approach overcomes an elemental drawback which he both identifies and admits. Earlier in his work, Callahan conceded:

A further, and critical, problem arises. Even if there is agreement that "the sanctity of human life" is worth affirming, indeed socially imperative to affirm, it appears to be singularly abstract and ambiguous as a principle. If it is possible to derive from this principle a huge variety of often divergent moral rules and duties, simply because it is open to human beings to interpret the principle in different ways, and, if, in practice, the widespread affirmation of the principle does not lead to any unified consensus on what it implies, and if each of the important words in the principle—"sanctity," "human," and "life"—is itself open to different and divergent definitions—then of what conceivable value is such a principle? Are we not perhaps deluding ourselves in trying to hold on to the principle, or in thinking that it can serve as a basis for consensus? Doesn't it just raise more problems than it solves?[193]

However engaging, Callahan's advocacy of the sanctity of life as a procedural ethic never does effectively surmount or overcome the "critical problem" of the principle's abstraction and ambiguity. Thus, Callahan's original questions remain apt. As a consequence, the sanctity of life, though widely affirmed by many secularists, continues to be open to divergent understandings that render it fundamentally incoherent and ultimately meaningless.

VIABILITY OF A SECULAR SANCTITY OF LIFE PRINCIPLE

It is tempting to think that some way might yet be found to lift a secular sanctity of life principle from the metaphysical mire into which it has sunk. The sheer optimism of secular liberals is proverbial: their commitment to the sanctity of life principle has been tenacious. Nevertheless, the real stumbling block or barrier to any universal acceptance of a secular sanctity of life principle may be the very modern society that it is meant to help. The whole idea of being bound by anything natural or even consensual seems to go against the present ideological grain of our society at large. As Daniel Callahan personally noted in addressing the abortion controversy:

> Alexis de Tocqueville's notion of civic republicanism—of a free people using their individual liberty to seek their common human end and destiny—seems merely quaint in a society that appears to believe that only individuals, not the community as a whole, can find or judge truth and goodness. A society [such as our own, today, which is] prone to say that right and the good must be private, not public, discoveries, is ill prepared to engage in common quests.[194]

Lacking a commitment to "common quests," modern secular society stands without the spiritual wherewithal to forge and sustain a consistent public ethic with regard to the sanctity of life.

There is a profound irony in this situation. The same corrosive forces of modernism that long ago began eating away at the moral hegemony of the Christian churches and all heteronomous religious institutions are now undercutting popular commitment to the secular morality that was offered as an alternative. The very Enlightenment which once made the sanctity of life seem "natural" and gave rise to a confidence that a truly moral society was rationally achievable without a defined religious cultus or a profoundly bonded community now appears to be bringing the curtain down on itself.

Although not necessarily appreciative or aware of all the historical dynamics and philosophical nuances involved, the controversial Helga Kuhse, who, along with animal rights activist Peter Singer, objects to the "speciesism" of humanists, is quite right in her critique of what fellow secularists have propounded as a defense against a utilitarian devaluation of human life: the secular sanctity of life doctrine has become highly "implausible" and improbable for our time.[195] Whether as a natural metaphysic or a consensual principle, a secular sanctity of life ethic can no longer be credibly argued or authoritatively maintained.

Perhaps not so surprising, Daniel Callahan, one of the more forceful advocates of a secular sanctity of life perspective, and still prominent and prolific as a scholar and writer in the field of secular ethics, has more recently qualified, if not moved beyond, his earlier embrace of human sanctity. Marked by an increasingly communitarian emphasis at odds with the highly individualizing focus of most sanctity of life talk, Callahan's current body of work stresses our collective need to recognize the inherent limits and finitude of human life.[196]

PART 2

What Makes Respect for Life a Viable Alternative?

6

The Recent Politics of Sanctity

From his prison cell in Nazi Germany during the 1940s, the German theologian and ethicist Dietrich Bonhoeffer wrote cryptically and prophetically about a "world . . . come of age." He foresaw a postwar era in which men and women would live autonomously without any sense of the transcendent God traditionally contemplated by Christianity.[1] How Bonhoeffer felt about this prospect and would have responded had he been spared execution for his role in a plot to assassinate Adolf Hitler is open to conjecture.[2] What is clearer, however, is the response made by many other theologians of his time.

Even before Hitler cast his long shadow upon world history, many Christian thinkers and church leaders were already disposed to adapt to the secular age and to channel in varying degrees their own religious impulses in defense of what seemed worthy within secular culture and society. As the horrors of what Hitler had wrought became more obvious and conspicuous, everything was speeded up. In a world where bureaucracy, technology, nationalism, and totalitarianism had combined to produce brutal warfare, concentration camps, and genocide, the lingering ambiguity of traditional Christian teachings on the value of temporal human life seemed grossly inadequate. Consequently, mainstream Christian thinkers and church leaders had fewer reservations about extending the rapprochement between Christianity and secular culture, begun earlier by more liberal Christians, to join with secular and religious humanists in a more direct and positive affirmation of human life.[3]

Further dramatic impetus for this rapprochement came a generation or more later as the United States embroiled itself in a Southeast Asian war. Media exposure of war-related atrocities, symbolized by the My Lai massacre, called into question the nation's moral integrity as well as its fundamental respect for human life. Some of the mainstream Christian churches felt compelled to respond critically.

One of the hallmarks of Western liberalism and humanism as they persisted in the twentieth century was their basic interest in protecting the individual from the threat of oppression and undue control by large institutions, especially the state. More and more, mainstream Christianity, both Protestant and Roman Catholic, from mid-century on came to subscribe to this specific cultural concern as well, increasingly, making clear its own willingness to help defend the individual. Accordingly, many Christian leaders embraced the secular humanistic preoccupation with individually centered human rights, a preoccupation that had already begun to dominate most moral discourse in the "public square," both in the United States and abroad. Moreover, seeking to make a contribution that would enhance the respect, credibility, and relevance of the theological enterprise in secular society, the theological leaders of mainstream Christianity soon mustered all the resources they could— namely, imago Dei doctrine, the Christian natural law tradition, and the notion of human life as a divine loan or gift—to add mystique and greater metaphysical depth to the secular sacralization of the individual. Out of these efforts emerged some new, very systematic statements of Christian anthropology.

Unfortunately, what no one, Christian or secularist, could or did foresee was the vulnerability of any Christian sanctity of life doctrine to confusion and outright corruption. Indeed, what seemed at the outset like such a straightforward Christian affirmation proved to be susceptible to multiple, mutually exclusive, and divisive interpretations.

By the last decades of the twentieth century, for instance, long-submerged conflicts between a sanctity of life perspective and older Christian teachings would gradually become more obvious, especially as interest in the actual opinions of the laity increased. In fact, polling of the Christian laity indicated that even when lay churchgoers professed a belief in the sanctity of life, they were not, issue to issue, consistently and comprehensively pro-life.

Far more serious and troubling, however, was the extent to which the sanctity of life doctrine proved susceptible to manipulation by conservative elements in the Christian churches, which had their own political and social agenda. Increasingly reduced to a crude human vitalism or a sacralization of nature, Christian sanctity of life doctrine came to be deployed by these conservative elements as a cudgel in their battle against aspects of liberal secular culture that they found noxious. The Roman Catholic hierarchy, for example, actually appropriated sanctity of life doctrine to help relegitimate its social teachings on gender roles and human sexuality. So too in their own way did some conservative Protestants.

Attempts have since been made to reestablish a Christian sanctity of life doctrine on a more positive and less reactionary basis and to enhance its overall persuasiveness by ensuring that it is as consistent and encompassing as possible. Nonetheless, as a Christian principle, sanctity of life remains highly questionable and controversial. Inconsistently upheld by the Christian churches and individual church members, the notion that human life is sacred appears neither coherent nor sustainable as a Christian teaching.

CHRISTIAN ACCOMMODATION TO HUMANISM

Christianity has claimed ancient origins for a sanctity of life doctrine and secular sources have reinforced this claim. In reality, however, the Christian churches did not really embrace sanctity of life doctrine until the late nineteenth and early twentieth centuries, when humanist ideals, shaping the wider culture, began to penetrate and overtake church life.

From the nineteenth century on, the challenge posed by humanism to the Christian churches was increasingly strong. Rejecting any profound concept of sin and human depravity and filled with positive visions of the future, humanism offered an attractive ideology. In many cases, humanism, combining an idealistic rhetoric with a pragmatic, can-do kind of compassion for the human race, was actually able to seize the high moral ground. The Christian churches, still suffused with otherworldly concerns, had to compete and cope.

The Christian churches did cope or respond in a variety of ways. One response was to ignore humanism as the *Zeitgeist* of the age, running the risk of appearing old-fashioned and anachronistic. A second response was to accommodate humanism by adopting some of its ideas, language, and popular organizational forms. A third response was far more drastic—a remaking or reformation of the entire church, theologically and organizationally, on a more enlightened, rational footing.[4]

Not infrequently, the Christian churches vacillated between these three responses on an issue-by-issue basis. In the end, however, no church was left untouched by the cultural ascendancy of humanism. Indeed, in differing measures and degrees most of the Christian churches began to inexorably shift from a nearly exclusive otherworldly focus to a this-worldly attentiveness, suggesting at least a partial reformation along humanist lines and an embrace of liberal culture.

As eighteenth-century Enlightenment ideals, embodied by humanism, overtook the Christian churches during the nineteenth and twentieth centuries, their estimate of human nature definitely became more sanguine. On the fringes of Protestantism, Christian Personalism emerged as a theological outlook, holding out the individual human person as sacred in God's sight. Although the outlook was never widely embraced, the Christian churches—liberal, mainstream, and conservative—generally became more committed to the amelioration of material conditions adversely affecting human life.[5]

In the United States, for instance, those Protestant churches most susceptible to humanism and the "modernist impulse" were fast attracted to the nineteenth-century abolitionist cause and, later, to the early-twentieth-century Social Gospel movement.[6] Though the Roman Catholic Church in Europe and America expressed considerable hostility to the modernist critique of its own theological doctrine and autarchic leadership, Pope Leo XIII was very much attuned to the *Zeitgeist* of the age with his promulgation of an 1891 encyclical, *Rerum Novarum*, affirming the rights of working men and women.[7]

Meanwhile, the Christian churches' attitudes towards other potential human rights issues also began to show change and evolution. Although the Roman Catholic and Protestant churches had been silent on the subject for the greater part of the nineteenth century, they began to criticize and oppose abortion as public opinion, shaped by a developing medical profession, increasingly inveighed against it. Emblematic of this change, the Roman Catholic Church in 1895 and 1897 issued several pronouncements that denounced abortion more strongly than ever before.[8]

All this accommodation to the humanism of the times may have ostensibly made the Christian churches seem more current and relevant. But conformity had its costs. As early as the 1920s, prominent Protestant leader Willard L. Sperry sensed that something important was being lost as the liberal Christian churches acceded to the optimistic anthropologies that were part and parcel of their fresh preoccupation with the rights of men and women. The traditional themes of sin and repentance, he noted, were being forgotten, and the Christian churches were weaker, rather than stronger, for it. Sperry saw this as a betrayal of the churches' heritage. "There is no point," remarked Sperry, "at which modern liberal Protestantism stands in sharper contrast to historic Christianity as a whole than in its indifference to this initial mood of Christian experience."[9]

Implicit in Sperry's critique was a recognition of the shift in emphases within the Christian churches from the spiritual to the material and the otherworldly to the this-worldly. In the ensuing decades of the twentieth century, as Christian belief in the sanctity of temporal life became ascendant, Sperry's critique would continue to gain, rather than lose, validity for Protestant, as well as Roman Catholic, churches.

POPE PIUS XI

It is ironic that even the Christian thinkers most hostile towards liberal thinking proved no less susceptible to its agenda of sacralizing temporal human life. More often than not, these critics, who sought to distinguish their own position from liberalism, actually legitimized the human sacralization process by contributing their own theological justifications for it.

The Roman Catholic Church provides a ready example. In 1931, Pope Pius XI, who was concerned that an "overrated independence of private judgement and that false autonomy of human reason" was undermining respect for the traditional moral teachings of the Roman Catholic Church, set out to reaffirm the procreative function of marriage and family life.[10] He proceeded to issue an encyclical, entitled *Casti Connubii,* which stressed the grave sinfulness of separating human sexuality from procreativity. Any act impeding generativity was a usurpation of God's authority over our bodies.[11]

While none of these assertions were in themselves novel, the language the pontiff used to demand absolute respect for the procreative nature of marriage and family life most certainly was. Marriage and family life were sacred, he argued. So too was the fetal life that emerged as a fruit of the marital relationship. Midway through the encyclical, Pope Pius XI chose to condemn the act of abortion with these words:

> But another very grave crime is to be noted, Venerable Brethren, which regards the taking of the life of the offspring hidden in the mother's womb. Some wish it to be allowed and left to the will of the father or the mother; others say it is unlawful unless there are weighty reasons which they call by the name medical, social, or eugenic "indication." Because this matter falls under the penal laws of the State by which the destruction of the offspring begotten but unborn is forbidden, these people demand that the "indication," which in one form or another

they defend, be recognized as such by the public law and in no way penalized. . . . As to the "medical and therapeutic indication" to which, using their own words, we have made reference, Venerable Brethren, however much we may pity the mother whose health and even life is gravely imperilled in the performance of the duty allotted to her by nature, nevertheless what could ever be a sufficient reason for excusing in any way the direct murder of the innocent? This is precisely what we are dealing with here. Whether inflicted upon the mother or upon the child, it is against the precept of God and the law of nature. "Thou shalt not kill." The life of each is equally sacred, and no one has the power, not even the public authority, to destroy it.[12]

Basically, in the interest of maintaining the procreative function of marriage and keeping the practice of abortion at bay, Pope Pius XI found it expedient to appropriate the sanctity of life rhetoric commonly used by an otherwise detested liberalism. Thus, here for the first time, the Roman Catholic Church identified "innocent" human life as sacred, including in that category fetal or embryonic life. Significantly, no commentator has heretofore been able to cite any earlier, comparable papal statement about the sacredness of human life, whether fetal or already born.

Since Protestantism did not share the Roman Catholic concern for the strictly procreative nature of human sexuality, it was not prone to invoke the sanctity of life on the same occasions. Nevertheless, mainstream and conservative Protestant leaders who otherwise took general exception to liberalism and its worldview still found their own reasons to subscribe to its sacralization of human life—or some variation of it.

Not least among these leaders were Emil Brunner and Karl Barth, two prominent German theologians associated with the Reformed Church during the middle third of the twentieth century. Brunner's commitment to the sanctity of human life was quite conscious, advertent, and explicit. For Barth, however, the endorsement of life's sacredness always remained veiled in a dialectical ambiguity. Despite these different responses, the larger picture was clear: sanctity of life was a liberal idea or notion that conservative and neo-orthodox Protestants, like their Roman Catholic counterparts, found increasingly difficult to resist.

EMIL BRUNNER

One of the hallmarks of Emil Brunner's work as theologian was his reworking of Christian Protestant anthropology as an alternative to liberal culture's emphasis on rational autonomy and radical individualism. Creatively revisiting imago Dei doctrine, which had either been dismissed or downplayed by all Protestant reformers except John Calvin, Brunner emphasized that men and women were made in the image of God. Though he conceded that a "material" part or dimension of this divine image, representing authentic being, had been lost because of a human "revolt" against God and an unwillingness to accept the reality of a creaturely status, Brunner did not regard men and women as beyond hope.[13]

However astray from their authentic being, men and women remained candidates for salvation and sanctification because they still retained the divine image in a "formal" sense and could thus hear the divine call to repentance and respond to it through acceptance of their relational dependence upon God.[14]

Clearly, Brunner's concept of "man in revolt" had a certain affinity with the outlook of Augustine and, perhaps, of Martin Luther. It could thus be counted as having orthodox precedent.[15] Similarly, Brunner could and did argue that a retention of the formal image after a mythic fall was also consonant with biblical and Reformed Church traditions.[16] More novel and controversial, however, was Brunner's further assertion that human life should be treated as sacred.

At first glance, Brunner's theology and anthropology would not seem amenable to sanctity of life claims. Quite unlike his contemporaneous Roman Catholic brethren, Brunner did not believe that the survival of the imago Dei in human beings, which he defended, conferred any intrinsic merit or virtue. Human life, Brunner contended, gains value only from being in relationship with God and participating in I-thou relationships with other human beings as empowered by God.[17] Yet in a move reminiscent of John Calvin in his more humanistically disposed moments, Brunner proffered an alternative basis for pronouncing human life as sacred.

Brunner stressed that life is a gift of God, which we need to honor by sanctifying our lives and dedicating them to God. For Brunner this meant "nothing less than the recognition of our existence as God's property" and our responsibility to "regard it and use it as God's possession."[18]

Brunner did not believe that life should be preserved at all costs—self-preservation was not an "unconditional duty."[19] Still, Brunner quickly counterbalanced this view by saying that "God does not require us to throw ourselves away" but, to the contrary, demands that we, as God's "possession" and "instruments," respect ourselves and have even "a grateful love of ourselves." Brunner added that while it was "always possible to conceive that it may be God's will that we should die," it was "impossible to imagine that God could will us to end our life by our own act."[20] Brunner's statements had potential implications for euthanasia and abortion as well as suicide.

In essence, Brunner was proposing a balancing act.[21] On the one hand, he freely acknowledged that, as those sanctified to God, it was not proper for us to worship life for its own sake. In life or death what was most crucial, according to Brunner, was that we strive to remain faithful to God's direction. On the other hand, Brunner was eager to maintain that the preservation of human life stood as an unequivocal Christian duty which God was not likely to countermand. Human beings, Brunner was saying, needed to cherish life as an "ultimate value" or risk violating what could reasonably be assumed to be God's own sovereign will.[22]

Here Brunner insisted that the "ultimate value" of men and women was not a function of "self-value" or any intrinsic merit on their part. Instead, the "high standing" of humankind was "due to the fact that God has rated us so highly." As Brunner further explained, men and women had reason to be "joyfully and proudly conscious" of their sacred dignity but strictly "with the pride of humility, which knows that we possess this value only as a gift" in the midst of our relationship with God.[23]

Overall, Brunner's "theocentric humanism" proved a peculiar blend indeed. While addressing humanist concerns, most notably the defense of the human person, it tried to remain loyal to an orthodox, God-centered Christian outlook.

Brunner accomplished this mix, however, only by resorting to the same extrinsic-worth account of the sacredness of human life that John Calvin had—and by perhaps misconstruing the "scriptural meaning of the word 'to sanctify'" in a way that similarly led him to view human life as divine property.[24] At the same time, Brunner took the sacralization of human life even further than Calvin: shorn from Brunner's arguments on behalf of the sanctity of life was any trace of Calvin's countervailing and restraining predestination doctrine.

Although Brunner's anthropology may have shown some measure of nuance and balance, it ultimately contributed to increasingly unequivocal arguments in support of the sacredness of life. Basically, the sacralizing tendencies in Brunner's "doctrine of man" proved to be a significant harbinger of the much more radical anthropological claims that were to follow within the Protestant Christian community.

KARL BARTH

During the 1930s, when Emil Brunner was approaching the height of his own success as a theologian, Karl Barth generated a major theological controversy by expressly criticizing Brunner for deviating from Reformation tradition and practice in his restatement of imago Dei doctrine. In an essay boldly entitled "Nein!" Barth rejected Brunner's distinction between a formal and a material image and the attendant anthropological claim that the formal image had survived the Fall. He virtually scolded Brunner for succumbing to something akin to substantialist Roman Catholic "relic doctrine" in which human merit or virtue is held to persist even in the aftermath of the expulsion from the Garden of Eden.[25]

While presenting himself as a true keeper of the faith, however, Barth was not impervious to the cultural pressures of his time. In his own fashion, Barth proved at least partly vulnerable to liberal arguments for the sacredness of human life. Indeed, this man and theologian, who viewed his own work as impeccably grounded in biblical revelation, revealed himself to be very much attuned to his times and susceptible to its expectations and hopes. This eventually prompted Barth to lean, as Brunner apparently had, on the isolated precedent of John Calvin and to make statements about the sanctity or sacredness of life which he thereafter found it necessary to endlessly qualify.[26] Whatever Barth may have actually intended, his qualified and noncomprehensive understanding of life's sanctity, which evolved over the course of his theological career, lent itself, just as Brunner's anthropology did, to some rather positive Christian claims about the absolute sacredness of human life.

Rather surprisingly, Barth's own outlook on the human condition and his Christian response to it were either directly or indirectly influenced by Albert Schweitzer. Barth evidently perceived Schweitzer's naturalistic philosophy as an intellectual challenge—a goad to develop his own respect for life stance.[27]

Some of Barth's initial responses to Schweitzer's philosophy were expressed in lectures on ethics that he delivered in 1928 and 1930. At the beginning of a lecture entitled "The Command of Life," Barth declared that God "wills something from me, he commands me to live." Barth added: "I cannot be told this without understanding that the life of the creature in general is willed by God and is an object of respect."[28] Issued by God to men and women, the command to live was preg-nant with divine expectation.

Subsequently, Barth developed the theme of respect for life as commanded by God. As he did so, Barth made clear that the divine command includes not only respect for our self but also for nonhuman life. Distinguishing his own position from Schweitzer's reverence for life, however, Barth offered some clarifications on what is commanded and what is to be respected in the command of life. Specifically, Barth advised his audience to remember that "my own life is not what is commanded as such but only a component of what is commanded," and, in addition, "the life at issue belongs only secondarily to me but primarily and originally to God, by whose command I have let myself be told how far it is in fact my own life."[29] Barth's pur-pose here was to affirm God's complete sovereignty and to place respect for life in the proper affirmative context. Barth saw the will to live as a "good will [only] inso-far as I will my life in the way that the Creator to whom it belongs would have it."[30] In short, we belong to God. From beginning to end, our lives should serve God.

Barth stressed that respect for life apart from our own existence is also divinely commanded. Here he felt that we could learn and take inspiration from none other than Albert Schweitzer. As Barth admiringly commented:

> His concept of reverence or respect for life expresses very beautifully and carefully what is at issue here. . . . In spite of his fatal mysticism . . . Schweitzer spoke felicitously, not of love, but of respect for life. Respect is in fact what alien life as such demands of us, or rather what is demanded for it by God the Creator. As we exercise our will to live, this life of others must be handled with awe and responsibility: with awe—we might also say piety, or, more deeply and basically, *sympa-thy*—because we know that the divine command can mean life and death at any time not only for our own life but also for all other life; and with *responsibility* because our attitude to this other life, by what we fail to do as well as by what we do, can mean its life or death, and thus represents God's own action towards it, so that, whether we admit it or not, we have to signify and know in some way the crisis of this alien life.[31]

Barth deeply appreciated Schweitzer's awe before nature. He concurred with Schweitzer that all life demanded from us a proper regard.

Nevertheless, true to his own theocentrism, Barth consciously went on to offer a quite different frame of reference in which faithful Christians might properly focus their own awe. Barth's stressed that the entire creation points to the creator and that the locus of our appreciation and veneration should reside there. Indeed, if creation, manifested in either human or nonhuman life, is worthy of our utmost respect or reverence—Barth seemed to use these two terms interchangeably—it is not due to any intrinsic worth or vitality but, rather, because the splendor we behold is God's creation and subject to God's continuing authority.[32]

Significantly, Barth insisted that the command to respect life is not the same as a command to preserve human and nonhuman life.[33] In God's command to respect life, death is not necessarily precluded. According to Barth, there could be situations where death might potentially serve the command to live best. Yet, not unlike Brunner, who issued a similar, even if sterner and more exclusive admonition, Barth warned that we need to be cautious and as certain as possible that it is God commanding death in such cases and not men and women usurping the prerogative that divinity alone should exercise. For Barth this warning was especially pertinent where human life was involved.[34]

Although Barth never spoke explicitly about it, he appeared to suggest that in God's command to live there is always a rebuttable presumption in favor of the preservation of life. He regarded as ethically dubious such acts as war, capital punishment, and killing in self-defense, which Christians of the Middle Ages sanctioned as morally licit.[35] Barth advocated great moral circumspection in any toleration of such actions.

Citing the constraints imposed by the lecture medium, Barth pointedly deferred any extended discussion of abortion and euthanasia in his talks on ethics.[36] But nearly twenty years later, in the aftermath of the Second World War, Barth did return to the topics of abortion, euthanasia, and related issues, in a very public fashion. They became the focus of considerable discussion in a section of his *Church Dogmatics*, entitled, "Freedom for Life."

Between "The Command of Life" from Barth's *Ethics* and "Freedom for Life" from his *Church Dogmatics* there are many affinities—as well as some fascinating changes and additions. Most important, Barth speaks not merely of respect for life as he did in 1928 and 1930 but also of life's sanctity and sacredness.

Right from the outset, Barth was clear in "Freedom for Life" on the basic themes that underlay his anthropology. "God the Creator," he stated, "calls man to Himself and turns him to his fellow-man" and "orders him to honour his own life and that of every other man as a loan, and to secure it against all caprice, in order that it may be used in this service and in preparation for this service."[37] This fresh emphasis upon God's call and human freedom was not necessarily at odds with Barth's stress on divine command in his earlier lecture, "The Command of Life." But it did suggest a slight shift in orientation. Likewise, the notion of life as a divine gift or loan was not new.[38] Yet it was suddenly accorded much wider prominence.

Barth employed the idea of human life as a divine gift or loan to counter the loud claims made on behalf of human autonomy and freedom in the modern era. Barth declared:

> God alone is truly independent. He alone belongs wholly to Himself and lives in and by Himself. Man's creaturely existence as such is not his property; it is a loan. As such it must be held in trust. It is not, therefore, under the control of man. But in the broadest sense it is meant for the service of God.[39]

Because life comes from God and belongs to God, human beings are expected to have appropriate respect for it and to be good stewards.[40] "Indifference, wantonness, arbitrariness or anything else opposed to respect," Barth insisted, "cannot even be considered as a commanded or even a permitted attitude."[41] Where there is a true respect for life, as commanded by God, there is consideration not only for one's own life but the existence of others as well.[42]

Where secularists and some of those who subscribe to natural law and natural religion believe that a "natural metaphysics" prompts a respect or reverence for life, Barth found a divine command at work. In a passage often quoted by sanctity of life advocates, Barth said:

> Those who handle life as a divine loan will above all treat it with respect. Respect is man's astonishment, humility and awe at a fact in which he meets something superior—majesty, dignity, holiness, a mystery which compels him to withdraw and keep his distance, to handle it modestly, circumspectly and carefully. It is the *respicere* of an object in face of which his attitude cannot be left to chance or preference or even clever assessment, but which requires an attitude that is particularly appropriate and authoritatively demanded. This compulsion does not derive from life itself and as such. Life does not itself create this respect. The command of God creates respect for it. When man in faith in God's word and promise realises how God from eternity has maintained and loved him in his little life, and what He has done for him in time, in this knowledge of human life he is faced by a majestic, dignified and holy fact. In human life itself he meets something superior. He is thus summoned to respect because the living God has distinguished it in this way and taken it to Himself.[43]

In the encounter with the divine command in the very midst of life, human beings realize how little they are, how great God is, and how marvelous is the gift of life that comes to them as a loan.

Barth openly criticized all Christian churches who relied on "general religious expressions" and "assertions of non-Christian humanism" to defend or protect human life.[44] He was particularly harsh with regard to past Christian reliance upon non-Christian humanism:

> The assurances of the latter [i.e., non-Christian humanism] that the value of human life rests on a law of nature and reason sound quite well. But on this basis they are extremely insubstantial, and it is clear that nature and reason can always be used to prove something very different from respect for man. They also have the disadvantage that by "human life" they understand either his very one-sided intellectual existence, "the infinite value of the human soul," on the one side, or his equally one-sided material existence and prosperity on the other. They have the further drawback of always being bound up with illusory overestimations of his goods, abilities and achievements which can only prove detrimental to the respect which ought really to be paid. And somewhere there obviously lurks the ambiguity that, although reference is made to man, humanity, the dignity of man, etc., it is not really man himself who is intended but all sorts of things,

ideas, advances and aims which in effect man has only to serve, for which he has only to let himself be used, and for the sake of which he can at any moment be dropped and sacrificed.[45]

Given the unspeakable crimes of Nazism in the years immediately preceding much of the writing of *Church Dogmatics*, Barth's concerns about the susceptibility of natural law arguments to perversion, even when invoked on behalf of respect for life, seem entirely warranted.

In their place, Barth emphasized the testimony provided by the Incarnation. In the birth of Jesus Christ, Barth saw a definitive revelation of God's command "as that of respect for life."[46] For Barth, the Incarnation gave human life "even in the most doubtful form the character of something singular, unique, unrepeatable and irreplaceable."[47] In contrast to the vagaries of natural law, the spirit-body dynamics of the incarnation also established, according to Barth, that human beings are to be respected as an inseparable union of body and mind.[48] By God's command the total human being was to be treated with respect.

Very significantly, in a departure from his *Ethics* lectures of earlier decades, Barth took the unusual step of adopting some of the rhetoric of secular and religious natural law proponents, as well as that of John Calvin, with whom he was not always in agreement.[49] Barth began talking in terms of the sanctity of life:

> All men know, either in an obscure and feeble or perhaps a clear and forceful way, that they are ordained and disposed to respect human life, and this in a far more original form than can be said of the evil readiness to kill. In this respect, too, man has been created good and not evil. At bottom, he knows very well that the life of his fellow-man is sacred and protected against him, and that he ought not to murder. Even if he does kill, and kills arbitrarily, criminally and murderously, whether from hunger for bread or money, from exotic lust or passion, or from revenge or pure delight in killing, he does not do so without at least trying to justify himself by one or other of these motives. The outbreak of the wolf in him does not take place directly, but as he believes the exceptional case has been reached when he may let the wolf howl and then break loose.[50]

From Barth's remarks flow several implications. First of all, Barth's earlier argument with Brunner notwithstanding, all human beings have been created sufficiently good to hear God's command to one extent or another. Not even the Fall or the fact that men and women have the "wolf" in them alters this. Second, the divine command proclaims that human life is sacred. As a result, human life is to be protected. Finally, because men and women know that human life is sacred, they feel automatically compelled to rationalize and justify their own transgressions against it.

Rather curiously, Barth chose to blame the massive violation of the sanctity of life on "legalism." Emphasizing human rebelliousness, Barth argued that men and women opt not to respect and protect life because ecclesiastical authorities are so morally earnest and legally exacting in trying to compel them to do so. Barth's own response, offered as an alternative, was to stress God's benevolence in the midst of the divine command and to emphasize the positive freedom, rather than the constraints, that accompany it:

> This Church knows and has the Word of the free mercy of God which also ascribes and grants freedom to man. It could and can tell and show a humanity which is tormented by life because it thinks it must live it, that it may do so. It could and can give it this testimony of freedom, and thus appeal effectively for the protection of life, inscribing upon its heart and conscience a salutary and resolute No to all and therefore to this particular destruction of human life. Hence it neither could nor can range itself with the Roman Catholic Church and its hard preaching of the Law. It must proclaim its own message in this matter, namely, the Gospel. In so doing, however, it must not underbid the severity of the Roman Catholic No. It must overbid its abstract and negative: "Thou shalt not," by the force of its positive: "Thou mayest," in which, of course, the corresponding: "Thou mayest not," is included, the No having the force not merely of the word of man but of the Word of God.[51]

By focusing attention on the gift of life and the freedom to live, provided by God, Barth hoped that the Protestant churches could avoid the alienating legalism of the Roman Catholic Church.

While his *Church Dogmatics* liberally invoked sanctity rhetoric, Barth simultaneously made clear that he did not regard human life as an absolute good. Reiterating both the tenor and the substance of his earlier *Ethics* lectures, Barth remarked:

> The protection of life required of us is not unlimited nor absolute. . . . [This] does not mean that there exists a standpoint from which a callous negation and destruction of human life may still be regarded as legitimate or even imperative. In no sense, then, does it imply a limitation of the commandment. It simply refers to the fact that the human life has no absolute greatness or supreme value, that it is not a kind of a second god, but that its proper protection must also be guided, limited and defined by the One who commands it, i.e., by the One who is a real God, the supreme good, the Lord of life. It simply means that the required protection of life must take into account its limitation in relation to that which is to be protected. It cannot try to have only one mode, or to express itself only in the assertion, preservation and defence of life.[52]

Such statements by Barth about the relativized value of human life in the divine command of God were not isolated but persistent.[53] For Barth, like John Calvin and Emil Brunner, human life had an extrinsic, rather than intrinsic, sanctity, and a very qualified sanctity at that. Human life, he insisted, was not to be wantonly violated. Yet this was because it belongs to God and has been created for God's ends rather than for manipulative human purposes.

Truer than many modern theologians to traditional Christian teaching, Barth emphasized eternal life as our ultimate prospect. In Barth's schema, this too contributed to the relativization of temporal human life. Not unlike John Calvin, who similarly admitted that the sanctity of life had to be viewed in the limiting context of God's purposes for us in life and death, Barth wrote:

> The commanded respect for life includes an awareness of its limitations. . . . [God] has determined [the human being] for eternal life, for the life which one day will finally be given him. He is leading him through this life to the other. The respect for life commanded by Him cannot then be made by man a rigid principle, an absolute rule to be fulfilled according to rote. . . . It will not consist in an absolute will to live, but in a will to live which by God's decree and command . . . may perhaps in many ways be weakened, broken, relativised and finally destroyed. Being prepared for this, it will move within its appointed limits. . . . Respect for life without this closer definition could be the principle of an idolatry which has nothing whatever to do with Christian obedience.[54]

Here again Barth is saying that respect for life cannot be equated with the mere preservation of life. Given the fact that we are meant for eternal life, both suffering and death might also serve the purposes of the Lord of Life. To cling to life, rather than God, is idolatry.

Barth's emphasis on respect for human life and his qualification that it can never be an absolute good in the midst of our paramount relationship to God constantly resurfaced in his discourse on such increasingly topical issues as health care, abortion, euthanasia, and suicide. At one point, Barth actually warned that in the "frontiers" where such issues get addressed, "respect for life and the will to live can assume in practice very strange and paradoxical forms."[55] Subsequently, Barth used his dialectical style to express the inherent paradoxes. Out of respect for life, for instance, Barth spoke up for health care and decent living conditions.[56] To give into illness without a fight is disobedience to God.[57] Nevertheless, Barth balanced this with a reminder that health for the sake of health alone is wrong and tantamount to idolatry because human life is intended as a "limited possession."[58]

A similar dialectic can be found in Barth's discussion of abortion. On the one hand, he talked about "the wicked violation of the sanctity of life which is always seriously at issue in abortion."[59] He insisted that we must recognize that "every deliberate interruption of pregnancy, whatever the circumstances, is a taking of human life."[60] He bemoaned abortion in his times as a "rising flood of disaster."[61]

On the other hand, Barth expressed profound ambivalence about the worth of legal or civil prohibitions against abortion and regarded abstract moral prohibitions as too "forbidding and sterile."[62] While Christian churches needed to encourage men and women to listen to the divine command, which disposes us to have awe and respect for life, they should, Barth asserted, simultaneously permit abortion if there are compelling physical, mental, economic, or environmental reasons to terminate a pregnancy.[63] In Barth's view, the life of the fetus was not automatically more important than the health, well-being, and survival of the mother.[64]

With great diligence, Barth outlined his criteria for making an appropriate moral and spiritual decision about abortion:

> 1. For all concerned what must be at stake must be life against life, nothing other nor less, if the decision is not to be a wrong decision and the resultant action murder either of the child or the mother. 2. There is always required the most scrupulous calculation and yet also a resolute venture with a conscience which is bound and therefore free. Where such thought as is given is only careless or clouded, and the decision weak and hesitant, sin couches at the door. 3. The calculation and venture must take place before God and in responsibility to Him. Otherwise, how can there possibly be obedience, and how can the content be good and right, even though apparently good human reasons and justification might be found in one direction or another? 4. Since the calculation and venture, the conviction that we are dealing with the exception, are always so dangerous, they surely cannot be executed with the necessary assurance and joy except in faith that God will forgive the elements of human sin involved.[65]

According to Barth, no abortion can be morally licit that is idly pursued or motivated by selfishness and self-centeredness. Abortion is permissible, however, if informed by a larger, more encompassing respect for life and commanded by an intention to serve God's purposes. Moreover, Barth regards abortion pursued for less than appropriate reasons as a forgivable sin.[66]

The powerful conviction about God's forgiveness that informed Barth's discussion of abortion inevitably touched his perspective on euthanasia and suicide as well. In the process of his own moral discernment, based upon respect for life, Barth always retained a clearly pastoral perspective, expressing great sympathy and compassion toward those faced with difficult moral choices.[67] Against the utilitarian reductionism of the age, Barth maintained that the value of a person's life, particularly when he or she is profoundly disabled or incapacitated, is "God's secret."[68] A community, he added, was not strong if it did not carry and care for the weak.[69] With this in mind, Barth expressed some wry reservations about the "humanitarianism" of euthanasia advocates.[70] Ultimately, Barth said, it was up to God alone to make an end to human life. Men and women should help only when there is a clear command from God to do so.[71] Yet he acknowledged that the artificial prolongation of human life that technology was making possible could be a "torturing." Though he could not support the practice of euthanasia as matters then stood, Barth did not rule against the morality of euthanasia for all time. He remarked that in the face of medicine's life extension efforts "we must await further developments in this sphere" before we can grasp the command of God.[72]

Meanwhile, in Barth's view, a person who commits suicide is not to be held condemned, because God can command men and women to take their own lives. Since we are never privileged to know how God may have addressed the person who has committed suicide, Barth refused to preclude the possibility that a particular death by suicide might actually be justifiable for God's purposes. Consequently, in response to suicide, Barth suggested that true humility and compassion were in order: respect for life in the divine command of God is simply not served by being judgmental in such instances.[73]

Barth's thoughtfulness and sensitivity here and throughout his discourse on critical moral issues remain a testimony to the capacity of his theology to accommodate morally complex, ambiguous human situations. Nevertheless, for all the theological dexterity that Barth displayed, a question remains: Were his statements regarding the sanctity of life really central to his perspective—or merely a concession to the age?

The fact that Barth in his post–Second World War writings chose to adopt sanctity of life language when it had so little basis in Christian tradition and added so minimally to Barth's own work—even making it at times seem more inconsistent—suggests one of two things. Either Barth, like John Calvin before him, continued to be more enraptured with the liberal, humanistic thinking of his era than he let on or, alternatively, he simply felt obliged to profess a conviction about the sanctity of life position in order to maintain credibility as a participant in twentieth-century theological dialogue dominated by the ethical and moral constructs of secular culture.[74]

Whatever the case, there can be no doubt that Barth, alongside Brunner, did contribute to the post–Second World War theological climate which eventually saw so many of the nuances and complexities of Christianity's earlier affirmation of human life stripped away. While Barth, as theologian, always remained cautious in his embrace of any sanctity of life claims, his personal invocation of sanctity rhetoric blessed and legitimated its wider use by Christians: the net effect was a reinforcement of the larger sacralization trend within both liberal culture and not so liberal Christian churches.

Thus, in the end, the man so eager to say "Nein!" to the merit of men and women apart from Christ helped foster Christianity's subsequent co-option by a humanistic ideology. This ideology, which had non-Christian origins, increasingly prompted Christians to join in the hubristic inflation of humanity's importance. It also led Christians to constrict or compromise their churches' earlier gospel message about an eternal human destiny transcending the present world.

CHRISTIAN APOCALYPTICISM

In the aftermath of the Second World War, a new generation of Christian theologians and ethicists, heirs to Pope Pius XI, Emil Brunner, and Karl Barth, found themselves in a quandary. While they were intensely sympathetic to liberal society as an alternative to totalitarian fascism or communism, they began to perceive problems with it as well.

Already in the immediate postwar period, photographs of the dead and living from Auschwitz, Dachau, Buchenwald, and other notorious concentration camps were being widely circulated in the West. So too were the images of the bombed-out, rubble-strewn cities of Germany and Central Europe. Yet all this was carnage which, directly or indirectly, could still be blamed on Hitler. Far more horrific and unsettling were the published accounts of the desolation of Hiroshima, describing the literal incineration of a vast civilian population wrought by American atomic blast.[75]

Further compounding the distress of mainstream Christian theologians in the post–Second World War period were such subsequent developments as the Cold War, which divided East and West; the nuclear arms race, diverting and draining national resources for defense; the Vietnam War, in which the destructive potential of liberal democratic societies was further highlighted; and the astonishing development of the double-helix model for DNA, which opened up future possibilities of genetic manipulation. Fear and anxiety among enlightened Christians—a sense of Western civilization standing at the edge of an abyss—became quite palpable in the writings of numerous Christian theologians and prominent Christian laity.[76]

Speaking to the postwar experience which he and others were living, Protestant theologian J. Robert Nelson, for instance, complained that "just when it [seemed] for the first time conceivable that most persons on earth might have a chance for that enhanced life which deserves to be called 'good,' there has come a tidal wave of debasement and destructiveness."[77] Writing retrospectively from the vantage point of the early 1970s, Nelson went on to offer his own rather grim account of what life had become in the secularized and secularizing "Age of Man":

> Often in these days it is said that the primary question is just that of human survival. The threats to the whole, or most, of the human race are neither fictional nor hypothetical. More than three decades after the invention and military use of the deadly atomic bomb—decades of wild proliferation rather than firm control—many scientists and political savants are convinced that we live on borrowed, and possibly brief, time. The apocalyptic vision of a barren, radioactive, peopleless planet haunts the minds of young people especially. It is they, or their children, they fear, who may be the victims of instant cremation or inexorable, agonized death. Albert Einstein's life and achievement have been feted enthusiastically and universally; but the somber warning he gave to the nations in 1945 has gone unheeded.[78]

For Nelson and others who had clearly bought into Western society's promise of a "good life" for all, the prospect of a nuclear doomsday was very disconcerting indeed.

Still, atomic destruction was not the only foreseen peril taking the bloom off the rose of modern Western society and its cornucopic promises. The threat to men and women in their nature as human beings was equally worrisome. Exposure of the experimentation conducted on living human beings in the guise of science under the Nazi German and Imperial Japanese regimes during the Second World War era had already aroused the conscience of the world. Theologians of the latter half of the twentieth century were concerned that the bodily and spiritual integrity of human beings could be just as readily undermined by far more friendly and seemingly innocuous procedures developed by modern medical research.

Outlining a litany of threats to human dignity,[79] the Roman Catholic theologian Bernard Häring observed that in the new age "the wholeness of the human person is in jeopardy."[80] Joan O'Donovan similarly opined that a "pervasive assault on the dignity of human being" was under way, "coming from recent developments in the modern sciences and technologies."[81] In a not dissimilar tenor, Langdon Gilkey, borrowing a phrase from the historian Arnold Toynbee, described the recent decades as a "time of troubles" because of assaults on the human and the humane.[82] Meanwhile, C. S. Lewis, the popular Christian writer, spoke apocalyptically of the "abolition of man through genetic and pharmacological experimentation."[83]

Eventually Pope John Paul II joined the chorus of those offering warnings about the extent to which human life was being undermined through *"scientifically and systematically programmed threats."*[84] In *The Gospel of Life* he announced:

> The twentieth century will have been an era of massive attacks on life, an endless series of wars and a continual taking of innocent human life. False prophets and false teachers have had the greatest success. Aside from intentions, which can be varied and perhaps can seem convincing at times, especially if presented in the name of solidarity, we are in fact faced by an objective "conspiracy against life," involving even international institutions.[85]

Casting aside circumspection, John Paul II charges that an immoral—or amoral—cabal is at work undermining a proper valuation of life.

Not all those wary about the scientific and technological endangerment to human life shared the pope's "paranoid style" in preaching about it.[86] At liberal Protestant ecclesial gatherings in the 1970s and '80s, the words of Pogo, a cartoon character, were often quoted by preachers and became a virtual mantra, if not an outright cliché, for such occasions: "We have met the enemy and he is us."[87]

Frequently, as J. Robert Nelson's earlier statement suggests, the sense of Western civilization in peril was accompanied by acute disappointment and feelings of betrayal. Disenchantment with liberal Western society, however, did not necessarily get the better of all Christian theologians and ethicists. Although their own opinions seemed to carry less clout and influence in a secular culture increasingly apathetic to religion, many struck a prophetic pose and steeled their own resolve to be part of the solution.[88]

While traditional Christian theology had a strong "vertical" focus, and even the theologies of Brunner and Barth had sought to balance both vertical and horizontal concerns, the focus of many postwar Christian theologians was unrepentantly horizontal. "Man's inhumanity to man" became a major preoccupation—an urgent problem in an age when mass destruction was a possibility. It was in this fertile ground, already watered and seeded by Pius XI, Brunner, and Barth, that the Christian sacralization of life truly began to flourish and overtake mainstream and even so-called conservative Christian churches.

THE CRITIQUE OF MODERN LIBERAL SOCIETY

Perhaps too modest and tactful, or perhaps just too afraid of their own further marginalization, the Christian churches in the post–Second World War period initially avoided any kind of direct attack on liberal society. While it must have hurt to see their own influence wane, there was no comprehensive reprimand of liberal culture for its withdrawal from a Christian worldview.[89] When Christian theologians wanted to critique liberal culture for its lack of charity and its real and potential destructiveness, they seemed to cast about looking for the least offensive and most palatable way to do so. Almost invariably, the course they chose led them to out-liberalize liberal society: they ended up criticizing liberal society for the shallowness of its appreciation for the human person and for the dehumanizing forces it had consciously or unconsciously unleashed.[90]

Although Christian theologians were not all of one mind, there was a considerable overlap in their diagnosis of what was going wrong. Some were inclined to blame the callousness of liberal society on the rise of moral relativism. From this perspective, Pope John Paul II was to later condemn the "progressive weakening in individual consciences and in society of the sense of the absolute."[91]

Others looked towards even more systemic issues. Bluntly calling our modern society "sick," Bernard Häring laid much of the responsibility for its disregard for human life at the door of technology and its abuses.[92] Behind the technological impulse, Häring contended, was a lust for power and control.[93] In Häring's view, scientists were being allowed to biologically manipulate men and women in the guise of fostering human freedom and dignity.[94] With a sense of urgency Häring argued that new ethical norms needed to be formulated to prevent abuse of technological power and avert a new holocaust.[95]

Häring was not alone in this critique of science and technology. For instance, French Reformed Church theologian Jacques Ellul penned an exhaustive and withering account of technology as a dehumanizing, out-of-control enterprise. His work offered an almost apocalyptic scenario of a technologically manipulated humankind.[96] Protestant church historian George Hunston Williams, concerned especially about abortion, complained about a possible reversal of a "perceptible moral evolution" after two millennia of civilization "in the name of human dignity and freedom (!) by a technologically potent, and affluent, and strangely harsh generation."[97] Once again, the abuse of technological power was seen as the root cause of liberal society's destructive propensities.

Addressing the precarious condition of Western civilization at a still later juncture, the Roman Catholic liberation theologian José Comblin continued to blame it on the emergence of a new "scientism" which "furnishes a pretext for all manner of manipulation of human creatures: manipulation by the state, by ideologies, by systems of communication, manipulation by medicine and genetics, manipulation by educational systems, and so forth."[98] Ordinarily, Comblin remarked, "scientific information is an enormous help, once it is subordinated to an overall view furnished by other sources." But from the moment that these other sources fail to provide necessary guidance and a scientific mentality prevails, "scientific knowledge of human beings leads to the manipulation and destruction of the human element in them."[99] The problem, as Comblin presented it, is that scientific knowledge, "being objective and external, fails to grasp the basic makeup of the human body" and rejects the idea of an inexpressible, mysterious human soul.[100]

Other commentators, before and after Nelson, Häring, Ellul, and Comblin, also remarked on the nefarious effects of an unchecked technology or technological mentality. Still, they were inclined to look beyond the evils of a technological imperative to explain why they felt Western civilization was going awry, compromising humanity's future prospects.

Protestant David Cairns, who was formulating his own statement on the Christian doctrine of humankind only a few years after the atomic bombing of Hiroshima, blamed the degradation of humankind in the modern era on the combined influences of Marxism, Freudianism, and liberalism.[101] Marxism, he noted, was contemptuous of individual human rights.[102] Freudianism taught that men and women had not fallen but were innately brutal and selfish.[103] Finally, liberalism sometimes exaggerated the power of human reason and gave men and women an inflated sense of self that also led to human degradation. Indeed, for all his sympathy towards liberalism, Cairns believed that its single-minded pursuit of the rational was undermining both the present and future moral and spiritual well-being of Western society. Only a renewed reverence for human life could turn things around.

Others, far more theologically conservative than Cairns, came to share his anxieties about liberalism and its use of rationality. Like Cairns too, they expressed hope that the rapacious excesses of liberal society could be put back into the bottle, like a bad genie, so that human life could, correspondingly, be protected.[104]

While compassion for fellow human beings and concern for their spiritual integrity and material well-being are clearly mandated by the dictates of Christian faith, the attentiveness of mainstream and conservative Christian leaders to the challenge of defending and preserving human life in the face of a misapplied technology and the excesses of instrumental reason was remarkable. Overall, it represented a changed orientation on the part of the Christian churches they served.[105]

Once preoccupied with the eternal destiny of the human soul, these mainstream and conservative Christian churches were revealing an underlying emotional attachment to the ideology of the very liberal culture they were critiquing. Rather than dispense with liberal culture and chalk up the demise of its ideology to the insufficiency and impermanence of all temporal worldviews that are not grounded in an eternal gospel, the Christian churches became engaged in trying to reform and save liberal culture and ideology—or whatever was left of it. In their view, as it subsequently developed, a Christian affirmation of the sanctity of life was the last best hope for doing so.

ALLIANCE WITH SECULAR HUMANISTS

Given the trends of the times, which had long since deposed theology as the "queen of the sciences" and increasingly sidelined churches as a moral influence, Christian theologians by the 1960s were convinced that they could not do effective battle against the self-destructive forces infecting liberal society on their own. Consequently, as a matter of either conscious or unconscious decision, or both, they forged tactical alliances with secularists who, besides sharing their sense of liberal society's perilous condition, were not entirely averse to the insights of a Christian critique. No doubt reflective of this decision to seek out secular partners, there was a simultaneous commitment on the part of theologians to rearticulate Christian concerns using secular concepts in order to render Christian theological and ethical concerns less intimidating and more culture-friendly. Out of these two circumstances emerged the real momentum for a more general and widespread Christian affirmation of the sanctity of life.

Alliance with sympathetic secularists was not always directly or immediately talked about.[106] All the same, it was implicit in the way that Christian theologians conducted their work. Rather emblematically, Bernard Häring noted that Christian humanists and secular humanists were not so far apart, observing that Christian humanists shared with secular humanists a concern for "increasing hominization," or fulfillment of human beings.[107] At heart the attitude that Häring was proposing for secular and Christian humanists alike was Jesus' own: those who are not against us are with us.[108]

Further suggesting their willingness to make common cause with secular humanists, a number of theologians freely adopted humanist themes, motifs, and language to proclaim their version of Christian kerygma or message and to assert the continuing moral and spiritual authority of the offices, institutions, and traditions they represented. Like the apostle Paul, the theologians of the period showed a willingness to become a Jew to the Jews and a Gentile to the Gentiles.[109] It was in this context that rhetoric about the sacredness of life, once a secular liberal province and only marginally a Christian one, except among liberal Christian Personalists, started becoming especially prominent.

The theologians' defense of humanity quickly became loud and sometimes extravagant. As one of them asserted, the inhumane development of contemporary science and technology not only threatened the biological integrity of human life but also represented a contravention of the two-thousand-year culture and history of Western civilized society. To break with the sanctity of human life, he added, was to condone and promote a new and unrelenting wave of barbarism.[110]

By an odd twist, the theologians, who were relatively new to the sanctity of life affirmation, argued that Christianity—or at least a religious viewpoint—was utterly essential in holding back instrumental rationality and a utilitarian ethic. It was also indispensable, they averred, if the sacralization of human life was to be properly maintained and extended.

Conservative Protestant theologian and ethicist Paul Ramsey proclaimed: "Only a being who is a sacredness in the social order can withstand complete dominion by 'society' for the sake of engineering civilizational goals—withstand, in the sense that the engineering of civilizational goals cannot be accomplished without denying the sacredness of the human being."[111] He subsequently went on to argue that the sanctity of life was best anchored as a Christian conviction.

Although identified with the more liberal end of the Protestant spectrum, Langdon Gilkey expressed remarkably similar sentiments. "Only some religious or semi-religious valuation of the person as *intrinsically* of worth, as *inalienably* a subject and not an object; as an 'end in him/herself,'" Gilkey said, "can guard us here from great sin." Moving on to a theological testimonial, Gilkey added that the "symbol of the 'image of God' in *each* human, however apparently worthless to us or even clearly guilty according to our laws and standards, best expresses (for me) this intrinsic, elusive and yet absolutely crucial integrity of the human."[112]

In the tenor of his own remarks, Pope John Paul II concurred with both Ramsey and Gilkey. But over and against those secularists who argued that a closer adherence to a philosophical Kantianism, where human beings are always treated as an "end" and never a "means," would protect men and women from manipulation and abuse, the pope insisted that Kant's largely secular doctrine of the human was not adequate for the challenges posed by the late twentieth century.[113] Among many other problems, Kantianism lacked the ability to command any deep and resonant loyalty that might motivate people to defend human life. Only a religious doctrine of the sacredness of life could accomplish this.

Through all these statements Ramsey, Gilkey, and Pope John Paul II were essentially drawing a line in the sand. In their view, a sanctity of life principle needed to be upheld if humankind was to have a viable future. Meanwhile, only Christianity could ensure that the principle was maintained. Therefore, Christianity had to irrevocably commit itself in support of the sanctity of life. An early advocate of the sanctity of life as a Christian principle expressed the feisty mood that came to prevail among his comrades-in-arms when he declared that Christians had to defend the sacredness of life against all comers.[114]

ENHANCING CHRISTIAN SANCTITY DOCTRINE

In arguing that Christianity was indispensable for the defense of the sanctity of life, theologians simultaneously contended that the "sacredness of man is an integral part of Christian faith."[115] Pope John Paul II was speaking rather typically when he insisted that "the absolute inviolability of innocent human life is a moral truth clearly taught by Sacred Scripture, consistently upheld in the Church's Tradition and consistently proposed by her Magisterium."[116]

Yet no sooner was this latter claim made than a problem arose: apart from the twentieth-century contribution of Pope Pius XI, Emil Brunner, and Karl Barth, the larger record of mainstream and conservative Christianity did not overtly support it. Consequently, those who now endorsed a sanctity of life principle were left to insist that the principle had been implicit within Christianity all along, even as they quickly set about to ground it at last in explicit anthropological doctrine.[117]

One theologian and ethicist, James M. Childs Jr., very frankly alluded to the creative task at hand in developing a Christian anthropology that would truly embrace the sanctity of life. He described the task in terms of a "search for a Christian understanding of man."[118] Childs's own anxiety was that a failure to develop a Christian anthropology which embraced the sanctity of human life would allow other ideologies to prevail—ideologies that were not so inclined to protect human life from manipulation and abuse and which would be only too glad to further shunt Christianity aside. Childs was among those who did not hesitate to propound a Christian anthropology of his own which he felt would suitably defend men and women as sacred beings.

Rather than starting from scratch, most Christian theologians, like Childs, leaned on traditional church doctrines or concepts to elucidate anthropologies affirming the sanctity of human life. Their accounts of the sacredness of human life variously incorporated interpretations of imago Dei doctrine, updated conceptions of natural law, and the notion that human life is a divine gift or loan.

Although Christian sanctity of life advocates did not always see eye-to-eye theologically, they agreed to disagree and go on together. For example, Paul Ramsey expressed complete amenability with regard to the coexistence of different Roman

Catholic and Protestant thinking on imago Dei doctrine and its implications for the sanctity of life they might mutually affirm.[119] In a similar spirit of bonhomie another Protestant writer, Joan O'Donovan, remarked that even though, in her opinion, "the transcendent-relational, Christological-Trinitarian conceptualisation" was "the most theologically adequate and efficacious defence of human being against the contemporary assault on its uniqueness," those advocating an "immanent-structural and rationalist approach to safeguard the invariable, unique humanity of man" had an "impressive claim."[120] In short, when it came to different theoretical approaches maintained by sanctity of life advocates, disagreement was relatively restrained and polite. A mutually shared commitment to the sanctity of life discouraged any undue public emphasis upon differences.

All the same, public politeness and restraint among sanctity of life advocates did not rule out a more quiet partisanship. Over time, the disagreement in outlook among sanctity of life advocates, particularly over imago Dei doctrine, became more pronounced and defined. Based upon divergent understandings about the survival of the imago Dei, a transcendent-relational view of the sanctity of life continued to compete with an immanent-rationalist version for loyalty and support among the Christian churches.

Since its earliest years, the Roman Catholic Church had held that in spite of the Fall, human beings had retained a remnant of God's image—a remnant which, besides being carnal, included human reason. This led Roman Catholics to identify themselves with immanent-rationalist arguments for the sanctity of human life. They simultaneously believed that the surviving remnant enabled all human beings to have access to knowledge available through natural law.

While the same immanent-rationalist position received at least partial support from the theology and anthropology of Protestant Emil Brunner, most other Protestants did not follow suit.[121] Instead, in keeping with Martin Luther, who objected to the possibility that there might be salvific merit in human beings apart from their relationship to Christ, the predominant Protestant position was that God's image had been all but effaced from human beings, who ceased to possess any inherent worth.

Nevertheless, this conviction about the fate of the imago Dei did not prevent Protestants from formulating an alternative basis for affirming the sanctity of life. Taking what they believed to be cues from Karl Barth, who had stressed that God had chosen to continue his relationship with men and women in spite of their fallenness, Protestants gradually elaborated a full-fledged transcendent-relational explanation for human sanctity. Simply put, the fact that a gracious Creator God had maintained a covenantal relationship with men and women through Christ meant for these Protestants that human life needed to be affirmed or respected as inviolable even in the absence of any intrinsic human merit.

PAUL RAMSEY

Next to Karl Barth, the theologian most instrumental in the development of the transcendent-relational account of human sanctity was the conservative Protestant theologian and ethicist Paul Ramsey. Presenting himself as one of Karl Barth's major interpreters, Ramsey converted Barth's "respect for life" statements, plus occasional references to the sacredness of life, into a more fully developed rhetoric about the sanctity of human life that could stand as an alternative approach to the intrinsic or inherent worth model.

Paul Ramsey's first major contribution to a sanctity of life discussion came in 1950 with the publication of his work *Basic Christian Ethics*. However, it did not offer any substantial clue to the role he would subsequently play as an outspoken sanctity of life advocate. In fact, his energy at that point appeared to be directed towards demolishing the very idea that anything about men and women could be called sacred.[122]

Despite this lack of enthusiasm for the notion that human life is sacred, it is clear that by the late 1960s Ramsey had definitely staked out a sanctity of life position. Specifically, Ramsey spoke on behalf of a relational or extrinsic worth account of the sanctity of life in an article on abortion ethics, initially published in the *Dublin Review* for spring 1967.[123]

Shortly before Ramsey's article appeared, *Life* magazine had published a series of rather spectacular embryological photographs by Lennart Nilsson.[124] While Ramsey's article emphasized the public impact of the photographs, he denied being personally affected or swayed by them in his own ethical judgments about in utero life.[125] Nevertheless, the fact that Ramsey chose to address the sanctity of fetal life so promptly after the photographs' publication suggests a certain synchronicity.[126]

In the *Dublin Review* article, Ramsey started out cautiously by saying that "the time of birth would in many ways seem the least likely account of the beginning of life that has dignity and sanctity."[127] But then with greater resolution Ramsey went on to elaborate a fresh doctrine about the sanctity of life that was readily inclusive of fetal life without regard to its developmental limitations:

> The sanctity of life in the first of it, if this has any sacredness, must be an overflow backward from or in anticipation of something—some capability or power—that comes later to be a man's inherent possession. One grasps the religious outlook upon the sanctity of human life only if he sees that this life is asserted to be surrounded by sanctity that need not be in a man; that the most dignity a man ever possesses is a dignity that is alien to him. From this point of view it becomes relatively unimportant to say exactly when among the products of human generation we are dealing with an organism that is human and when we are dealing with organic life that is not yet human (despite all the theological speculations upon this question). A man's dignity is an overflow from God's dealings with him, and not primarily an anticipation of anything he will ever be by himself alone.[128]

In true Protestant fashion, Ramsey proposed that since our merit as human beings comes not from our own ability and accomplishments but only from the fact of our createdness in God and our continuing relationship to God, no distinctions on the basis of moral worth can be made between us and a yet undeveloped fetal life. All of us enjoy merely an "alien dignity" and an "overflow" sanctity from God. Ramsey later reiterated and further elaborated his position:

> The value of human life is ultimately grounded in the value God is placing on it. . . . According to the religious outlooks and "on-looks" that have been traditional to us, man is a sacredness in human biological processes no less than he is a sacredness in the human social or political order. That sacredness is not composed by observable degrees of relative worth. A life's sanctity consists not in its worth to anybody. What life is in and of itself is most clearly to be seen in situations of naked equality of one life with another, and in the situation of congeneric helplessness which is the human condition in the first of life. No one is ever much more than a fellow fetus; and in order not to become confused about life's primary value, it is best not to concentrate on degrees of relative worth we may later acquire.[129]

Both quickly and deftly, Ramsey conjoined his perspective with a very resolute sanctity of life affirmation for all stages of human life, including fetal life. According to Ramsey, a "religious" outlook—not specified in this case as either Christian or Protestant—militated that all who share the same human genus are to be regarded as completely equal in sacredness without any distinction being made between them.

Not surprisingly, Ramsey invoked Karl Barth in support of an extrinsic worth, overflow sanctity perspective. Still, Ramsey, who was eager to claim the seminal twentieth-century theologian as his own mentor, did not always represent Barth faithfully in the latter's dialectical complexity.[130] Indeed, as an interpreter and popularizer, Ramsey may have often imputed more to Barth's words than Barth intended. Recapitulating Barth's perspective on "respect for life," for instance, Ramsey put his own distinctive spin upon it:

> For the greatest Protestant theologian of this generation, the congeneric human situation is that ours is a "fellow humanity" held in trust. Respect for life means that a man should "treat as a loan both the life of all men with his own and his own with that of all men." "Respect" is indeed too pale a term to use for the attitude and response of those who "handle life as a divine loan." Or rather—since Barth uses the term—we must allow the word "respect" to be filled full of the meaning and awe derived from the fact that whenever a man's life is in question the primary affirmation to be made about it is that from all eternity God resolved not even to be God without this particular human life.[131]

For all that Ramsey professes admiration for Barth, he finds Barth's affirmation of human life "too pale." He thus proceeds to supply enhanced meanings for Barth's own words. Most noticeably, Ramsey's presentation of Barth's outlook omits any account of the Swiss theologian's total aversion to legalism in ethics.

While cursorily acknowledging Barth's openness to abortion, Ramsey avoids delving into the many different circumstances under which Barth regarded abortion as morally licit and permissible.[132] Ramsey's representation of Barth's views on euthanasia is also highly tendentious,[133] failing to do justice to Barth's open-mindedness or pastoral pragmatism on the subject. Further slighted is Barth's radical theocentric perspective, which was always concerned with the idolatry implicit in many human moral judgments about euthanasia and other life-and-death issues.

Generally speaking, Ramsey, who was so eager to vindicate and establish a distinctive Protestant account of the sanctity of life, may have succeeded in his task. More than anyone else, he certainly appears to be responsible for the sanctity of life perspective which did come to prevail in some Protestant quarters. Yet Ramsey's success cannot obscure the fact that the foundation for a sanctity of life affirmation, based upon an "alien dignity," an "overflow," or an extrinsic worth perspective, was less firmly and authoritatively anchored within the Protestant Christian tradition than he claimed.

CONTENDING THEORIES WITHIN THE SANCTITY MOVEMENT

Since the late 1960s and early 1970s, Christian sanctity of life doctrines have largely become what Paul Ramsey and others argued they should be—namely, the orthodox or officially endorsed teaching of various Christian churches. Indeed, a number of Christian organizations and bodies in Europe and North America, presenting themselves as the intellectual conscience of the Christian churches, have become increasingly outspoken and defensive about the sacredness of life.

Representative of the new orthodoxy is an editorial statement issued by the *Christian Century*, a respected mainstream periodical. In prompt response to a just-published "how to" manual for suicide penned by Derek Humphry, founder-leader of the Hemlock Society, editor James M. Wall declared:

> [We] must not ignore the religious imperative that human life is the sacred responsibility of both individual and community. . . . The religious community must take the side of the absolute sacredness of life, with a commitment to the principle that the life we are privileged to live is given to us by God. To be responsible stewards of life is not just a suggestion but an obligation. Our eagerness to be sensitive to the special circumstances surrounding terminal illness does not relieve us of our responsibility to God and to the network of relationships we are privileged to share.[134]

The passion with which Wall embraces the sanctity of life as a Christian doctrine has been echoed through a host of other Christian declarations and pronouncements.[135]

Of course, neither the newfound orthodoxy of the sanctity of life concept among Christians nor the shared vehemence with which it has come to be upheld by many of them should mislead anyone into thinking that it is a coherent doctrine or that it enjoys an unambiguous consensus. To the contrary, the success which the sanctity of life concept has enjoyed in the abstract has simply masked divisions among its supporters. In addition to ongoing disagreement on whether human dignity is intrinsic or extrinsic, as related to the imago Dei, sanctity of life supporters within the Christian churches do not see eye-to-eye on the circumstances under which human life is to be held sacred.

Beginning in the nineteenth century, Christian Personalists contended that human personhood was sacred and inviolable. In this tradition the eminent Anglican prelate William Temple was led, midway through the twentieth century, to affirm the "sanctity of personality" even as he refused to deem sacred mere biological life for humans.[136] More recently, contemporary Christian Personalists have affirmed that it is only human life with a relational capacity that should be defended as inviolable.[137]

Other sanctity of life advocates have insisted that any biological life with a full complement of human chromosomes is to be held a human person and regarded as sacred. Subscribing to a traducianist perspective, for instance, Pope John Paul II and Protestant theologian Paul Ramsey have argued that a fetus is a "person" from its conception because, genetically speaking, it contains the "germ" of everything he or she will need to develop into a mature and maturing human being.[138] Likewise, at the other end of life, a brain-disabled individual who lacks any relational capacity retains in their view full personhood because he or she continues to contain the genetic essence of what makes us human.[139]

In the midst of all the debates, no one has articulated the competing views on the sanctity of life more succinctly than the conservative Christian ethicist Robert Wennberg. Although he has his own biases, Wennberg objectively outlines three completely distinct "right to life" theories or outlooks:

> These theories might be labeled, respectively, the *actuality principle*, the *potentiality principle*, and the *species principle*. And if we were to stipulate that a *person* is an individual with a developed capacity for self-reflective intelligence (admittedly a narrow construal of the term), then we can state the three principles in the following way: (1) The actuality principle: only persons have a right to life. (2) The potentiality principle: both potential and actual persons have a right to life. (3) The species principle: all members of the human species have a right to life, whether or not there is a potential for personhood.[140]

In Wennberg's analysis, the actual presence of a self-reflective intelligence, a real or immediate potential for such self-reflective intelligence, and mere species membership are alternative criteria for determining whether human life is to be protected as sacred. Needless to say, the gap between these competing "principles" can be huge.[141]

Wennberg does not pull any punches. As a personal opponent of abortion, he rejects the actuality principle. He also takes issue with the potentiality principle, which he finds too susceptible to different interpretations. As Wennberg candidly observes, "Should we ultimately convince ourselves of a gradualist or developmental understanding of the right to life (and it is tempting), it will become much more difficult to be a crusader on the abortion issue."[142] Under the circumstances, Wennberg contends that only the species principle provides a solid basis for a true sanctity of life affirmation.

Wennberg's advocacy of the species principle in order to hold back abortion underscores the partisanship that is part and parcel of the sanctity of life movement. It also offers a glimpse of the way in which passionate convictions about particular issues may actually be energizing, if not driving, the entire sanctity of life controversy.

SANCTITY AS A NATURAL LAW AND RIGHT

For sanctity of life advocates of somewhat conservative stripe the importance of prevailing in the public square with their own ideas has loomed large. Even as these advocates from the late 1970s and onward sought to marshal the entire Christian community into their own ranks by arguing that the sanctity of life is axiomatic to Christian thought, they remained profoundly attuned to both the possibility and the necessity of a wider audience in the encompassing secular culture. Indeed, there seemed to be a conviction, especially among those subscribing to the species or potentiality principles, that the sanctity of life, as an overarching concept, would rise or fall according to its secular acceptance. There was little or no confidence that it could be widely and effectively maintained in the long run as a Christian ethic alone.

Consequently, the most forceful sanctity of life advocates, those who favored the "potentiality principle," conservatively interpreted, or the "species principle" in toto, embarked upon the challenge of persuading the enveloping secular culture as to the merit and truth of their particular positions. To this end, attempts were made to frame the rationale for the sanctity of life principle so as to make it convincing to those thoroughly secularized or those on the margin between a purely secular point of view and a religious or quasi-religious outlook. One of the rationales invoked was natural law.

Clearly, natural law and natural rights possess an extensive historical basis within Christianity. Both are notions which Christianity early borrowed from ancient Stoicism and incorporated into its own systems of thought. Natural law, discerned by the faculty of reason, was treated as a supplement to biblical law and revelation.[143] Even in the Protestant churches natural law and natural rights continued to have a respected place, albeit more limited and truncated than in the Roman Catholic Church.[144]

Still, Christianity, Roman Catholic or Protestant, never accorded natural law or natural rights the same measure of moral authority and prestige that liberalism so freely did as it emerged from the European Enlightenment.[145] It was only as the Christian churches' support for the sanctity of life gained momentum that their commitment to natural law and natural rights theory also deepened. By expressing their sanctity of life convictions in terms of natural law and natural rights, which were respected liberal concepts, Roman Catholics and Protestants hoped to disarm their potential critics and communicate more effectively with a wider liberal culture that did not necessarily subscribe to a species principle or a conservative potentiality principle as a criterion for determining inviolability.[146]

Unfortunately, the Christian churches' invocation of natural law and natural rights was both manipulative and dissembling. Marching forward with their own idiosyncratic and authoritarian agenda, alongside their avowed commitment to uphold human life, the Christian churches read into natural law whatever served their own purposes. In the process they unwittingly exposed natural law as other than "natural," inherent, or universal.

ROMAN CATHOLICISM AND NATURAL LAW

As early as the 1950s, Glanville Williams noted that natural rights doctrine was increasingly being used as the theoretical basis for the Roman Catholic Church's opposition to abortion.[147] Other commentators later remarked upon the same thing, regarding it as a triumph of liberal values within an otherwise anti-liberal citadel. Although the larger significance of what was happening was not fully appreciated at the time, the strengthened focus on natural law and natural rights meant that the Roman Catholic Church's more traditional theocentric emphasis was being eclipsed.[148]

Rather than abating, the emphasis upon natural law and natural rights persisted and deepened in the 1960s and '70s, especially as support for the sanctity of life became pandemic within the Roman Catholic hierarchy. It reached a crescendo in the Roman Catholic Church during the tenure of the present pontiff, John Paul II, who proceeded to make every effort to formally integrate rights talk into the theology and teaching of the church. Not without reason, the introduction to an early collection of essays by Pope John Paul II, entitled *Sacred in All Its Forms*, pointedly commended the pontiff for an "originality [demonstrated in] his capacity to see the dramatic uniqueness and wonder of classic Christian doctrine about the worth of human life" as expressed through the concept of human rights.[149]

The pope, an ostensibly conservative man, claimed precedent for his own emphasis on natural rights in biblical scripture, as well as in the Roman Catholic Church's earlier defense of the "sacrosanct rights of the worker as a person."[150] Indeed, he asserted that he was only vigorously reaffirming the value of human life and its inviolability as previously established within the Roman Catholic Church.[151] Yet at other moments Pope John Paul II was much more candid, admitting that the human rights perspective, which he espoused in his encyclical *The Gospel of Life*, represented a new teaching or at least one that had distinctly evolved under both his recent predecessors and himself. As he tactfully put it, "In facing the challenges of the present situation, the Church is becoming more aware of the grace and responsibility which come to her from her Lord of proclaiming, celebrating and serving the *Gospel of life*."[152]

Significantly, the pope acknowledged that a major component of the Gospel of life was strictly furnished by the reasoned discernment of natural law:

> In Christ, the *Gospel of life* is definitively proclaimed and fully given. This is the Gospel which, already present in the Revelation of the Old Testament, and indeed written in the heart of every man and woman, has echoed in every conscience "from the beginning," from the time of creation itself, in such a way that, despite the negative consequences of sin, it can also be known in its essential traits by human reason.[153]

Since natural law is accessible to all by the gift of reason John Paul II claimed that everyone, whether Christian or not, should be bound by it as well. Consequently, the Gospel of life, grounded in elements of natural law and the sense of rights that flow from it, also deserved universal respect.

In at least one measure the pope presented himself as a quintessential liberal. He echoed Kant's categorical imperative. "Individual human beings," he insisted, "are not 'means' for some 'higher' good." Instead, he said, "they are already the higher good."[154] But the pope also moved beyond Kantian and liberal orthodoxy with some additional idiosyncratic assertions that suggested a heteronomous or authoritarian agenda.

While the pope conceded that the gift of reason may be necessary for our cognizance of natural law, he did not regard it as a condition of our personhood or as a higher good. Indeed, the pope perceived a "surprising contradiction" in the way in which liberal states understand human rights.[155] They have, he argued, wrongly made the capacity for autonomy a prerequisite for human rights.[156] From the pope's perspective, the human rights entertained by liberalism had promoted a callous, irresponsible kind of freedom that did not properly protect everyone.

In the view of the pope—and other Roman Catholic theologians simpatico with his thought—true freedom was dependent upon the acknowledgment that every individual life is inviolable.[157] Offering a corrective to liberal individualism, the pontiff and his theological cohorts contended that all freedom is necessarily conditioned by a duty to uphold the inviolability of innocent human life.[158] On this point John Paul II chose to speak with great firmness:

> Precisely for this reason, civil law must insure that all members of society enjoy respect for certain fundamental rights which innately belong to the person, rights which every positive law must recognize and guarantee. First and fundamental among these is the inviolable right to life of every innocent human being. While public authority can sometimes choose not to put a stop to something which—were it prohibited—would cause more serious harm, it can never presume to legitimize as a right of individuals—even if they are the majority of the members of society—an offence against other persons caused by the disregard of so fundamental a right as the right to life. The legal toleration of abortion or of euthanasia can in no way claim to be based on respect for the conscience of others, precisely because society has the right and the duty to protect itself against the abuses which can occur in the name of conscience and under the pretext of freedom.[159]

At the heart of this particular encyclical statement was a claim that John Paul II had reiterated many times before—namely, the "first right of man is the right to life."[160] Here, however, the pope was actually trying to rally both natural law and natural rights to his church's commitment to the species principle, whereby human life in any form or stage is deemed sacred and inviolable.

The same portion of the papal statement also made several other points clear. Specifically, from the pope's perspective the right to life was so transparent and fundamental in natural law that nothing impugning or challenging it could be allowed to stand. In addition, monitions of conscience which contradicted the right to life of any human, regardless of condition or development, were misguided.[161] Finally, democratic majoritarianism, as exemplified by a parliamentary vote, was also not to be trusted if it was disposed to lend itself to a violation of the natural right to life in any degree or measure.[162]

In the same encyclical, the pope asserted that democratic societies are always tempted to make allegiance to their own form of government an idolatry with potentially catastrophic results. In the pope's view, it was imperative that a moral commitment to the right to life of all human beings without regard to stage or development outweigh all other considerations and provide the content for all democratic deliberation:

> Democracy cannot be idolized to the point of making it a substitute for morality or a panacea for immorality. Fundamentally, democracy is a "system" and as such is a means and not an end. Its "moral" value is not automatic, but depends on conformity to the moral law to which it, like every other form of human behaviour, must be subject: in other words, its morality depends on the morality of the ends which it pursues and of the means which it employs. If today we see an almost universal consensus with regard to the value of democracy, this is to be considered a positive "sign of the times," as the Church's Magisterium has frequently noted. But the value of democracy stands or falls with the values which it embodies and promotes. Of course, values such as the dignity of every human person, respect for inviolable and inalienable human rights, and the adoption of the "common good" as the end and criterion regulating political life are certainly fundamental and not to be ignored.[163]

Somewhat paradoxically, the pope thus presented himself as the friend of democracy, seeking to help it "rediscover those essential and innate human and moral values" which it needs to remain sound.[164] What the pope did not acknowledge, however, was his own strongly authoritarian bent. Also ignored by the pope was the possibility that thoughtful people of great moral integrity could "reasonably" disagree over the rights he regarded as so certain and absolute.

At one point the pope actually ventured to say that a legal toleration of abortion or euthanasia could not claim to be based on respect for the conscience of others, precisely because "society has the right and duty to protect itself against the abuses which can occur in the name of conscience and under the pretext of freedom."[165] Essentially, the pope was suggesting that there could only be one "right" conscience on the sanctity of life issue. Expounding on his own views, the pope stated that "abortion and euthanasia are . . . crimes which no human law can claim to legitimize" and there "is no obligation in conscience to obey such laws." Quite the contrary, the pope declared, "there is a *grave and a clear obligation to oppose them by conscientious objection.*"[166] According to the pope, any democracy which permitted abortion and euthanasia did not deserve respect and had lost the very basis for its authority. The pope was supported in these specific sentiments by other Roman Catholic theologians.[167]

Overall, Pope John Paul II's ambivalence and wariness with regard to freedom of conscience, majoritarianism, and the authority of the democratic state were highly revealing. While he deployed natural law and natural rights theory to support his own understanding of the sanctity of life and to legitimate the Roman Catholic Church's stance on particular issues, such as abortion, he simultaneously demonstrated in practice a profound distrust of natural law and natural rights, plus any of the noneccesial institutional mechanisms that might express them.

His readiness to preempt with dogma any outcome of natural law and natural rights thinking that disagreed with his own conclusions raised the question whether his affinity for natural law and natural rights was anything other than tactical—a matter of political utility. In the end, the Roman Catholic Church was put in the incongruous position of professing to uphold natural law and its attendant rights even as it actively and conspicuously focused on seeking to contain, delimit, or undermine any fruits of autonomously rational discernment and moral decision that were not in agreement with official church teaching.

PROTESTANTISM AND NATURAL LAW

Given their more acute sense of human depravity, mainstream and conservative Protestants have never professed the same degree of trust in the monitions of natural law that their Roman Catholic brethren ostensibly have. Nevertheless, mainstream and conservative Protestants have not been entirely immune to the temptation of natural rights thinking and talk. Indeed, Protestant thinkers have leaned upon both in more than one pinch. In some cases, natural law claims have actually served as a cover for personal dogmatic beliefs that cannot otherwise be justified as a part of the Christian tradition.

While such an emblematic Protestant theologian as Paul Ramsey could claim a biblical basis for sanctity of life assertions, the iconic nature of such biblical concepts as the divine origins of human life, the image of God, and the divine-human covenant has meant that details have always needed to be worked out according to human reason or whatever seems self-evident—in short, whatever jibes with natural law.[168] The Protestant resort to natural law and natural rights has not always been announced, but it is no less real for that fact.

Significantly, Ramsey did not talk about a right to life. Yet he employed language akin to this. All human beings, including children, he made clear, possess life as a sacred entitlement:

> Because it is the Lord who has beset him behind and before, the child is a bit of sacredness in the temporal and biological order—whether it is in the womb of the mother, in the arms of its father, playing hopscotch on the sidewalk, a professional football player, or a scientist at work in his laboratory (or whichever one you value most). Each has the same title to life immediately from God. . . . Protestant Christians and everyone of whatever profound religious outlook must join the

> Roman Catholics in experiencing extraordinary anguish in the face of
> situations that throw life against nascent life, each of whom has *equal*
> title to protection.[169]

Coupled with the talk of entitlement, the fact that Ramsey believes that anyone of "profound religious outlook" would join Roman Catholics in their anguish over abortion indicates that Ramsey implicitly subscribes to either a natural law or natural metaphysic perspective. More specifically, he seems to regard the species principle as one of the obvious dictates of natural law.

Ramsey's proclivity for natural law is further evidenced by his conviction that there is also a fundamental harmony between biblical revelation and non-Christian moral codes:

> Many of God's life and death decisions are inscrutable to us. People
> are born and die. . . . But there is no indication at all that God is a
> rationalist whose care is a function of indicators of our personhood,
> or of our achievement within those capacities. He makes his rain to
> fall upon the just and the unjust alike, and his sun to rise on the abnor-
> mal as well as the normal. Indeed, he has special care for the weak and
> the vulnerable among us earth people. He cares according to need, not
> capacity or merit. These images or shadows of divine things are the
> foundation of Western medical care, together with that "Pythagorean
> manifesto," the Hippocratic Oath.[170]

Here Ramsey's reference to the "images or shadows of divine things" seems to stand as a euphemistic reference to a natural metaphysic accessible to both Christians and non-Christians. While there may be a certain inscrutability to God's purposes and workings, he believes them to be at least partially decipherable to Christians and non-Christians alike. Thus, Ramsey appears to have adhered to what could be called a modified or partial natural law and rights perspective.[171]

Unfortunately, Ramsey's embrace of a natural metaphysic or some form of natural law, which he saw underlying Christianity, as well as other religions and secular moral codes, seems to have made him less, rather than more, tolerant. Ramsey perceived something amiss with others who did not share his own particular moral convictions with regard to the sanctity of life. Not unlike Pope John Paul II, who charged modern society with being a "culture of death," Ramsey was quick to literally demonize those who disagreed with him. Using highly inflammatory rhetoric, for instance, Ramsey condemned the "apostasy of most Protestant churches [in their departure] from the common Christian tradition concerning the sanctity of unborn life."[172] Once again, we have an attempt by a sanctity of life advocate—in this case a Protestant—to use natural law to legitimate a preconceived moral position and to anathematize those who do not concur.

Intolerance of this sort, which represents a strange tyranny of "reason," has actually prompted a number of respected moral philosophers and theologians to pull back from any carte blanche affirmation of natural law.[173] In fact, theologian Kenneth Vaux expressed surprise that any Christian churches should rush to embrace natural law and natural rights rhetoric so totally when cultural, social, and political circumstances were simultaneously combining to discredit and repudiate them.[174]

What Vaux did not grasp was the extent to which convictions about the sanctity of life, going back to Stoicism, have always been intertwined with natural law. Also not understood or appreciated by Vaux was how badly Christian sanctity of life advocates, including Paul Ramsey, needed the long-popular rhetoric of natural law and natural rights to help them rehabilitate certain moral and spiritual beliefs concerning human salvation and human sexuality which, given modern sensibilities, had become too irrational and anachronistic to be palatable.

Some assorted intellectuals and cognoscenti, like Vaux, might suddenly shrink from any expansive natural law claims. But the public enchantment with natural law and natural rights had not yet crested. Both remained appealing and authoritative in most Western societies, especially the United States. Thus, Christian sanctity of life advocates rode the wave of natural law and natural rights for their own cause. From the start, they proved able to use the language of natural law and natural rights to substantial polemical and strategic advantage.

LIFE ON LOAN FROM GOD

Quite beyond any claim that sanctity of life is based on an immutable natural law, Roman Catholic and Protestant leaders continued to be eager to establish, if possible, a more distinctively Christian basis for their stance. Not surprisingly then, they rallied behind an expansive interpretation of the sovereignty of God to undercut any autonomous human initiative that might intrude upon the inviolability of human life. Consequently, the "lordship" of God was constantly emphasized, along with such corollary concepts as life as a gift and human beings as mere stewards of their own embodied lives. The vehemence with which the sovereignty of God came to be preached in the twentieth century was probably unprecedented. A burgeoning concern on the part of conservative Christian theologians about the sanctity of life and a desire to check human freedom fired the sovereignty of God, as a concept, with fresh force and energy.

Among modern Roman Catholic theologians, Pope John Paul II's reaffirmation of the sovereignty of God is particularly noteworthy and illustrative. This late-twentieth-century pope quickly delimited his profession of respect for human autonomy by an overarching emphasis upon divine sovereignty. As the pope expressed himself, "Man is ruler and lord not only over things but especially over himself. . . . Man's *lordship* however is not absolute, but *ministerial*: it is a reflection of the unique and infinite lordship of God. Hence man must exercise it with *wisdom* and *love*."[175] For all his pleasantness about it, the pope was determined to constrain any sense of freedom which men and women might claim for themselves.

Subsequently, the pope was even more specific in countermanding or at least qualifying his allowance for any kind of autonomous human authority. "God," Pope John Paul II declared, "proclaims that he is absolute Lord of the life of man, who is formed in his image and likeness."[176] The pope elsewhere elaborated: "*God therefore is the sole Lord of this life*: man cannot do with it as he wills."[177] Plainly, the freedom and autonomy that the Pope was willing to concede to human beings were not nearly as great as initially appeared. The Vatican's Congregation for the Doctrine of Faith, a body obviously attuned to papal thinking, mostly echoed John Paul II's sentiments.[178]

While other Roman Catholic theologians appeared more sincerely accepting of human autonomy than either their pontiff or the Vatican's instrumentalities, their subsequent rhetoric rendered their true stance ambiguous. Those who extolled human freedom felt obliged to simultaneously redouble their emphasis upon the sovereignty of God.

Roman Catholic theologian Bernard Häring was typical. On the one hand, he exalted human freedom and dignity, even calling men and women "co-creators" with God. On the other hand, Häring was also disposed to use rhetoric uncongenial to human autonomy. For instance, in the *Ethics of Manipulation*, Häring described "the freedom of mankind as the summit of all evolution and of all history, if it is truly freedom for God, for our neighbour, for genuine love, justice and peace."[179] Nevertheless, Häring could and did write in a fashion less friendly towards human freedom and autonomy:

> Our bodily life does not belong to us but to the One who has entrusted it to us for ourselves and for the service of our brethren. "For no one of us lives, and equally no one of us dies, for himself alone. If we live, we live for the Lord; and if we die, we die for the Lord" (Rom. 14:7–8). . . . The Old Testament looks upon a long life as a gift of God, a blessing often inherent in the right use of this earthly life. "Honour your father and your mother, that you may live long in the land" (Ex. 20:12; Eph. 6:2–3). . . . Man's bodily life is entrusted to his freedom as its most precious talent. He is not the independent lord of his life but only a steward subject to the sovereignty of God.[180]

Clearly, Häring imputes more to his cited biblical verses than is really there. There is also a latent incongruity between his accent on human freedom and his sharp restriction of it as he admonishes that our bodily life "does not belong to us" but is owned by God.

The same incongruity was palpable in pronouncements made by conservative Protestants, identified with a sanctity of life position. Although they still spoke in terms of human freedom, their celebration of the sovereignty of God essentially cut back on any allowances for the autonomy of human life. In many respects, Karl Barth and Emil Brunner led the way. Barth's "command theology," which claimed a biblical mandate, spoke of human life as a mere "loan" from God.[181] Not too dissimilarly, Brunner's own neo-orthodox theology appropriated the pagan-Thomist notion of human life as divine "property" or chattel.[182] Although other Protestant sanctity of life advocates did not always expressly adopt the "loan" or "property" language invoked by these theologians, the sensibility communicated by such rhetoric did seep into language that most subsequent Protestant sanctity of life advocates employed.

For conservative Protestants following in the wake of Barth and Brunner, the preferred language to describe the standing of humanity vis-à-vis God involved the concept of stewardship. Men and women, it came to be said, did not own their own lives, but instead were stewards of them on God's behalf.[183] What was this if not a way of reaffirming human lives as divine property? Naturally, a biblical warrant was also claimed for the notion of human beings as stewards in relationship to their own lives.[184]

Ignored by those viewing human life as a total exercise in stewardship, however, were many contrary currents in Old and New Testament scripture, plus church tradition. A careful reading of the book of Genesis, for instance, reveals that God charges men and women with stewardship responsibilities over the rest of creation.[185] There is no indication in the biblical text that God meant that those distinctively made in God's own image should regard themselves as mere stewards over their own embodied lives too. In fact, as historian Elaine Pagels has noted, the early Christian churches perceived the entire Genesis story concerning creation and the subsequent human departure from the Garden of Eden as a parable about how men and women acquired their personal freedom in relationship to God.[186]

Further contradicting the notion of human beings as mere stewards over their embodied lives is the larger Old Testament emphasis upon divine-human covenant.[187] The covenantal tradition of the Old Testament actually presupposes an important measure of human autonomy and liberty of action at odds with any standard conception of the steward's role.[188] While human beings remain unequal to God, they nevertheless stand in a relationship of true mutuality with God, free to say yes or no to God's plan and purposes in a way that would be unthinkable for someone limited to the office of steward or household manager, a position not infrequently filled in ancient times by indentured servants or slaves.[189]

New Testament scripture does not sanction the notion that human beings are mere stewards over their own embodied lives either. Though the concept of stewardship surfaces in three Gospel parables, Jesus employs it only in calling his disciples to be responsible and accountable evangelists for the good news of God's coming kingdom.[190] Not once does Jesus speak of our bodies as God's property. Nor does the apostle Paul do so. Quite the opposite, Paul's admonition to the Christians of Rome "to present your bodies as a living sacrifice, holy and acceptable, to God" seems to anticipate an entirely voluntary faith decision.[191]

Protestant sanctity of life advocates, joined by their Roman Catholic counterparts, attempted to mask the severity of their stewardship claims by conjoining it with gift language. It was said, for instance, that human beings need to be good stewards of their physical, embodied lives because God provides life to men and women as a gift. The emphasis in such instances was upon God's generosity. Yet what sanctity of life advocates did not recognize was the fundamental inconsistency in being both a gift recipient and a steward.[192]

In custom and in law, a gift involves the relinquishment of ownership by a donor to a donee.[193] As Paul Camenish has observed, examining the notion of gifts in the light of ethics, the donor may expect the donee to use the gift he or she gives in respectful, rather than wanton, ways, creating through the giving, in effect, a moral obligation.[194] The donor may also have an expectation that the donee will show "grateful conduct" towards him or her.[195] But unless the donor expressly and formally conditions the gift, the donee may do with the gift whatever he or she chooses without formal penalty, apart from alienating the generous donor.[196]

The circumstances of stewardship are quite different: the original owner remains owner, only relinquishing the management and care of his or her property to another. Unlike the gift recipient, the steward cannot do what he or she likes with the property at hand. Ultimately, all stewarded property must be returned to the owner intact, if not enhanced.[197]

Considering the overall tenor of the Genesis story, the notion of gift and the kind of donor–donee relationship that goes with it are not inappropriate motifs to describe the creaturely human condition and the measure of accountability that men and women have towards God for their lives. Gift language makes room for the kind of covenantal autonomy contemplated by the Old Testament, especially in the aftermath of the Garden of Eden. If properly understood, however, such gift talk presents an alternative to the idea that human beings are mere stewards over their own bodies, enjoying life as a loan or temporary commission.

Obviously, such an alternative was not what either Protestant or Roman Catholic sanctity of life advocates had in mind. Accordingly, their conflation of gift-holding and stewardship persisted, but with stewardship of physical life serving as the sine qua non of their particular outlook.

Scrutiny of simultaneous arguments concerning the sovereignty of God, the stewardship of the physical body, and life as a gift makes it clear that Roman Catholic and Protestant sanctity of life advocates could be intellectually lax and inconsistent as they set about to curtail the exercise of human autonomy, applying Christian concepts in ways no more consonant with traditional Christianity than the tenuous monitions of natural law.

SACRALIZATION AS MORAL CAP AND GENDER CONSTRAINT

In some respects, amid all their talk of stewardship, sanctity of life advocates were greatly enamored with medical technology. In its potential for preserving life, they viewed it positively as serving God's purposes. On the other hand, true to their suspicions of human autonomy and its fruits, sanctity of life advocates were also quick to anticipate in modern technology no shortage of demonic possibilities. Persuaded that there was a clear convergence between God's purposes and the workings of the natural order, they looked for and found limits within nature that could not be crossed without also transgressing against the sovereignty of God and the moral order which God had ordained and built into nature.

Small wonder then that Pope John Paul II complained of "a certain Promethean attitude" at work in the present day.[198] The divine plan of the Creator, he alleged, was being undermined by those "intoxicated" with the power of technology.[199] Technology, he added, was tempting men and women to go *"beyond the limits of a reasonable dominion over nature, jeopardizing the very survival and integrity of the human person."*[200] Scientific advances, he concluded, were not the highest good or value: limits were needed for science and technology.[201]

A similar concern for limits to scientific and technological intervention was echoed by Paul Ramsey.[202] But he also expressed concern about the "intervention" that could occur where scientific and technological procedures were deliberately withheld by those charged with providing medical care:

Physicians are not appointed to remove all life's tragedy, least of all by lessening medical care now and letting infants die who for social reasons seem fated to have less care in the future than others. . . . If physicians are going to play God under the pretense of providing relief for the human condition, let us hope they play God as God plays God. Our God is no respecter of persons of good quality. . . . A true humanism also leads to "an equality of life" standard.[203]

Ramsey's message was that we should be scrupulously egalitarian in any intervention we do attempt and leave all qualifying judgments to God, via natural biological processes.[204]

In varying degrees, what most of the sanctity of life advocates fell prey to in their affirmation of God's sovereignty was a worship of sheer biological vitality. Indeed, Roman Catholic theologian Bernard Häring, who noted that sanctity of life advocates could not help but look with horror upon anything that thwarted or impeded the course of nature, perceived a clear tendency to sacralize nature.[205]

It was precisely this kind of sacralization of biology that was so evident in insistent arguments by sanctity of life advocates that all human sexuality must remain oriented towards procreation. Advocating a "theology of the body," Pope John Paul II offered repeated paeans to human procreation.[206]

In *The Gospel of Life*, for instance, Pope John Paul II asserted that humanity's greatest responsibility is procreation—giving birth to those who are in the image of God.[207] Thereafter, he lauded parents and procreation and attacked the "caprice" of couples who through artificial contraception betray the intended "fruitfulness" of the marriage union.[208] "It is," he wrote, "precisely in their role as co-workers with God *who transmits his image to the new creature* that we see the greatness of couples who are ready 'to cooperate with the love of the Creator and the Saviour, who through them will enlarge and enrich his own family day by day.'"[209]

In his own brand of "naturalism," the pope rejected contraception except by means of a natural rhythm method.[210] He contended that the study of nature by modern genetic science "offers clear confirmation" that personal human life begins with a fertilized ovum. He went on to say, "Even if the presence of a spiritual soul cannot be ascertained by empirical data . . . 'how could a human individual [as represented by the fertilized ovum] not be a human person?'"[211] It was the responsibility of Christians not only to cherish sexuality in all its generative potential but also to respect the sanctity of all its fruits.

While the pope did not overtly sacralize sex, some of the more devout members of his own flock did. One commentator did not mince words. "Because many prolife people see sex as literally sacred," she remarked, "they are disturbed by values that seem to them both to secularize and to profane sex." For them sex was to be held "sacred because in their world view it has the capacity to be transcendent—to bring into existence another human life."[212] The perception of human sexuality as sacred on a de facto, if not a de jure, basis illustrates how susceptible Roman Catholic sanctity of life advocates continued to be to a radical divergence from any traditional Christian orientation.

Meanwhile, there was no shortage of statements from John Paul II reinforcing the importance of maintaining traditional distinctions between masculinity and femininity as a part of a wider sanctity of life affirmation. In "The Mystery of Woman Revealed in Motherhood" and other similar addresses, the pontiff stressed that the "woman-wife" expresses the "very depth of her femininity" only by giving herself over to the "creative peculiarity" of her own "female organism" which serves for "the conception and begetting of the human being."[213] The overall message was clear: an embrace of a pro-life position for Roman Catholics entailed an allegiance to sex and gender roles designated by the church hierarchy as foreordained and natural.[214]

Although not always as conspicuous or encompassing, the same tendency to sacralize the natural procreative sex act, plus other aspects of human biology, found expression in the arguments of a bevy of Protestant theologians, among them George Hunston Williams, Paul Ramsey, and J. Kerby Anderson. Commending the Roman Catholic Church for keeping to the "embryological facts" in its account of the beginnings of human personhood, George Hunston Williams called upon Protestants to "rally . . . to the Catholic position concerning the fetus."[215] The elaborateness of Williams's total scheme to regulate pregnancy and abortion, plus his sympathies for Roman Catholic traducianism, revealed his own inclination to sacralize the biological processes involved. Meanwhile, Ramsey's own sacralization of human biology translated into opposition to artificial insemination or use of surrogate mothers. Both in his view violated "a yoking of loving and begetting."[216] He too took up the traducianist position, arguing that human personhood began with the fertilized ovum, thereby sacralizing fetal life.[217] Following suit, Protestant evangelical John Stott expressed his own profound wariness about in vitro fertilization (IVF). He explained:

> IVF may involve an *intrusion into the process of procreation.* Some Christians are just able to come to terms with IVF and ET [embryo transfer] when they concern the husband's sperm and the wife's ovum and womb. Yet even in this case, when no external donation is involved, the sacredness of human reproduction has been moved from the bedroom into the laboratory, and from a God-designed process to a human technique, as fusion takes place no longer unwitnessed within the mother's body but on a glass dish carefully monitored by scientists. . . . Moreover, IVF separates what God has united. His purpose from the beginning was that marriage, love, sex and procreation should belong together, and in particular that "baby-making" (better, "baby-begetting") should be the consequence of "love-making."[218]

Fellow evangelical J. Kerby Anderson was even more explicit and adamant in terms of his opposition to in vitro fertilization. He criticized it on the grounds that it would encourage deviant, nonbiblical lifestyles—perhaps parenting by unmarried persons or homosexual couples.[219] Not unlike Pope John Paul II, Anderson saw technology opening a Pandora's box that needed to remain tightly shut.

In their arguments for a hands-off respect for human life, these theologians joined a long line of sanctity of life advocates who have ignored nature's underlying profligacy—a profligacy which, as several commentators have suggested, calls into question any divine endorsement for life's sacredness.[220] Their stances on in vitro fertilization in particular illustrate the way that the entire sanctity of life movement, usually as a means of maintaining the status quo and keeping a cap on social mores, has shunned some technological interventions that involve provocative moral choices.[221] To this day, there continues to be a highly conservative, authoritarian social agenda underlying the entire Christian sanctity of life movement, similar to what sociologist Kristin Luker observed in the anti-abortion movement fifteen or more years ago.[222]

CARDINAL JOSEPH BERNARDIN'S CONSISTENT ETHIC

As more conservative Christians stepped forward to embrace the sanctity of life as an explanation for their own moral agenda, critics were quick to note that their affirmation of the sacredness of life seemed to include only human life deemed innocent. To be more specific, critics made much of the fact that the sanctity of life movement opposed abortion and euthanasia but had little or nothing to say about the defense and protection of human life imperiled by the possibility of nuclear war, capital punishment, or sheer material poverty.[223]

Not all sanctity of life advocates were blind to some of the strains and weaknesses underlying their own arguments and postures. Responding to the complaints of their critics, which challenged the credibility of their whole movement, a handful of leading sanctity of life advocates earnestly sought to make their doctrine more respectful and encompassing towards all human life. Yet, ironically, these best efforts floundered when it came to winning genuine support from either the official leaders of the Christian churches or the supposed rank and file of the sanctity of life movement.

Insistently opposed to abortion, Roman Catholic theologian Germain Grisez was clearly among those who came to believe that the moral credibility of a sanctity of life argument in the wider culture depended upon casting a bigger net. He took a stand against the destruction of all innocent human life, whether through abortion, war, or euthanasia.[224] Similarly, Protestant evangelical theologian Lewis Smedes called for a more comprehensive sanctity of life ethic—one potentially embracing pacifism.[225] However, the single greatest impetus towards any clear and resolute articulation of a more encompassing sanctity of life doctrine came from a Roman Catholic prelate, the late Cardinal Joseph Bernardin of Chicago.

Following up on a pastoral letter issued earlier that same year by American Catholic bishops, linking the issues of nuclear warfare and abortion, Cardinal Bernardin boldly called for a "consistent ethics of life" in a December 1983 Fordham University address.[226] Citing the Catholic bishops' pastoral letter, Bernardin explained:

> The central idea in the letter is the sacredness of human life and the responsibility we have, personally and socially, to protect and preserve the sanctity of life. Precisely because life is sacred, the taking of even one human life is a momentous event. Indeed, the sense that every human life has transcendent value has led a whole stream of the Christian tradition to argue that life may never be taken. That posi-

tion is held by an increasing number of Catholics and is reflected in the pastoral letter, but it has not been the dominant view in Catholic teaching and it is not the principal moral position found in the pastoral letter.[227]

Treating the Catholic bishops' pastoral letter as a starting point, Bernardin argues for a sanctity of life standard more absolute and encompassing than any previously endorsed by the Roman Catholic Church—one which would preclude the taking of human life under any circumstances. But Bernardin did not even stop here. He went on to suggest that a consistent sanctity of life stance involved more positive duties too. Sanctity of life advocates needed, he said, to embrace a "heroic social ethic," committing themselves to fight on behalf of social support programs for those in need. In a burst of eloquence, Bernardin proclaimed:

> I contend the viability of the [sanctity of life] principle depends upon the consistency of its application. . . . Consistency means we cannot have it both ways: We cannot urge a compassionate society and vigorous public policy to protect the rights of the unborn and then argue that compassion and significant public programs on behalf of the needy undermine the moral fiber of the society or are beyond the proper scope of governmental responsibility.[228]

According to Bernardin, the sanctity of life concept would lose moral credibility if it did not address the socioeconomic needs of those struggling in the midst of life. Mere preachments about socioeconomic justice would not be sufficient. In its defense of the sanctity of life the Roman Catholic Church needed to develop a pro-life constituency that would array itself in practical, concrete ways against a full gamut of social evils that cause human distress and impugn human sacredness.[229]

Over the course of several subsequent addresses, Bernardin expanded upon his arguments for a consistent ethic of life, metaphorically describing the sanctity of life as a "seamless garment":

> Nuclear war threatens life on a previously unimaginable scale; abortion takes life daily on a horrendous scale; public executions are fast becoming weekly events in the most advanced technological society in history; and euthanasia is now openly discussed and even advocated. Each of these assaults on life has its own meaning and morality: they cannot be collapsed into one problem, but they must be confronted as pieces of a larger pattern. . . . A consistent ethic does not say everyone in the church must do all things, but it does say that as individuals and groups pursue one issue, whether it is opposing abortion or capital punishment, the way we oppose one threat should be related to support for a systemic vision of life.[230]

Bernardin closed his remarks by declaring that the church has an "open moment" in which to "demonstrate the strength of a sustained moral vision,"[231] a unique opportunity to provide a positive example for others and to shape overall public opinion in the enveloping culture.

Not unexpectedly, Bernardin's consistent ethic drew praise, even acclaim. It could not help but mollify some of the critics of a Christian sanctity of life stance. Underscoring the fact that Bernardin's consistent ethic was compatible with liberal intellectual sensibilities, Stephen D. Johnson and Joseph B. Tamney commended it for exemplifying the highest stage of moral development—at least as contemplated through a schema outlined by Harvard University psychologist Lawrence Kohlberg.[232] In addition, educated Roman Catholics with special insight and interest in this controversy were also impressed. James R. Kelly contended, for instance, that the "pro-life or consistent ethic sector of the [anti-abortion] movement is likely, in the long run, to achieve the most lasting cultural presence."[233] He even noted the emergence of a "larger interreligious network called The Seamless Garment Network which promotes a consistent ethic of life."[234] He further cited research which found that educated Roman Catholics largely affirmed a consistent ethic approach.[235]

Despite this positive reaction, however, other equivocal statements by Christian leaders soon indicated that a consistent ethic of life would never really make it very far from the starting gate. Although Bernardin was the influential chairman of the Pro-Life Activities Committee of the National Conference of Catholic Bishops, his consistent ethic approach to the sanctity of life never garnered the enduring support that might have been expected from the hierarchy of his own Roman Catholic Church. Nor did Protestant church leaders who advocated a strict sanctity of life stance rush to support Bernardin's consistent ethic approach.

On the one hand, the pronouncements of Pope John Paul II increasingly adopted a consistent ethic flavor. On the other hand, the pope did not remain consistent about the consistent ethic. For instance, in *The Gospel of Life* the pontiff affirmed that the direct and voluntary killing of innocent human life is always gravely immoral, and that this applies to abortion and euthanasia.[236] But, quite unlike Bernardin, he never widened this to include a ban on capital punishment and the protection of not-so-innocent life.[237] Nor did he address in specifics or at length the immorality of war from a sanctity of life perspective.[238] In the case of the death penalty and war, the pope chose to remain as noncontroversial as possible by suggesting that opposition to each is a still evolving sensibility.

Further absent from the papal encyclical was Bernardin's ringing opposition to degrading poverty and his emphasis on developing social support programs that address the human condition in terms of bodily material needs. Instead, Pope John Paul II called for individual acts of charity with political and legislative action mostly reserved for laws that protect an "innocent person's natural right to life."[239]

The pope's most radical statement concerned changes in the social sphere to uphold the sanctity of life focus on family. He contended that a "*family policy must be the basis and driving force of all social policies.*"[240] Here, the pope did add that "solutions must be sought on the global level by establishing a true economy of *communion and sharing of goods.*"[241] Still, apart from these statements, the pope proved vague. Overall, his willingness to commit the church to a full-fledged confrontation against economic inequities which bear down upon a respect for life seemed tepid.

The lack of resounding support from the pope or the hierarchy of the Roman Catholic Church for Bernardin's consistent sanctity of life ethic was matched by the continuing ambivalence of others, Roman Catholic and Protestant, who, demonstrating profound social concerns of their own, might have been expected to be sympathetic towards what Bernardin hoped to accomplish. Almost immediately, for instance, John R. Connery, author of a detailed history of Roman Catholic doctrine on abortion, took issue with Bernardin's support for a ban on capital punishment. Connery argued that the need to combat sin in the world should not be forgotten or overlooked. Accordingly, Connery insisted, Bernardin's consistent ethic would be more helpful in the face of present realities if it refocused more narrowly upon prohibiting any direct killing of the innocent.[242]

By contrast, another Roman Catholic theologian, Richard A. McCormick, seemed to be more open to Bernardin's consistent ethic. He applauded Bernardin's efforts and endorsed his "general thrust."[243] Nevertheless, he too had difficulty with the lack of nuances in Bernardin's consistent ethic approach as it affirmed the sanctity of human life.[244] Specifically, McCormick noted the "problematic character of translating the presumption against taking life into viable derivative applications for practice."[245] In addition, he felt compelled to reject the consistent ethic understanding of human life as an absolute good in favor of a view that treats our continued existence as a more qualified basic good.[246]

Meanwhile, mainstream Protestant theologians were no more inclined than some of their Roman Catholic brethren to climb aboard the wagon for a consistent life ethic. For instance, while Protestant theologian Stanley Hauerwas seemed eager to help the Christian churches develop a consistent ethics promoting peace and non-violence, he too expressed skepticism about attempts to uphold human life as an absolute good. Quite pointedly, he also declined to speak of human life as sacred.[247]

Thus, however promising it initially seemed, Bernardin's consistent ethic approach to the sanctity of life remained practically stillborn. The limitations and inconsistencies of sanctity of life doctrine that Bernardin sought to correct also continued to stand as before.

POPULAR AMBIVALENCE ABOUT SANCTITY DOCTRINE

Right from the outset, regardless of official theological opinion, there has been comparatively little support for a consistent ethic on behalf of the sanctity of life among the Christian laity, Roman Catholic and Protestant. A slew of opinion polls, taken among Christian laity, indicate that Marvin Kohl was close to the mark when he described the sanctity of life concept as "chameleon-like" and argued that, instead of a consistent ethic, there was "a family of related but differing principles . . . hidden under the rubric of the SLP [Sanctity of Life Principle] in order to give the impression of moral consensus."[248]

The tenuousness of support for the consistent ethic approach, even among lay sanctity of life proponents, was tacitly conceded by the same *Origins* publication that faithfully reproduced Cardinal Bernardin's several addresses on the subject. As an *Origins* editorial note stated:

Fears that anti-abortion efforts in the political sphere may suffer through the consistent-ethic-of-life approach recommended by Cardinal Joseph Bernardin were expressed in a number of quarters after the December address by the cardinal at Fordham University. A chief concern appeared to be that linking life issues would weaken or compromise action against abortion. Joe Scheidler, director of the Chicago-based Pro-Life Action League, said in a January interview that he felt the bishops were "trying to give a new definition to pro-life to bring some people into their camp who are not really pro-life." The Ad Hoc Committee in Defense of Life said after Bernardin's Fordham Address that a survey of abortion opponents found that 99 per cent "oppose the cardinal's conglomerate." If people in the anti-abortion movement can't "keep their issue the premier 'single' one in the political spectrum, then it may well sink into the gooey swamps where yesterday's causes fester," the committee suggested.[249]

For many identified with the sanctity of life position, a ban on abortion remains the paramount, if not exclusive, concern.

While the partisanship of the Ad Hoc Committee in Defense of Life might make their own poll results suspect, other surveys also established beyond a doubt that most Christians do not think in terms of a consistent ethic on the sanctity of life. In his own assessment based upon opinion surveys, J. Stephen Cleghorn described the overall Roman Catholic community as "lukewarm" about Bernardin's seamless garment approach to sanctity of life. Consequently, he stated, church leaders must not assume wide agreement about the sacredness of life.[250] Cleghorn and others found complex factors shaping both Christian and non-Christian opinion on issues associated with sanctity of life. In almost every instance, responses to abortion, euthanasia, and assisted suicide were more pluralistic and varied than the pro-life Christian leadership has wanted to acknowledge.[251]

In line with what might be anticipated, Elizabeth Cook, Ted Jelen, and Clyde Wilcox observed that religion is "a very important source of abortion attitudes" and that religious involvement and a high view of scripture (where the Bible is regarded as the literal, inerrant word of God) are the best predicators for an anti-abortion stance.[252] Yet they went on to note that "even among evangelicals and Catholics, there are more pro-choice than pro-life citizens." Their conclusion was that the Roman Catholic hierarchy had "failed to mobilize" the support it often claims in its pro-life, anti-abortion crusade.[253] According to the same sociologists, Protestant churches, whether evangelical or mainline, were no more successful in garnering pro-life support—often they lagged behind their Roman Catholic counterparts in cultivating a pro-life constituency within their own ranks.[254]

Similarly surveying the situation in the Netherlands, researcher Henri Hilhorst obtained somewhat mixed results. On the one hand, he was able to report that "religiosity and other religious indicators are negatively associated with pro-euthanasia attitudes."[255] In other words, religious individuals were less in favor of euthanasia than nonreligious individuals.[256] However, Hilhorst's data indicated that religious individuals were still "more in favour of euthanasia than religious institutions and organizations, the latter being the 'gatekeepers of established morality.'"[257]

In an additional twist, polling research suggested that religious belief or doctrine per se might not be the actual source of the anti-abortion or anti-euthanasia stances that have been lumped together under the sanctity of life. Specifically, it was found in a country like the Netherlands that anti-abortion attitudes are twice as prevalent among churchgoing Christians as among non-churchgoing Christians.[258] This prompted a set of analysts to conclude that "conservative conceptions strongly inter-reinforce among church-members. . . . From this combination of a conservative culture that reinforces itself and the absence of a direct effect of religion [among non-churchgoers], it seems that in the churches religion functions at least partly as a legitimation of a conservative culture."[259] The anti-abortion and anti-euthanasia stance of some Christians may represent an "internalized group norm" that is consciously or unconsciously used by church communities to define themselves and reenforce their own discrete identity over and against the rest of the culture which may, morally speaking, be looser and more liberal. This is certainly true in the United States, as further research has indicated.[260]

Such studies in the Netherlands and the United States confirm what some theologians and moral philosophers have surmised—namely, that no real consensus exists on sanctity of life issues.[261] Moreover, the evidence ratifies another related suspicion: that communities associated with a sanctity of life perspective do seem more intent on either limiting or controlling illicit sex than recognizing or defending in any absolute way the intrinsic value of fetal life—or any other human life form.[262]

Based upon his own surveys, for example, Cleghorn has determined that church attendance does not correlate to opposition to either capital punishment or the arms race.[263] Simultaneously, Cook, Jelen, and Wilcox maintain on the basis of their polling efforts that "much of the opposition to legal abortion seems based on a desire to increase the risks associated with nonmarital sex" and the "desire to punish sinners."[264] Sociologists Stephen Johnson and Joseph Tamney roughly concur in this assessment, as do Eric Woodrum and Beth Davison. In their collective view, a preemptive concern with sexual morality shapes and determines abortion attitudes on the part of many Christians.[265] With this array of survey statistics available, it is clear that Susan Teft Nicholson is not off the mark when she declares that "even if the fetus were not a human being, Catholics would still view abortion as evil."[266] The same could probably be said about the sensibilities of conservative pro-life Protestants.

Of course, the limited popular commitment to any thoroughgoing sanctity of life principle or a consistent life ethic turns out to be conspicuous in still other ways. Indeed, no matter how loudly Christians may protest something as specific as abortion, practice proves another matter. In a study following up actual behavior, rather than stopping at expressed opinion, it was found that "women reporting conservative religious affiliations were no more likely than those reporting other or no affiliations to reject abortion in response to problem pregnancy."[267]

Even more compelling, a similar lack of commitment to any absolute sanctity of life principle is encountered in polled attitudes on the withholding of medical treatment, euthanasia, and physician-assisted suicide. For instance, in one study with regard to the treatment of newborns, eighty-two percent of the pediatricians and pediatric surgeons surveyed said no to saving the life of every newborn without regard to condition. Furthermore, this no prevailed among doctors of every kind of religious affiliation.[268] Meanwhile, half or more of the physicians surveyed in many areas of the United States viewed active euthanasia as morally justified and felt that physician-assisted suicide should be made legal.[269] Comparable poll results have been obtained in surveys of the nursing profession.[270] General public opinion in the United States on the same issues is equally, if not more favorably, disposed towards euthanasia and physician-assisted suicide.[271]

Naturally, those who continue to subscribe to a strict sanctity of life perspective might see in these poll results nothing more than evidence of the deteriorating regard for the value of human life. In fact, however, another possibility must be considered: such statistics may not represent any moral deterioration at all but, rather, a certain moral continuity with the past when there was less tendency to absolutize the value of human life and a greater inclination to uphold it in the context of a wider range of considerations. Indeed, the only real fault of medical professionals and the lay public who hold opinions at odds with some of our society's religious leaders may be their "failure" to give themselves over wholeheartedly to what started out in the eighteenth century as a purely liberal doctrine and ended up by the late twentieth century as conservative Christian dogma, unevenly upheld.

Rather than ignoring or condemning the moral judgment of its own laity, which may depart from what church leadership finds theologically appropriate, church prelates, pastors, and self-appointed ministers from the pews might simply benefit from being more attentive to popular insight and wisdom on all life-and-death issues. What the Christian churches could gain is an old-fashioned dose of realism.

SANCTITY AS A SWORD OF DISCORD AND CONFUSION

Long before the sanctity of life rhetoric acquired its momentum or developed its present fervor and pitch, the Christian churches, apart from some idiosyncratic attitudes towards sex, had the capacity to deal with real life-and-death situations in ways that combined principles with pragmatism and morality with compassion. If the Christian churches are to provide effective moral leadership, consonant with its own tradition, they need to recover that capacity.

As matters stand right now, all signs point to one unassailable fact: the sanctity of life is a principle that can only hobble the Christian churches in their gospel mission. Largely born for the Christian churches out of a late-nineteenth-century accommodation with liberal secular culture, the Christian concept of sanctity of life has never cohered with other eschatological or anthropological traditions of Christianity, which traditionally relativized the value of embodied human life by means of a larger view of each individual's eternal destiny.

Furthermore, today, as indicated by Wennberg's threefold "right-to-life" typology and the controversy surrounding Cardinal Bernardin's "consistent ethic," there is no widespread, let alone universal, agreement about what the sanctity of life means and how it should be applied as a principle amid the complicating and compelling circumstances of particular cases. As J. Robert Nelson has correctly summed up the current situation:

> In current disputes over capital punishment, abortion, infanticide and assisting in the hastening of death, it is remarkable how frequently people on opposing sides appeal to the same standards of the intrinsic value, dignity, sacredness, or sanctity of human life. No sensible, moral person wants to be regarded as antilife or lenient towards killing. Yet, it seems to be just as possible to argue for the death of a fetus, a "defective" newborn, a comatose patient, one with a terminal illness, or even a criminal by claiming respect for the sanctity of life as it is to defend life by the same claim. Sissela Bok muses on the evidence "that everyone, including those who authorize or perform the most brutal killings in war, can protest their belief in life's sacredness." If all the disputants could agree on what is meant by value, dignity, sacredness, and sanctity, most such arguments could be settled forthwith. It is not these evaluative words as such that divide people, but the diverse senses in which they are used. And not only the definitions of the words, but the total concepts of life, both general and human, which are at variance, constitute the barriers to understanding and agreement.[272]

As Nelson makes clear, so many different perspectives are readily and regularly clustered under the sanctity of life rubric that it ceases to be, if it ever was, a clear, coherent doctrine.

While splendidly high-minded, the sanctity of life concept seems high-handedly destined to generate further acrimony, conflict, and polarization among the Christian churches, as well as within Western society at large. Ultimately, judgment cannot be avoided: the whole sanctity of life principle, however interpreted or rendered, is more hurtful than helpful in the quest to maintain and extend an appreciation for the proper valuing of human life. Indeed, the Christian churches need to be on guard lest the sanctity of life concept that they have enshrined become an outright fetish, diverting and displacing a true faith in God and leading Christianity to get caught up in lines and divisions quite contrary to the unity that Jesus Christ calls us to seek.

7

Respect for Life as an Alternative to Sanctity

No one can entirely challenge the good intentions of those who have espoused the sanctity of life as a principle or doctrine for the Christian churches. Proponents of the sanctity of life principle are no doubt sincere in their opposition to the utilitarian calculus they see overtaking more and more of liberal society.

Unfortunately, however, the whole sanctity of life principle, as endorsed by some Christian churches, ends up as a case of metaphysical overreach. Besides being divisive for the Christian churches themselves, support for the sanctity of life principle represents an attempt to impose heteronomous or authoritarian solutions on a crisis of values within an autonomous liberal culture. Given the many inconsistencies inherent in the sanctity of life principle, the Christian churches need to moderate it sharply or replace it altogether with a different and more pragmatic appreciation for the value of human life.

ENDING THE IDOLATRY OF THE SANCTITY PRINCIPLE

The extent to which sanctity of life doctrine contravenes traditional Christian anthropological convictions and threatens the integrity of the Christian faith should not be underestimated. Indeed, in a time when sanctity of life advocates, despite occasional disclaimers, have increasingly absolutized the value of human life, an impressive contingent of Christian theologians have voiced the profoundest concern, warning against the danger of idolatry where, in the prophetic words of Karl Barth, human life is treated as a "second God."[1]

Although his ties to the Roman Catholic Church might dispose him to be cautious in his pronouncements, theologian and ethicist Richard McCormick has not equivocated in discussing the dangers that allegiance to the sanctity of life poses for Christian faith. McCormick notes that "idolatry is elevating a fragment of the world into the position of God." It is, he adds, "to take something out of its place and invest it with divinity."[2] He goes on to remark:

The characteristic temptation of the ethos of the medical profession is to make life and the profession's ability to preserve it an idol. The symbol of this is patient-abandonment when cure is no longer possible and death is imminent. ("I can do no more.") For many physicians death is defeat. ("No one dies on my shift.") This can skewer and distort the ministry of health care, decontextualize its instrumentalities, technologize its value judgements, and bloat its practitioners—to say nothing of limitlessly expanding its cost.[3]

Observing that "excessive concern for the temporal is at some point neglect of the eternal," McCormick suggests that the example of Christ's sacrificial life and death is the best defense against an idolatry of temporal life and the perception of death as a defeat.[4] McCormick recalls the wisdom that had traditionally determined the Christian perspective on life and death. Among the "themes that give shape to our ethical deliberations" as Christians, he states, are the related convictions that "life is a basic but not an absolute one" and that "death is an evil but not an absolute or unconditioned one."[5] In McCormick's view, life is a value to be preserved only insofar as there is some potentiality for human relationships.[6]

Another prominent Roman Catholic theologian and ethicist, Bernard Häring, has expressed similar reservations about sanctity of life doctrine with its attendant danger of idolatry. At the outset, Häring acknowledges the importance of the human body. It is the means by which we are present in the world as persons.[7] Disparagement of the human body would not only contradict Christian beliefs but also deny something fundamental to personal existence.[8] Nevertheless, Häring makes clear his own antipathy toward any tendency to equate human life with mere biological functions. Reflecting a concern about idolatry, Häring has in fact called for a "desacralization of the biological."[9] From Häring's perspective, measures to prolong biological life can demonstrate a contempt for human life in its true meaning and purposes in relationship to God.[10] For Häring human life is present where there is capacity for personhood and the exercise of freedom, however limited or constrained.[11]

Typical of the Protestant objection to sanctity of life doctrine are the views expressed in their "Declaration of Faith and Health," by Jan Van Eyck and Kenneth Vaux. Although Kenneth Vaux has elsewhere described sanctity of life as a "newfound and unprecedented human conviction" that needs to be safeguarded, he has joined with Jan Van Eyck in asserting that the health crisis now besetting the United States is a "crisis of faith and theology," precipitated by "heresy" and reflecting "an idolatry that threatens the very fabric of our society and the rightness of our relationship with God." Together, they proceed to say that the cult of perfection and the idolatry of medicine needs to be corrected by a return to God's sovereignty.[12]

Also concerned with the diminution of God's sovereignty, Howard Moody rails against an absolutizing sanctity of life affirmation in an article entitled "Life Sentence":

> This medical warfare against death is highly dramatized in media events
> of artificial organ transplants and the heart of a baboon in the body of

a newborn baby. A medical and scientific hubris promises a seemingly unending and miraculous control of the life process, foretelling the time when death is a curable disease and immortality a medical commodity. . . . Listen to the language of "right-to-lifers." In their fanatical semantics God is no longer ultimate but life is the ultimate. And if life becomes God, then the death of a life is deicide. A fetus must not be allowed to die no matter what pain, sorrow, or suffering may result from the consequence of its birth: Likewise, a brain-dead 80-year-old must be kept alive no matter the pain and expense to family and society. . . . But surely, the absolute deification of life is an idolatry for the followers of a Master who said "Greater love hath no man than he who lays down his life for a friend" or "she who loses life will find it." For people of faith, life is meaningful and precious (sometimes), but not the only value in this world.[13]

Just as Karl Barth warned long before, Moody contends that the obsession with physical health and well-being and the preservation of life at all costs is a sign not of good stewardship, but of faithlessness. Moody remarks, "If Christians really believed in life after death, we could save the billions of dollars in health care spent in the last six months of life, trying to rob death of a few more days, weeks, or months."[14]

Roman Catholic sociologist Ivan Illich would seem to concur wholeheartedly with Moody's assessment. "Through the medicalization of death," Illich writes, "health care has become a monolithic world religion whose tenets are taught in compulsory schools and whose ethical rules are applied to a bureaucratic restructuring of the environment."[15] Illich sees this idolatry tied up with a loss of conviction among ordinary people about the prospect of an afterlife or an eternal life. He cites, for instance, research by Pierre Delooz, which "shows that contemporary French public speakers have effectively separated belief in God from belief in the hereafter."[16]

In basic agreement with the critique offered by Moody and Illich, Stanley Hauerwas stresses the importance of reaffirming God's sovereignty and the human vocation in order to bring an end to such idolatry. "The Christian," he posits, "is concerned not with life as an end in itself, but rather as the medium for service in God's kingdom."[17] Hauerwas goes on to express skepticism about both the validity and the helpfulness of sanctity of life claims.[18] He cites with favor Protestant theologian John Howard Yoder, who, though associated with one of the historic Peace Churches, denies that human life is sacred.[19] Hauerwas quotes Yoder to the effect that "the idea that human life is intrinsically sacred is not a specifically Christian thought."[20] Hauerwas takes exception to sanctity of life parlance, whether disposed toward an intrinsic or an extrinsic view of human sacredness, as an idolatrous intrusion upon God's sovereignty:

Appeals to the sanctity of life beg exactly the question at issue, namely, that you know what kind of life it is that should be treated as sacred. More troubling for me, however, is how the phrase "sanctity of life," when separated from its theological context, became an ideological slogan for a narrow individualism antithetical to the Christian way of life. Put starkly, Christians are not fundamentally concerned about living. Rather their concern is to die for the right thing. Appeals to the sanctity of life as an ideology make it appear that Christians are committed to the proposition that there is nothing in life worth dying for.[21]

Basically, Hauerwas sees problems for the sanctity of life doctrine whether maintained in a religious or a secular context. In Hauerwas's estimation, it has the potential to mislead or corrupt Christian faith.

An assortment of ethicists and theologians standing elsewhere on the theological spectrum have come to nearly identical conclusions about the perniciousness of sanctity of life doctrine for Christian faith. Averse to the excessive individualism that sanctity of life doctrine promotes, James M. Gustafson rejects physical life as an absolute value.[22] He joins in warning that a respect for human life, even personal human life, can become "dogmatic and idolatrous."[23] Beverly Wildung Harrison is of a similar mind. Very specifically, amid sanctity of life arguments against abortion, she sees a "fetishizing of fetuses."[24]

Process theologians Charles Hartshorne, John Cobb, and Charles Birch are even more resolute in their conviction that sanctity of life doctrine is counterproductive and wrong. Hartshorne states: "God, not an individual [human] animal, is sacred."[25] Cobb and Birch similarly make known their opposition to any absolutizing sanctity of life doctrine. While observing that the sanctity of life principle has sometimes "worked in praiseworthy ways against the casual destruction of people perceived as socially useless," it has also, they add, "forced discussions of abortion into artificial distinctions from which these discussions need to be freed" and "led to judgements about abortion and medical practices with the dying which need to be challenged."[26] Cobb and Birch are persuaded that the disadvantages of the sanctity of life principle outweigh the advantages of retaining in any form.

In the final analysis, however, it is an outward secularist and one-time partisan of the sanctity of life doctrine who is the most outspoken about the idolatrousness of the sanctity of life stance and the harm to human life, materially and spiritually, it has caused. Daniel Callahan, a former Roman Catholic who has never lost his sensitivity to theological issues, severely criticizes the doctrine he once espoused.

Essentially, in the sanctity of life doctrine Callahan sees an unfortunate, even disastrous, meeting between traditional religion, a quasi-religious respect for the individual, and modern medicine. As Callahan describes the "strange, often bizarre" results:

> In the name of the sanctity of life, many who would consider themselves conservatives and supporters of traditional religious values are forced into a slavery to medical possibilities, held in thrall by the false god of technology. The value of life is in practice defined, not by religious or moral principles as traditionalists wish, but by technical capacities. . . . As long as a treatment itself is beneficial in sustaining life and not burdensome, there is [now] an obligation to use it . . . even if it leaves the patient as a person worse off than before, and even if it enhances the likelihood that a later death will be worse than the one

averted. . . . Supporters of the view that only treatment burdens should count have been beguiled into acting as if a failure to use technology is tantamount to deliberate killing, an act inimical to life's sanctity.[27]

In Callahan's view the medical imperative has overtaken both custom and common sense when it comes to our responses to the beginnings and endings of human life. Christianity and other religions have become subject to a technological enchantment. Accordingly, he blames the excesses of sanctity of life proponents not on anything inherent in their stance, but on their bondage to scientific medicine:

> I do not believe that either the most central religious or nonreligious traditions of the sanctity of life hold life as such to be the ultimate value. . . . Yet, somehow, that principle has become distorted and misused. This could not have happened had not the principle come under the sway of the promise of medical power and progress. That promise made it seem plausible for the presumed corollary of the respect for life, the judgement that death is an evil, to have a feasible end point, its elimination by science. Thus was created the perfect double-bind: If you are serious about the value of life and the evil of death, you must not stand in the way of medical science, our best hope to eliminate it. If you hesitate to use that science to its fullest, to give it every benefit of doubt, you are convicted not only of failure of hope for the efficacy of science, but also a lack of seriousness about the sanctity of life.[28]

Here Callahan is underscoring a basic fact: in the late twentieth century, when imposing hospital buildings and massive medical complexes proliferate just as cathedrals and religious edifices did in the past, major segments of the Christian churches feel obliged to kowtow to medical science. As conscious or unconscious heirs of St. Augustine and Martin Luther, who viewed death as a punishment, these same Christian elements have proven highly susceptible to modern medicine's view of death as an unmitigated evil which must be conquered or held at bay.[29] Under the circumstances, they simply cannot say no to medical science in its life-extension efforts even when the hubris in such vitalistic enterprise contravenes what the Christian tradition has simultaneously taught about the right valuing of human life.

    In critiquing the rise of a new vitalism or worship of biological life, as promoted by modern medicine, Callahan properly attributes the religious embrace of it to a perversion of basic religious principles—another way to speak of idolatry. Despite Callahan's confidence to the contrary, however, it is not clear that a Christian sanctity of life principle—or any religiously held sanctity of life doctrine—can be divorced from biological vitalism and the consequent idolatry while remaining meaningful as a concept. Nor is it certain that the sanctity of life concept in its present form—or a more theologically tenable revision—could ever gain the wide support and following it needs in order to become the universal ethic it has claims or pretenses of being.

THE CHALLENGE OF A NEW CIVILITY

For all its gravity, the danger of idolatry is not the only reason why sanctity of life doctrine needs to be sharply moderated and set aside by the Christian churches. As the doctrine is presently elaborated it has the ready potential to damage, if not sunder, whatever unity the Christian churches have been able to forge across old denominational and doctrinal lines.

Although a few staunch sanctity of life advocates have called for "realism in the political arena" and civil courtesy "in dealing with those who do not share the same pro-life position," such a prospect does not appear likely.[30] Some of the suppositions upon which sanctity of life doctrine has been built would seem to encourage dogmatism and militate against civility and tolerance for other sincerely held viewpoints. In a strange twist, the same sanctity of life advocates who are so eager to extend the influence of the Christian churches over secular culture jeopardize by word and deed the moral credibility of the entire Christian community.[31]

Advocates for the sanctity of life position have argued very adamantly that the principle is revealed in the Bible, which is compelling for every Christian, and in natural law, which is universally accessible and thus binding upon all. The fact that the sanctity of life concept is peripheral to scripture and that popular and public rhetoric about it did not gain real currency among Christians until relatively recently in this century does not faze its supporters. With their distinctive understanding of history and divine revelation, they have an unfortunate capacity to rationalize any discrepancies away.

In the introduction to the 1930 papal encyclical that introduced the term "sacred" to describe embryonic life, the Roman Catholic Church's sense of historical dynamic in the formal exposition of doctrine was neatly summarized:

> Doctrine is rarely, if ever, defined until widely denied. The wide denial of doctrine when accompanied by unyieldingness is called heresy. If then the history of the Church's dogma teaches us that heresy has been the constant preliminary of authentic definition, we may expect the arrival of a widespread moral heresy to be the next episode in the world of spiritual values.[32]

As it talks about a process of "authentic definition" for church doctrine, the papal statement appears to be informed by a couple of underlying assumptions. First, the papal statement suggests that Christian teachings, whether grounded in biblical or natural revelation, are constant, unchanging, and eternal even if rendered obvious over time only through the heretical choices of a few and the need of the church to formally rebut them. Second, it seems to presuppose that biblically or naturally revealed Christian teachings, no matter how ancient, possess an inherent capacity to anticipate and conclusively answer any moral dilemmas or exigencies that might develop over time.

Totally lacking is any recognition of the possibility that there could arise circumstances never contemplated by holy writ or earlier established church doctrine. Also absent is any sense of scripture or church doctrines as historically conditioned artifacts that must undergo periodic reinterpretation or outright change if they are to remain pertinent.

It is this same largely static historical perspective on biblical and natural revelation which continues to prevail today among both Roman Catholic and Protestant sanctity of life advocates. Not surprisingly, then, advocates regard the santity of life as a principle that has been mostly fixed from the beginning of time for all time. They contend that, as something integral to God's will, the sanctity of life has been tacitly accepted by Christians and non-Christians all along. If the sanctity of life is more consciously and conspicuously affirmed today, it is, they say, only because more grievous and extensive assaults on human life have necessitated such openness: the growing perfidy and sinfulness of human society means that Christians can no longer take the sanctity of life for granted. For Christian sanctity of life advocates, there is simply no basis for doubting the immutable truth and antiquity of their doctrine.

The intolerance fed by such a conviction has not been focused only on those within the Christian circle of faith who disagree with them. The same animus has been directed against those beyond and apart from the Christian community. In the eyes of Christian sanctity of life advocates, those not disposed to accept the authority of a biblical mandate to respect life as sacred remain morally bound to do so as a monition of conscience informed and directed by natural law.

While natural law in both a religious and a secular context has been lauded as giving rise to modern human rights, it often generates high expectations of social conformity. Indeed, within the orbit of natural law theory, a belief that certain truths are self-evident can make it harder for some people to understand why other "reasonable" men and women do not automatically concur with them and behave accordingly. In the attendant confusion, personal resentment, moral anathematization, and social recriminations can quickly follow. Although called to be charitable, Christians have sometimes given way under the influence of natural law to their own worst impulses.[33]

An imperious confidence about the positive, unequivocal, pro-life content of natural law has led Pope John Paul II, for instance, to virtually demonize as "forces of evil" those who do not perceive the "grave moral error" of abortion, euthanasia, and assisted suicide, or who would adopt a more accepting and tolerant attitude to any one of these practices.[34] Other Christian sanctity of life advocates have just as plainly spoken of euthanasia supporters as reverting to "barbarism."[35] The most charitable thing said about those who would allow "mercy killing" is that they have "compartmentalized consciences."[36] Such loud vituperation has been matched on the streets of the United States with actual assassinations and bombings conducted by those identified with the Christian sanctity of life cause.

The intolerance often expressed by sanctity of life proponents has led a number of theologians to challenge their static sense of history and the validity of their biblical and natural law defenses. Very pointedly, the Christian theologian and ethicist Beverly Wildung Harrison, who regards the sanctity of life as a not-so-Christian dogma, has warned that "those who believe that Christian theology . . . can live untouched by change end up equating Christian theology with an ideology of the status quo"—retrojecting present prejudices and biases onto a hallowed Christian past.[37] While she does not concede that holy writ supports an absolutist sanctity of life ethic, Harrison remarks that even if it did, the biblical tradition should not be allowed to substitute "for creative and intelligent moral action in the present. . . . New circumstances confront the norms of received tradition."[38]

Meanwhile, others have been outspoken about the weaknesses of the natural law which sanctity of life advocates have come to hold so dear. Protestant theologian James M. Gustafson has been especially thoughtful and provocative on this score. Gustafson notes that natural law arguments "can too readily fall into a rationalization for desires and interests of both individuals and human communities."[39] In other words, natural law can amount to little more than another human projection upon the divine. Gustafson even challenges Karl Barth's biblical command theology, which, in spite of its alleged rejection of natural law, is actually dependent upon the same kind of human intuition and discernment that are part and parcel of natural revelation.[40] What is needed on everyone's part, Gustafson avers, is greater theological humility.[41] As Gustafson explains, natural law does not disclose as much as most claim. "The signals of the divine ordering," he states, "are not as loud and clear as might be preferred."[42]

Gustafson is by no means alone in his reservations about natural law claims. In a surprising aside, Roman Catholic ethicist Joseph V. Sullivan qualifies the universality of natural law—or at least the depth of discernment that is universally possible through it.[43] Meanwhile, Stanley Hauerwas is very forthright about his personal skepticism concerning natural law claims and mandates. For him the conflict and dissension rampant in contemporary Western society is evidence that there is nothing natural about natural law. Instead, it is a consensual artifact, a medium for expressing certain traditional moral beliefs generated by the Christian community.[44] Unfortunately, according to Hauerwas, right to life and right to die talk is indicative of a culture that has lost any common moral language, vision, and consensus.[45]

Those who share with Gustafson, Sullivan, and Hauerwas a wariness about any explicit commands of natural law do not necessarily agree with Hauerwas's sense of a moral meltdown in contemporary society. Ethicists and theologians such as James F. Childress still believe that moral agreement and consensus on life and death issues can be rationally worked out.[46] Childress's confidence is more or less endorsed by another Protestant theologian, J. Robert Nelson, who believes that something specific like the fractious abortion debate "could be softened or avoided" if we recognized that "it is human value, not life, that is being contested."[47] Nevertheless, though they may even express some pro-life views, none of these theologians regard a sanctity of life position as either reasonable, sustainable, or theologically correct.

The simultaneous rigidity and zeal with which the battle for the sanctity of life is being waged by its advocates would appear to illustrate the kind of "moral imperialism" which Childress, for one, believes must be constrained.[48] The sanctity of life position also involves the kind of abstractions that process theologian Charles Hartshorne regards as unhelpful and untenable. Specifically, Hartshorne writes:

> For moral or legal rules to have much importance in a society they
> must be supported by the traditions of that society. History shows that
> on the basis of pure reason, or what can be demonstrated by manipu-

lating abstractions (such as the "beginning of life"), human beings tend to disagree more or less hopelessly.[49]

Not only does Hartshorne implicitly reject any natural law basis for the sanctity of life. He also asserts that the traditional ethical practices of Western society do not support sanctity of life claims.[50]

In the absence of any natural law constraints or a truly universal ethic, a number of commentators suggest that moral pluralism must be accepted. Secular moral philosophers and ethicists speaking to the Christian community, along with the rest of society, are especially emphatic about this. Yet so are numerous Christian theologians.

On the secular side, H. Tristram Engelhardt Jr. has observed that there "is far from any agreement, or near-agreement, about how one can establish or identify as canonical a particular normative view of the moral life."[51] Here and elsewhere he argues that all religious groups must be ready and willing to negotiate a common ethic.[52] Constitutional legal scholar Lawrence Tribe is inclined to agree. He remarks that what defines a human being is a religious opinion and presumes a morally unitary world that does not exist.[53] K. Danner Clouser is even more specific. While sympathetic to a religious perspective, he plainly states that the world is too pluralistic for the sanctity of life doctrine to singularly prevail: it must be acknowledged as simply one perspective among many.[54]

Some Christian theologians and ethicists second the assessment and conclusions of their secular counterparts on both the subject of pluralism and the sanctity of life. Commenting generally on contemporary moral life, Stanley Hauerwas suggests that Christians can and should accept a certain measure of moral diversity even among themselves. "[There] is no inherent reason," he says, "that Christians must agree about every issue." What is uniquely required of Christians, however, is that "their agreements and their disagreements reflect their theological convictions" and that "the discussion is governed by love."[55]

Basil Mitchell believes that Christian churches will only hurt themselves if they do not acknowledge and accept a diversity of moral outlooks. Though Christian churches that support sanctity of life may not want to surrender the principle's claim to universality and a singular moral correctness, they have a choice: accommodate other perspectives or forfeit their "controlling influence in the culture" altogether.[56] As Mitchell makes clear, the future of the Christian churches hangs in the balance. Unless an alternative to the heteronomous dogmatism and intolerance of the sanctity of life movement prevails, the authority of the Christian churches in the wider society could be further discredited.

THE DESACRALIZATION OF NATURE AND THE ACCEPTANCE OF DEATH

Although sanctity of life advocates have always been quick to criticize the real or imagined inconsistencies of others, they have been prone to miss or overlook the irrational elements in their own thought. This myopia is certainly apparent in their dogmatic insistence on the preservation of human life at all costs. In America, for instance, sanctity of life advocates have encouraged citizens to regard the most expensive medical technology as a birthright in spite of the fact that a third of our global population has barely sufficient means to feed, clothe, and shelter itself and not much prospect, given continued population growth, of improving upon its fortunes.

Even more problematical, however, has been the obliviousness of sanctity of life advocates to their own strangely asymmetrical outlook on nature. In the guise of maintaining the sovereignty of God, sanctity of life proponents have virtually sacralized nature. They have persistently argued that human beings should let God's will, as revealed and expressed through nature, prevail. On this basis, active euthanasia and assisted suicide have been condemned as an intrusion upon divine prerogatives. At the same time, sanctity of life advocates have allowed themselves to be co-opted by modern medicine's own obsession with the conquest of human mortality. Thus, quite incongruously, sanctity of life advocates have consistently supported radical interventions against nature in order to hold back death and prolong whatever life is possible. The significance of such a dichotomy with regard to nature and its workings cannot be overestimated: it provides further illustration of the general illogic of the sanctity of life position.

Even if sanctity of life advocates have remained blind to their own self-contradictions, other fellow Christians have not. Indeed, a whole host of highly respected theologians and scholars have directly or indirectly noted the lack of symmetry and consonance in the sanctity of life stance on nature. They have further observed that the sacralization of nature and the hubris of trying to defeat death are each in their own way antithetical to everything a true Christian faith teaches. Stressing the importance of humility, faithful discernment, and reasonable judgment, as personally exercised by Jesus, these critics of the sanctity of life stance have argued on behalf of a more realistic understanding of both our freedom and finitude in the face of nature.[57]

One of the great moral challenges of our times lies in assessing anew the proper relationship between divine sovereignty and human autonomy. In an earlier age, so much more seemed fated and divinely willed. Yet, thanks to the power of technology and science, human beings today have a greater sense of their own authority and their capacity to give direction to nature, thus determining their own future. This capacity includes our ability to manipulate not only our external environment but also ourselves as human beings.

Fortunately, some theologians have stepped forward with fresh anthropologies that more positively acknowledge humankind's unprecedented manipulative powers. James M. Gustafson, for instance, declares that for some it is still "a matter of debate" whether "the weight of the accountability for the ordering of life has shifted, in a sense, from God to man." For him, personally, however, the matter is clearer. "Certainly," he says, "the balance has shifted to some degree since primitive times, and it is shifting more rapidly in this century than in all the previous centuries of human culture combined."[58] According to Gustafson, the shift is especially conspicuous in the impact technology has had on the continuation or termination of human life:

> Karl Barth, Thomas Aquinas, and even Kant, in his precritical ethics, stated in effect that the moment of termination of life was for God to

decide, not man. Technology clearly has made such statements obso-
lete; it is in human power to sustain human life under increasingly desperate circumstances. Yet in the end the powers that create and sustain
life also bear down upon it and destroy it.[59]

While Gustafson remains wary of technological hubris, he does not lament what some
might regard as an intrusion upon divine prerogatives in matters of life and death.
From his perspective there is no going back to what was: our technological prowess
is a fact of life. What this means is that as human beings we truly stand on fresh
ground in our relationship to God and nature.

Gustafson paradoxically notes that it is an older conception of nature and of what
is natural that have become artificial. Today, he specifically states, "the 'natural order'
is less natural." Even though humankind has "not dominated nature," we control
"more aspects of it than was possible in previous times" and "our capacities to intervene into it mean that 'nature' does not provide the kind of blueprint for proper
human conduct that is more strongly the case in the ethics of Thomas [Aquinas]."[60]

Gustafson's refusal to regard human nature as inexorably fixed and delimited is
hardly unique. The Roman Catholic theologian Karl Rahner has also emphasized
human nature and existence as dynamic, rather than static. In essays entitled "The
Experiment with Man" and "The Problem of Genetic Manipulation," Rahner
insists, for instance, that God did not intend that nature should be untouchable.[61]
Quite the opposite, it is within the very nature of human beings, whom God created, to constantly transcend nature. "Man," Rahner declares, "is fundamentally
'operable' and legitimately so" and "it would only be symptomatic of a cowardly
and comfortable conservatism hiding behind misunderstood Christian ideals and max-
ims if at the outset one were to simply condemn the approaching age of self-manip-
ulation as such; to break out into lyrical laments on the theme of degrading
barbarity, the cold, technological rationalism, the destruction of what is 'natural'
. . . etc." While Rahner agrees that Christians have to fight with the "greatest deter-
mination" against "radical catastrophes and threats to man's existence," it is important to accept that "tomorrow's world will be different from that of today."[62]
Rahner concludes:

And in this coming world man will be the one who, both as an individual and as a society, plans, controls and manipulates himself to a
degree which was previously both undreamed-of and impracticable.
He must do so; he can do no other if he wishes to exist on the Earth
side by side with many thousand millions of other human beings.[63]

According to Rahner, the consistent human transcendence of nature is utterly essential for our survival. It is the proper role of Christian faith to provide positive guidance for this transcendence, rather than to automatically and reflexively impede or
obstruct it.[64]

Rahner is not the only major theologian to argue that intervention in nature has
become natural. In his own theology and ethics, Bernard Häring emphasizes that
Christian faith is often pointing us in a direction beyond nature as we presently

know it. While alert to possible abuses, Häring believes that God gives men and women freedom to change themselves, as well as their surrounding circumstances. Essentially, Häring's position is that it is within the nature of human beings to manipulate nature for their own self-enhancement in God's likeness and image.[65] Indeed, elsewhere, Häring pronounces human beings to be co-creators with God.[66] He further declares that men and women should feel free to alter themselves in fundamental ways providing there is no demeaning intent or result:

> It is my thesis that [a human being] has to interpret his stewardship in the light of his noblest vocation. In that interpretation, he can freely interfere with and manipulate the functions of his bios and psyche in so far as this does not degrade him or diminish his own or his fellowmen's dignity and freedom. Not only nature around him but his own natural being—his biological, psychological reality—calls for his free stewardship, his creative cooperation with the divine artist.[67]

As one commentator has noted, Häring does not regard human nature as "sacred in the sense of being unalterable and beyond every modifying biomedical intervention."[68] Instead, Häring views men and women as divinely created to be self-transforming and self-transcending. For Häring "man himself is an unfinished work, called to be an even better image of God."[69] In the process of manipulating nature, Häring sees human beings becoming ever more like God.[70]

Häring's sense of human malleability clearly puts him at odds with sanctity of life advocates. But his divergence from their outlook does not stop there. He further distinguishes himself from a sanctity of life stance by his simultaneous concern about undue efforts to subjugate and control the course of nature. Even as Häring argues for active intervention in nature to enhance, prolong, and preserve human life, he regards any desperate manipulation of nature as a sign of lost eschatological hope.[71] While Häring is most obviously addressing obsessive efforts at genetic manipulation, his critique would seem to apply just as readily to those who would use all available technological means to push back or hold off the death of an individual human being.

Häring's insight on lost eschatological hope is fully ratified by Southern Baptist theologian Paul D. Simmons. Simmons, who asserts that "death belongs to creation," notes that any posture of despair in the face of death stands contrary to a biblical Christian faith with its professed confidence in the resurrection.[72]

In the end, however, it is secular ethicist Daniel Callahan who is perhaps the clearest and most cogent about the numerous problems engendered by lost eschatological hope. In several of his works, Callahan calls attention to the exalted expectations that men and women have developed with regard to the control of nature and the longevity of human life. Though never attacking the concept of sanctity of life directly, Callahan nonetheless suggests that its advocates have gotten caught up in the wider confusion about how we should understand the proper interrelationship between nature and humankind.

Without pulling any punches, Callahan states what he regards as one of the most crucial questions of our times—namely, does nature still have any independent reality apart from human manipulation and artifice, or has it become totally subject to human control?[73] As a discerning social observer, Callahan sees pervasive support for the illusion that nature has ceased to possess an independent existence. He finds liberal philosophers and theologians increasingly operating under the premise that "there is no moral difference between allowing a patient to die from an underlying disease and killing that patient directly by, say, an injection." Simultaneously, he notes, a large complement of conservative philosophers and theologians now subscribe to the idea that "allowing a patient to die by stopping treatment is a discreet way of intentionally killing that patient." Meanwhile, Callahan finds among physicians of every stripe a pronounced tendency to construe death as a "medical failure" rather than "an inevitable biological denouement."[74]

Callahan's remarks suggest that it is, perhaps, the sanctity of life advocates who have bitten deepest into the apple of humbug and hubris about human power and the possibilities afforded by medical technology to subjugate nature:

> For whatever mischievous historical reason, the ideas of scientific progress and the sanctity of life have come to hold each other in mutual captivity, and to the mutual detriment of both. For its part, by treating all the causes of death as avoidable evils, equivalent as evils to death itself, medical science has held out the hope that the causes might be eliminated—and has made the promotion of that hope a moral imperative. For its part, a capacious notion of the sanctity of life is ready to play along with scientific ambition: if life is sacred, and death an evil, then it becomes our common duty to support whatever will reduce or eliminate death and enhance life.[75]

Thus, the sanctity of life doctrine makes itself the handmaiden to a scientific imperialism.

Not surprisingly, Callahan believes that the effects of a "vanishing nature," reinforced by a peculiar partnership between technologists and sanctity of life advocates, have been pernicious. To the extent that religious groups have accepted the idea of a technologically subjugated nature in their affirmation of life's sanctity, they have unwittingly compromised their own heritage and values which, generally speaking, have viewed the telos of human existence as something other than self-perpetuation of physical human life. Callahan speaks of the compulsion to use technology as a "technological monism" or a "technological imperative."[76]

Under the circumstances Callahan advocates a "return to nature"—in other words, a recognition that nature, while subject to human manipulation, is not entirely within human control. In this "return to nature" Callahan also believes that we must accept death as an inevitable fact of nature, rather than a human failure:

> We cannot return to a premodern world, nor should we want to. Yet we must restore nature to put the human responsibility for death into a more fitting focus. We need a plausible and useful interpretation of nature, one free of the conceit that nature has disappeared, and free in particular of its medical corollary, a technological monism that can

find no boundary to human responsibility for life and death. A peaceful death can never be ours if we let that view hold sway.[77]

As Callahan makes clear, he is not encouraging passivity in the face of nature, nor a renewed sacralization of it. Instead, he is calling upon men and women to come to terms with the simple truth that control of nature, including death, will always elude our grasp.

For Callahan, the conceit that nature and death can be subject to human control is like a hydra-headed monster: it must be challenged and refuted in all its ramifications. Laying out a strategy, Callahan says:

> The necessary place to begin is with three fundamental errors that have made their way into common thinking, both medical and lay. Taken together, they tell the story of the way nature has been distorted. The first is the pervasive belief that, although death may be inevitable, none of the medical causes of death need be accepted; all are in principle curable. The second error is the widespread conviction that there is, in the end, no fundamental moral difference between killing a person and allowing a person to die. The third error is that a commitment to the sanctity of human life is best expressed and pursued through medical science and technological aggressiveness against death. . . . The third error helps to make clear why a commitment to the value and sanctity of life has often ended in a captivity to technology, which is tacitly allowed to dictate moral standards.[78]

Not one to mince words, Callahan is calling for a complete change in our present intellectual and moral landscape as earlier shaped by liberalism and a techno-medical ethic.

A fresh recognition that natural processes, including death, have an autonomous momentum eluding any ultimate human control, regardless of whatever interventions we may attempt, cannot help but affect all sides in the controversy about human responsibility in either prolonging or ending human life. It would certainly pose a challenge to those ethicists, such as Peter Singer and Helga Kuhse, who regard any distinction between positive and negative euthanasia as a matter of hypocrisy, bad faith, and moral irrelevance.[79] Yet even more challenged would be current sanctity of life advocates. Indeed, if our society as a whole was inclined to set all technological and medical hubris aside and to acknowledge death as an inexorable reality, sanctity of life doctrine would not make as much sense or be able to maintain its present appeal. The net result might be a renewed quest for eschatological hope. For Christians this might also mean a properly restored and focused faith with God as both its telos and basis for confidence and trust.

RESPECT FOR LIFE ON A NONSACRAL BASIS

Contrary to what may be claimed by its advocates, the sanctity of life principle is not the only possible safeguard against the degradation of human life. A simpler, less absolutist respect for human life in which no claims about sanctity or sacredness are made could be just as effective in defending against a utilitarian reductionism.

While Roman Catholic theologian Richard McCormick may once have subscribed to the belief that human life is an inviolable good, he has since been among the most forthright in arguing against the absolutizing of human life that is at the crux of the sanctity of life position.[80] For him human biological life possesses a relative, rather than absolute, value:[81]

> The fact that we are (in the Christian story) pilgrims, that Christ has overcome death and lives, that we will also live with Him, yields a general value judgement on the meaning and value of life as we now live it. It can be formulated as follows: life is a basic good but not an absolute one. It is basic because it is the necessary source and condition of every human activity and of all society. It is not absolute because there are higher goods for which life can be sacrificed.[82]

According to McCormick, our Christian faith teaches us that our capacity for loving relationships is a higher good that our biological life should serve. When and where this capacity ceases or is radically impaired because of physiological failure, it is not necessary to continue efforts to preserve life.[83]

Lisa Sowle Cahill has credibly summarized McCormick's attitude and approach in particular situations that help define his understanding of "relational capacity" and his ethical application of it as a criterion for continuing or discontinuing treatment:

> [McCormick] expands the criterion of relational capacity into four guidelines extendable to other patient classes: (1) lifesaving interventions ought not to be omitted because of burdens they impose on the family or others, who are owed assistance by larger social bodies; (2) even relatively significant retardation is not alone adequate reason for nontreatment; (3) life-sustaining interventions may be omitted in cases of excessive hardship for the patient, especially if combined with a poor prognosis; (4) they can be omitted if the anticipated life span is brief and if it requires artificial feeding.[84]

As Cahill's summation suggests, McCormick essentially endorses quality of life considerations. Nevertheless, he opposes the direct taking of human life.[85] He finds no convincing reasons to override a ban on it.

McCormick attributes recent popular support for mercy killing and euthanasia to a shallow understanding of human dignity and a misguided view of the human individual as autonomous with an absolute personal right to determine how, when, and where we should die. In contradistinction, McCormick is an advocate of interdependence—or interpersonal dependence—as a more adequate foundation for human dignity. Furthermore, in death as well as life, he sees us called by our Christian faith to be responsible to others, not just follow our own preferences and desires. As Christians, in other words, we do not have the option of dying unto ourselves alone.[86] Overall, McCormick's ethical stance offers formidable testimony to the fact that a refusal to espouse a sanctity of life position does not open the floodgates to a disrespect for life.

Equally prominent Protestant theologian and ethicist James M. Gustafson similarly avoids all sanctity of life claims. In its theocentricity, Gustafson's own ethic of life represents a reassertion of an older Christian piety. At the same time, it is not afraid of being unconventional or responding to novel circumstances. Speaking of the moral context provided by Western society, Gustafson states:

> There are perduring principles such as distributive justice and respect for individual life; there are almost absolute values such as that of physical life. But these are not sufficient as a basis to determine what courses of action are preferable in the light of finite and changing natural and cultural conditions. . . . To relate human activity to the ultimate ordering power is to see that various conditions must be met or created in order to avert potential suffering to present and future generations of humans, and to avoid irreversible and deleterious outcomes for the natural world of which we are a part.[87]

With his theocentric perspective, Gustafson calls upon us to consider human life in the broadest possible context. Of critical importance to him is that we listen to what God may be saying to us through present circumstances. For Gustafson too, moral judgments must be pronounced in a spirit of humility. Our human powers of observation are too limited, constrained, and fallible to justify dogmatic or absolute moral declarations on anyone's part.

Elsewhere, Gustafson is explicit about his attitude toward human life. "The preservation of physical human life," he writes, "is not an end in itself." Instead, its "almost absolute value stems from the fact that it is the condition sine qua non for the individual to value anything else and to make contributions as a participant in life."[88] Gustafson insists that physical life should not be accorded ultimacy.[89] Gustafson subsequently ventures his own opinion that "one does not need to affirm that human life is of supreme value in order to defend the view that it is of distinctive value."[90]

Gustafson takes issue with the anthropocentrism of many Christian theologians and ethicists, seeing God's principal concern as residing with the more encompassing order of creation and only secondarily with the salvation of humankind.[91] From Gustafson's perspective, humankind and the natural world are completely interdependent: human life must be informed by such an awareness. Ultimately, this "theological construal of the world requires that more than the good of the human species must be considered" in ethical decision-making.[92]

Gustafson's theocentrism and his stress on the interdependence of humankind and nature shape and qualify his attitude toward such issues as infanticide, abortion, and contraception. Although he regards infanticide as "a very grave matter" and "morally wrong," his total condemnation of it is conditioned on the availability of an "alternative means of birth control."[93] Likewise, he regards abortion as "a morally serious [choice] because fetal life has the possibility of developing into a unique human being" but would not ban it outright or judge it morally wrong in all cases.[94] Finally, Gustafson speaks up as an advocate for birth control. As he puts it, the use of contraception is not just licit. It has "an authority that is little short of an imperative."[95]

Generally, Gustafson is convinced that human beings need to limit their pro-creativity for the common good of all species of life on our planet. As Gustafson perceives matters, any continuing anthropocentrism which leaves population growth unchecked will imperil the future for all, including human beings. Thus, in Gustafson's view, respect for other species and respect for human life coalesce to a highly sig-nificant degree.

The fact that Gustafson does not treat any individual human rights as categor-ical may cause concern for some.[96] Yet the absence of such an affirmation does not mean that Gustafson is insensitive to the notion of individual rights as fostered by liberalism in our society's secular and religious spheres. For Gustafson, however, indi-vidual human rights are just one part of the equation in a "dynamic equilibrium of values" within a cosmos where, as one commentator explains Gustafson's outlook, there is no immutable ordering of life or harmony of values—no risk-proof or cost-proof morality.[97] In the end, just as he declines to regard physical human life or indi-vidual personal life as sacred, Gustafson refuses to sacralize nature as Albert Schweitzer and a more recent crop of ecologically oriented theologians have.[98]

While Gustafson avoids all sanctity of life rhetoric, he nevertheless offers a firm and well-developed respect for life ethic.[99] His theocentric ethics are very much in keeping with the Reformation tradition of returning the focus of our lives to God. In a genuine way, they are a healthy corrective to the narcissistic excesses engendered by an eighteenth-century liberalism, which, in various permutations, whether sec-ular, Christian, or other, continues to shape the modern world.

Of course, the distinctive life ethics offered in turn by McCormick and Gustafson are not the only alternatives to a sanctity of life perspective. There are other vari-ations possible which, while refusing to absolutize the value of human physical life by means of sacredness rhetoric, nevertheless display a serious respect for human life. For instance, Beverly Wildung Harrison, who has written extensively on abor-tion, bypasses the "alien dignity" arguments of some Protestants and speaks directly of the "intrinsic value" of human life, which, as she puts it, "we ought to acknowl-edge as worthy apart from any functional or use relation to us."[100] According to Harrison, however, the intrinsic value of human life must be understood within the context of a broader continuum. On one end the continuum is bounded by our sur-rounding natural environment, which, even though we often put it to use, has some intrinsic value. At the other end of the same continuum is God, who is the 'center of value,' grounding the valuation of all things."[101] Meanwhile, along this contin-uum of intrinsic value lie both physical human life and human personhood or per-sonal life. In Harrison's estimation it is human personhood or personal life, rather than mere physical human life, which may "most clearly and unambiguously . . . claim 'intrinsic value.'"[102]

The continuum that Harrison posits for the proper valuation of life is reflected in her willingness to regard abortion as a moral option. Fetal life, according to Harrison, does not possess personhood. Thus, the emotional, spiritual, and physi-cal well-being of a pregnant woman, who is clearly a person of unambiguous intrinsic worth, should override the concern we have for her fetus as human life. Nevertheless, the moral claim which the fetus has upon the mother and the wider community is not negligible. In principle, where carrying a fetus to full term would not conflict with the emotional, spiritual, or physical well-being of the woman, the moral claims of the fetus for the support necessary to see it to birth and beyond would be compelling, even paramount. In any decision regarding abortion, the respective moral claims based upon their relative intrinsic worth need to be thoughtfully weighed.[103]

Although Harrison does not regard human life as sacred and inviolable, she, like McCormick and Gustafson, is still able to articulate through the idea of an "intrinsic worth" continuum a highly reasonable and responsible life ethic. Harrison's approach is further testimony to the fact that there are viable alternatives to the sanctity of life position which demonstrate a respect for human life that can withstand any utilitarian reductionism.

In his own anthropology, developed long before the immediate controversy over the sacredness of life emerged, the process theologian W. Norman Pittenger spoke of human life as "sacramental."[104] What Pittenger meant is that as we grapple to understand human life in both its creative potential and its limitations we catch a glimmer of something ultimate both in the midst of it and beyond it. In other words, ordinary and mundane human life, along with other bodily life forms, serves as the medium and the occasion by which we encounter God. Rather than counting human life as sacred and holy, either inherently or on the basis of an alien dignity, perhaps the vision of human life as sacramental offers a truer foundation for an abiding Christian respect.[105]

OVERCOMING THE SLIPPERY SLOPE SCARE

Consciously or unconsciously, sanctity of life advocates have often been successful in garnering support for their own position by playing upon inchoate fears about the depravity of the unrestrained human will. They have continuously held out the specter of slippery slopes and wedge effects.

For example, Karl Barth apodictically forewarns of the "wolf" breaking out in human beings.[106] Likewise, Paul Ramsey expresses concern about a collective reversion to barbarism as our horror of Nazi atrocities, including medical experimentation on human subjects, recedes from memory.[107] Another Protestant, J. Kerby Anderson, sees the erosion of the sanctity of life principle as creating a slippery slope in which the movement from abortion, if permitted, to euthanasia will be an "inevitable" progression.[108] Meanwhile, Roman Catholic theologian Germain Grisez claims that contraception is sure to lead to a violation of life itself, undermining all convictions about life's sanctity.[109] In a similar vein, American Catholic bishops have declared that "a society which tolerates the direct destruction of innocent life, as in the current practice of abortion, is in danger of losing its respect for life in all other contexts."[110] Finally, there are theologians and ethicists leaning toward the sanctity of life perspective who are disturbed by the prospect of a slippery slope attaching to particular actions and deeds in medical treatment.

The wedge effect of discontinuing artificial sustenance is argued, for example, by Mark Siegler and Alan J. Weisbard, who generally fear that a right to die may, in time, shift to a duty to die.[111] In spite of the fact that he appears to have distanced himself from his earlier thoroughgoing sanctity of life stance, Daniel Callahan has similarly proffered wedge effect arguments against withholding life-sustaining food and hydration, insisting that a moral and "esthetic repugnance against deliberate starvation" must always be kept alive.[112]

Perhaps the fears of the slippery slope advocates should not be entirely discounted. All the same, while the possibility of a gradual and unwitting habituation to real evil and inhumanity always exists, the danger can be greatly exaggerated.[113] Theologian Paul D. Simmons has been especially eloquent in challenging not only slippery slope and wedge arguments but also the guilt-by-association tactics frequently deployed on behalf of the sanctity of life:

> Popular associations of euthanasia with the Nazi atrocities are both misleading and inaccurate. Those who oppose any form of euthanasia frequently make such allegations in a guilt-by-association tactic. There is no justification for arguing, however, that the first use of the term "euthanasia" was in Germany in 1920, which then becomes the rationale behind Nazi genocide. The unfortunate consequence of such arguments is the clouding of the legitimate issues at stake in the debate about medical technology and its relation to human dying. Hitler's gas chambers were not merciful but merciless; killing was by political coercion not voluntary consent; and the patients were not dying but, for ideological reasons, were judged undesirable.[114]

According to Simmons, it was the underlying Nazi ideology with its unchecked will to power and its non-Christian and undemocratic convictions about Aryan racial supremacy which led to atrocities against human life. For this reason, Hitler's Germany does not validate the slippery slope hypothesis that killing is seductive or contagious, especially where the situs for our own discussion of the proper respect for human life is a very different kind of society. In our era, quite apart from any belief in the sanctity of life, such Christian communal values as love, compassion, and justice can be said to remain intact and to serve as an ongoing check on the potential abuse of power.[115]

One evangelical Christian commentator has suggested that the use of slippery slope arguments by sanctity of life advocates to fuel the apocalyptic vision of a new barbarism reflects a personal inability to deal with moral ambiguity.[116] Whether or not this is true, their dark vision of Nazi medicine revisited, if sanctity of life fails to prevail as a principle, reveals a definite lack of trust in the general ability of men and women to morally cope with complex or even paradoxical situations. This lack of trust is unwarranted. Ignored is much evidence to the contrary, underscoring the human capacity for moral differentiation.

Very pointedly, James M. Gustafson observes that "the toleration of approximately 50,000 deaths by automobile accidents per year in the United States has not adversely affected respect for life in other circumstances."[117] Moreover, the Jewish community, which does not regard the fetus as a "sacred person," has permitted abortion without succumbing to a devaluation of all human life. In fact, while maintaining a tolerant stance toward abortion in keeping with Jewish tradition, the eminent rabbi and ethicist Immanuel Jakobovits has espoused a sanctity of life position.[118] Slippery slope arguments notwithstanding, such a paradox within the Jewish perspective shows that allowance for contraception, abortion, and other practices that Christian sanctity of life advocates condemn does not have to lead to a moral abyss.

James F. Childress further challenges the idea that total moral consistency is necessary to preserve a proper respect for life. He notes the ability of men and women to make significant moral differentiation, sometimes by resort to a positive compartmentalization of conscience.[119] For example, Childress has argued that it is possible to withdraw artificial hydration and nutrition where a patient, exercising his or her own autonomy, requests the withdrawal or where continuing artificial hydration and nutrition does not serve an incompetent patient's interests without impugning a wider and deeper respect for human life.[120]

Others who espouse an alternative to a strict, emphatic sanctity of life ethic would completely agree. Not unlike Childress, they view the Christian moral life in terms of a balancing act in which different, competing, and sometimes equally compelling interests for the patient must be weighed. While they might be concerned about undue medical zeal, which can afflict a patient with overtreatment that is as bad as or worse than any underlying disease, they remain sensitive, alert, and discriminating about any rash or capricious devaluation of human life. They would assiduously oppose any slide toward a truly utilitarian ethic.[121]

Naturally, beyond the Christian community and its distinguishing self-constraints some temptation may exist. Secular ethicists such as Marvin Kohl and Joseph Fletcher, for instance, have called for a new openness to what they respectively refer to as active beneficent euthanasia and direct, nonvoluntary euthanasia—in other words, "mercy killing."[122] Reiterating many of their arguments, another secular ethicist, Peter Singer, best known as an animal rights activist, has more recently advocated a new "Copernican revolution" in which, among other things, the moral distinction between passive and active euthanasia would be collapsed once and for all.[123] Like Kohl and Fletcher, Singer contends that directly dispatching someone and committing active euthanasia, where a patient's medical circumstances warrant, should morally be no more significant and grievous than facilitating passive euthanasia and withdrawing medical care.[124] Still, all these proposals on behalf of euthanasia have been adamantly and effectively rejected by the same mainstream Christian ethicists and theologians who simultaneously eschew any sanctity of life principle.

Critiquing Kohl, Fletcher, and Singer, mainstream theologians and ethicists insist that these secular ethicists are wrong in morally equating passive and active euthanasia. Passive euthanasia simply accedes in some cases to natural processes, which continue to have a direction and dynamic of their own. Active euthanasia, however, seeks to hubristically extend human control over nature by actively ending human life.[125] In the end, active euthanasia contravenes, as passive euthanasia does not, the ancient Judeo-Christian commandment "Do not kill"—an admonition to which even those not subscribing to the sanctity of life principle remain acutely sensitive.

Of course, at the heart of the rejection of active euthanasia by ethicists and theologians who challenge the sanctity of life principle is the belief that many who are chronically or terminally ill may be beyond cure but not beyond human caring and comfort. While those who espouse an alternative to the sanctity of life ethic would regard mercy killing as morally permissible in those care situations where a patient suffers intractable and irremediable pain, such allowance is neither extreme nor particularly distinctive. In the name of Christian compassion even sanctity of life advocate Paul Ramsey recommended a direct "dispatching" of patients who appeared to be beyond the reach of palliative care.[126]

Overall, the stance taken by many mainstream Christian ethicists and theologians demonstrates that a rejection of a sanctity of life ethic is not, as some would have us believe, a carte blanche for killing. It is possible to pursue a more moderate appreciation for the value of life without automatically plunging into a moral abyss where respect for life is totally lost. A realistic Christian worldview calls upon us to recognize the potential moral perfidy of men and women. But such Christian realism need not preclude us from affirming the positive human capacity for healthy, wholesome moral discernment and initiative in keeping with an abiding Christian faith.

SANCTITY DOCTRINE AS A CAUTIONARY TALE

In an extended essay on ethics the American theologian H. Richard Niebuhr once suggested that any responsible or truly responsive moral decision-maker needs to begin with a simple question: What is happening?[127] The preceding genealogy of the sanctity of life concept has sought to shed light on what is happening in one of the major controversies to touch Christian churches in the late twentieth century.

In many respects, the genealogy of the sanctity of life concept offers a profound and complex cautionary tale. In the midst of it, we variously encounter the manipulation of history, including biblical and ecclesiastical traditions; the limits of natural law doctrine; the misperception of secularism as a religiously neutral stance; the weakening of Christian conviction about an eternal life; the eruption of idolatry; and the continuing propensity of the Christian churches to resort to new forms of heteronomy when threatened by either the action or the apathy of the enveloping culture.

One of the frank conclusions of this genealogy is that the sanctity of life is not worth fighting for. In light of its history and evolution it hardly deserves to be called a Christian principle. Despite the fact that it is now part of common parlance within many Christian circles and is even regarded as axiomatic, the sacredness of human life does not have a particularly long or extensive Christian pedigree. To the contrary, except for John Calvin's isolated embrace of the sanctity of life as a part of his own response to Renaissance humanism, the doctrine is of fairly recent origin as a Christian dogma.

As its actual history indicates, the sanctity of life concept made its first inroads within the more liberal sectors of the Christian churches, which appropriated it from secular humanist sources grounded in the eighteenth-century Enlightenment. Only thereafter—most particularly in the twentieth century—did the idea of the sanctity of life win acceptance among more conservative Christian churches, Protestant and Roman Catholic.

In some respects, the growing Christian embrace of the sanctity of life was natural, almost inevitable, given the drift of popular sentiment. From the eighteenth century on, science, sanitation, and medical technology increased life expectancy for men and women. Mortal life came to feel less temporary, tenuous, and provisional. Instead of bowing to the vagaries of nature, men and women, Christians among them, could realistically pin their hopes on surviving illness and disease.[128]

Meanwhile, scientific rationalism generated growing skepticism toward religious claims of a heavenly afterlife. For many, life in this world began to seem like a surer bet than life in the next. While the Christian churches did not expressly alter their own thinking about temporal and eternal life, they had to deal at a practical level with a shift in their own adherents' confidence regarding each.

In the mid-twentieth century it was a cadre of secular humanists who gave fresh impetus to the notion of the sanctity of human life. Reacting to the modern horrors of Auschwitz and Hiroshima, as well as the prospect of the kind of anti-utopian future envisioned by Aldous Huxley and George Orwell, they sought to defend the human individual from technological invasions guided by strictly rational, utilitarian considerations. The Enlightenment ideals of human freedom and human rights figured prominently in this defense and attracted liberal Christian support.

Unlike their liberal brethren, the conservative Christian churches did not entirely subscribe to the secular humanist critique of technology. Nevertheless, they recognized that they did share with the protesting secular humanists a common foe—namely, a rationalist utilitarian ethic that also displaced conventional moral piety and religious beliefs.

Thereafter, to the chagrin of secular humanist advocates of the sanctity of life, who had sought to enshrine a respect for human personhood, conservative Christians actually began appropriating a liberal rhetoric of human freedom, human rights, and human sacredness to shape their own distinctive stance, which came to stress the bodily inviolability of human life. Further anchoring their position in a fresh interpretation of traditional imago Dei doctrine, conservative Christians proceeded to deploy the sanctity of life in public policy debates as a heteronomous principle to constrain human moral initiative, which they regarded as offensive to their own moral piety and theology. For the Roman Catholic Church particularly, arguments on behalf of the sanctity of life became a means of making more palatable to the contemporary age a highly negative, centuries-old sex ethic banning contraception and abortion.

On the basis of natural law, both Roman Catholic and conservative Protestants contended that their own opposition to acts such as abortion and euthanasia was part of a universal morality that should be binding upon the entire society. Thus, the sanctity of life doctrine, which had its origins in liberal theory and culture, came to be used as a cudgel by conservative Christians against those aspects of the same liberal culture which they had long seen as threatening to their own authority and worldview.

Although conservative Christians argued that the sanctity of life principle was a moral axiom over which reasonable men and women would not disagree, their particular interpretation of it did not engender wide loyalty, as public opinion polls continue to attest. Subsequently, the rancorous debate that emerged in medical ethics between sanctity of life advocates and quality of life proponents was often a dispute on what was sacred about human life. While some quality of life proponents cited an actual or imminent psychosocial relational capacity as a criterion to value human life, and viewed personhood and personal autonomy as sacrosanct, conservative Christian sanctity of life advocates were adamant in maintaining that the life of any being within the human genus, regardless of psychosocial development or relational potential, was to be held inviolable. Once again, appropriating the language of their adversaries, who distinguished between personal and nonpersonal human life, conservative Christians insisted upon a more expansive definition of personhood that would embrace all human life.

Secular humanists, who ultimately had to abandon sanctity of life rhetoric to conservatives, were not without a line of defense. Countering conservative Christian claims that their own conception of the sanctity of life was a universal moral principle deserving the sanction of specific public laws, the humanists argued that it was instead a parochial dogma which had no place in public policy, especially within a pluralistic nation with a firm constitutional rule about the separation of church and state.[129]

Some liberal Christians have endorsed this kind of rejoinder. Others have counseled Christian sanctity of life advocates to moderate their conduct, if not their views, within the public square or arena. Christian ethicist Basil Mitchell has stated matters plainly. Though the Christian churches may not be prepared to surrender their sanctity of life principle, they have a choice: come to terms with other perspectives or lose both moral credibility and influence.[130]

A NON-HETERONOMOUS RESPECT FOR LIFE

Right now, the whole sanctity of life controversy—sometimes punctuated by violence—is at a standoff in our society at large. To avert further polarization and conflict, all parties need to step back and thoughtfully reexamine their own public positions, including the theological and anthropological assumptions underlying them.

The responsibility of the Christian churches at this juncture is especially great. Quite apart from whatever obligations they may have as participants in society alongside other groups, organizations, and institutions, the Christian churches are more fundamentally accountable to their own gospel heritage. Rather than reifying a single idea or principle, they have a call and duty to uphold a wider Christian kerygma.

Popular belief notwithstanding, the sanctity of life principle does not represent this larger Christian heritage well. Functioning as a heteronomous principle, it consistently violates the anti-legalism of the gospel. What is needed in place of the sanctity of life principle is a more faithful basis for upholding the value of human life against unwarranted and unscrupulous intrusions.

The best hope for a faithful alternative to the flawed sanctity of life principle may lie in looking as much backward as forward. As some stalwart theologians have argued all along without the audience they deserve, Christianity would do well in resisting the utilitarian manipulation of human life if it simply refocused itself theocentrically, using such means as evangelism, education, compassionate outreach, ecclesial community-building, and public dialogue to foster a wider appreciation for the importance of seeing "all things in relation to God" as, in fact, earlier saints and reformers were inclined to do.[131]

Attendant to this kind of restored theocentrism would be a renewed vision of human life as sacramental, instead of sacred. Also incumbent would be a commitment to the preservation of human life as a penultimate and limited good, rather than the ultimate and absolute value that sanctity of life adherents have made it out to be. Indeed, while a Christian doctrine of creation may call us to cherish human life, the corresponding doctrine of redemption always requires that we weigh the value of mortal human life in a context that is conscious of the eternal. Only a more qualified, non-heteronomous respect for life, which seeks to keep the Christian doctrines of creation and redemption in appropriate balance, should command our loyalty.

In the face of the intra-religious conflict and confusion, all Christians—liberal, mainstream, and conservative—need to plumb anew the real fundamentals of the faith we ecumenically share with one another. Only as Christians recenter their faith in a relationship with God and recognize that dignity comes to men and women through the opportunity to serve God's dynamic purposes does a healthy respect for human life stand a chance of being defended in faith and sustained with integrity.

ROLE OF CHURCHES IN FOSTERING RESPECT FOR LIFE

Not surprisingly, some of the diverse theologians who advocate a Christian respect for life disentangled from neo-Stoic or liberal notions view the Christian churches, gathered as local communities, as critical participants in efforts to renew and maintain a respect for life ethic. Akin to secular ethicist Daniel Callahan, who believes that the "heroic self-sacrifice [necessary for a true respect for life] may be possible only if understood within the context of an entire way of life," they share a conception of the Christian churches as spiritual and moral powerhouses for present and future society.[132]

Kenneth Vaux and James P. Wind are perhaps typical of this breed of Christian ethicists and theologians in stressing that churches, as well as neighborhoods, are essential to the flourishing of human well-being.[133] This perspective on the important role of churches as communities teaching proper moral discernment is seconded by evangelical ethicist and theologian Dennis Hollinger. He encourages evangelicals and other Christians to see themselves as "resident aliens" and the church as salt, light, and leaven in the midst of the larger society and world.[134] Yet an even more thoroughgoing statement of the role that the Christian churches should play and the approach that Christian ethics should take in actualizing an uncompromising respect for life is offered by two other Christian theologians, Stanley Hauerwas and James M. Gustafson.

Hauerwas is eloquent in expressing his vision of the church as a morally acculturating institution and community. In *The Peaceable Kingdom* he writes that "to be a Christian is not principally to obey certain commandments or rules, but to learn to grow into the story of Jesus as the form of God's kingdom." He adds, "Ethics is not primarily about rules and principles, rather it is about how the self must be transformed to see the world truthfully."[135] The function of the Christian churches is not to inculcate rules but to help women and men of all ages to enter into a transforming relationship with Jesus Christ through the narrative account of his life, death, and resurrection, plus the story of the first apostles, disciples, and saints who gathered in his name. According to Hauerwas, this relationship with Jesus ultimately demands from us much more than could be reasonably expected if we were not relating to Jesus as Christ in faith.[136]

Hauerwas rejects the claims of natural law—claims about the universality of certain moral knowledge that have prompted some Christian churches, most notably the Roman Catholic Church, to hold non-Christians morally accountable in the same way as Christians.[137] Even more specifically, he believes that we need to resist the temptation to simply water Christian morality down so as to make it more comprehensible, palatable, and practical for those outside the circle of faith. As Hauerwas states, a genuine "Christian ethics can never be a minimalistic ethic for everyone, but must presuppose a sanctified people wanting to live more faithful to God's story."[138]

Instead of trying to increase a general respect for life by resort to coercive political and social pressures, Christian churches should, in Hauerwas's view, seek to embody the values they hold dear. The example that the Christian faithful provide for the rest of the society is crucial. Ultimately, it will be far more persuasive and compelling than any loud and vociferous exhortation. In tandem with this claim, Hauerwas reminds us that the responsibility of the churches is to bring people to Christ, rather than promote adherence to any particular doctrine, dogma, or ideal that might purportedly be derived from Jesus' teachings.[139]

Protestant theologian James M. Gustafson similarly assigns to the Christian churches the responsibility for promoting the relationship with God rather than prescribing or proscribing particular behaviors and deeds. Only a relationship with God can provide the basis for the moral discernment that properly respects life.[140] Like Hauerwas, Gustafson is very wary of those who would profess to know what God might command in any given situation:

> The history of religion is the history of human attempts to manage and manipulate the awesome power of God, who finally is beyond our capacities to know fully, to capture in human thoughts and words. It is the history of human efforts to nail down God's power and goodness, to avoid God's wrath and judgement. It is the history of efforts to control the times and places of God's presence, to create devices by which to make God serve our interests, to give God form and shape so that we can caress "him." Indeed, it is the history of human efforts to exercise sovereignty over God. . . . But God will not be manipulated. God will be God.[141]

For Gustafson, morality and ethics must always be exercised in a spirit of profound humility. The temptation to overstate the authority of all moral judgments must be resisted. There is no place in Christian ethics for dogmatism, especially of the kind witnessed in debates over the biomedical sciences. Though as Christians we are called "to relate all things in a manner appropriate to their relations to God," Gustafson reminds us that "there are no divinely initiated or infallibly revealed prescriptions of proper actions," or any "precise moral blueprint in nature to which actions are to be conformed." Rather than providing "an infallible moral guide," theology can at best "support an interpretation of life and of various ends and values that have to be taken into account."[142] Amid such frank statements Gustafson endorses a "theocentric piety" and a "theocentric ethics" shaped by "the senses of dependence, gratitude, obligation, remorse and repentance, possibilities, and direction" in relationship with God.[143]

The churches figure prominently for Gustafson in educating people for appropriate moral discernment.[144] In his earlier writings, Gustafson averred that it was "plausible to claim . . . not only that religious communities tend to form persons with certain preferences for values, including moral values, but also that a conscious awareness of the reality of God, a living of the life of faith, can alter the values that persons have come to hold."[145] He further observed that "the connections between religious believing and experience and moral activity are complex, not simple."[146] Though Gustafson believed that Christian ethics should be "intelligible" to non-Christians, he recognized that there is always going to be a "remainder" factor not rationally comprehensible to persons outside the faith.[147] For example, the self-sacrificial obedience unto death that is asked of Christians cannot be justified by the kind of rational, enlightened self-interest that grounds most purely secular ethics.[148]

Gustafson's more recent writings continue to stress the importance of church life in building up and sustaining this kind of theocentric piety and ethics. He details the complex ways in which Christian churches, as "communities of moral discourse," shape human beings for the good, cultivating a sense of interdependence and a profound and unselfish respect for all life:

> Our participation in the patterns and processes of interdependence enables and requires us for the sake of worthy wider ends and purposes to be self-giving. . . . To be such persons, communities, and institutions, however, requires our participation in communities that interpret or construe the world as ultimately brought into being, sustained, borne down upon, and provided with conditions of possibility by the ultimate power and orderer of all life. Herein lies the significance of . . . life in the Christian community with its symbols and concepts, its liturgies and communal life, and with its distinctive determination by the accounts given in the Bible and particularly, for it, those given in the New Testament.[149]

Gustafson regards the shared symbols, rites, and stories of the Christian community as shapers of human character. As he views matters, participation in communal Christian worship, whereby people open themselves to the power of religious symbols and imagery, not only enables them to see and sense their own relative insignificance. By presenting all things in "the light and power of the majesty of God," it inculcates appreciation for the relative insignificance of the entire "human venture." Through Christian worship, Gustafson adds, "we also see and sense our own possibilities and accountabilities, individual and communal, in the light of what the sustaining powers enable and require."[150] In short, participation in communal Christian life fosters a theocentric piety and an attendant sense of humility and responsibility. This kind of piety, personally embraced, internalized, and lived out in personal deeds and sacrifices, is more prone to result in a respect for created life than the many exogenous demands which the Christian churches try to impose on their own members and others.

No doubt the rhetoric about the sanctity of life will remain appealing to men and women who are appalled and frightened by the moral chaos of liberal culture, which in its relativism really does appear to be at loose ends. Those who cling to the sanctity of life as an antidote are likely to be impatient with the greater uncertainties inherent in a response to the crisis that, quite differently, stresses relationship to God and participation in the life of the church as a formative moral community first and foremost—and respect for life only secondarily.

Yet, before the ideas and concepts of the philosophical Enlightenment impinged upon Christian outlook and doctrine, this was the emphasis within the historic Christian churches, at least when they were not caught up in Constantinianism, neo-Constantinianism, or some other variation on the same theme.[151] Even today, a re-evangelization of our society based upon the positive example of Christians spiritually and morally living out a gospel faith dedicated to love and justice holds out more promise for creating a new society where human life is really respected than all the efforts to draw a line in the sand on behalf of the sanctity of life.

Almost in passing, the theologian Paul Ramsey, one of the persons most responsible for the genesis and propagation of the sanctity of life doctrine, quoted a leading British hospice physician, Dr. Cicely Saunders, as saying: "If you relieve a patient's pain and if you can make him feel like a wanted person, which he is, then you are not going to be asked about euthanasia."[152] While we should not minimize the pain which those at the edges of life often face, it is hard not to see a kernel of truth in the statement. Saunders got it more than halfway right.

Rather than standing on dogmatic principle or resorting to heteronomous authority in the face of a utilitarian, instrumental outlook that has little or no respect for the value of human life, our energies as Christians are better directed to a renewal of communal and individual faith. Respect for life can and will prevail if men and women have—thanks to a lively faith—a palpable, ongoing sense of their own worth in God's sight; a revived and abiding eschatological hope; and the spiritual insight and courage to accept their own death as a morally significant way station in the passage from life to life. To these ends and purposes, all our Christian churches need to turn.

Notes

PREFACE

1. Jack Brovins and Thomas Oehmke, *Dr. Death: Dr. Jack Kevorkian's Rx—Death* (n.p.: Lifetime Books, 1993), 24, 31.

2. Ibid., 49–50.

3. Ibid., 50–53.

1. IS HUMAN LIFE "SACRED IN ALL ITS FORMS"?

1. John Richard Neuhaus, *The Naked Public Square: Religion and Democracy in America* (Grand Rapids, Mich.: Eerdmans, 1984), 20–27.

2. Pope John Paul II, *The Gospel of Life (Evangelium Vitae): The Encyclical Letter on Abortion, Euthanasia, and the Death Penalty in Today's World* (New York: Random House, Times Books, 1995). Also see Pope John Paul II, *Sacred in All Its Forms and Selected Documents from the Holy See and Various Bishops*, ed. James Schall (n.p.: St. Paul Editions, 1984), 16–17.

3. John Paul II, *Gospel of Life*, 7.

4. See Joint Evangelical Protestant–Roman Catholic Statement on Abortion in "Evangelicals and Catholics Together: The Christian Mission in the Third Millennium," *First Things* 43 (May 1994). Reprinted in Charles Colson and Richard John Neuhaus, eds., *Evangelicals and Catholics Together: Towards a Common Mission* (Dallas: Word Publishing, 1995), xv–xxxiii. Though the joint statement makes no mention of the sanctity of life per se, its rhetoric clearly alludes to it. See ibid., xxiv–xxv. The sense of alliance and common cause between Roman Catholics and conservative or evangelical Protestants is also palpable in the discussion of the abortion controversy offered by John Stott, *Decisive Issues Facing Christians Today* (Grand Rapids, Mich.: Baker Book House, Fleming H. Revell, 1993), 308–15, and by Benedict M. Ashley, "Birth Issues: Pro-Life Evangelization," *The New Technologies of Birth and Death: Medical, Legal, and Moral Dimensions* (St. Louis and Chicago: Pope John Center and Franciscan Herald Press, 1980), 83–87.

5. James R. Kelly, "Learning and Teaching Consistency," *The Catholic Church and the Politics of Abortion*, ed. Timothy A. Byrnes and Mary C. Segers (Boulder, Colo.: Westview Press, 1992), 158. Also see Ronald Smothers, "Abortion Doctor and Bodyguard Slain in Florida," *New York Times* (late New York edition), 30 July 1994, 1.

6. See Ashley, "Birth Issues: Pro-Life Evangelization," 81.

7. See Paul Ramsey, *Ethics at the Edges of Life: Medical and Legal Intersections* (New Haven, Conn.: Yale University Press, 1978), 48. Also see Kelly, "Learning and Teaching Consistency," 159.

8. Alasdair MacIntyre, *After Virtue: A Study in Moral Theory*, 2d ed. (Notre Dame, Ind.: University of Notre Dame Press, 1984), 253–54.

9. Arthur Dyck, "Beneficent Euthanasia and Benemortasia: Alternative Views of Mercy," in *Beneficent Euthanasia*, ed. Marvin Kohl (Buffalo: Prometheus Books, 1975), 127. Also see C. Everett Koop, "The Challenge of Definition," in *Mercy, Murder, and Morality: Perspectives on Euthanasia, Hastings Center Report: A Special Supplement* (January/February 1989), 2.

10. Leon R. Kass, "Death with Dignity and the Sanctity of Life," *Commentary* 89 (March 1990): 34.

11. "Is Every Life Worth Living? To Take a Human Life Is to Take What Belongs to God," *Christianity Today* 26 (19 March 1982): 13.

12. J. H. Channer, Foreword, *Abortion and the Sanctity of Life*, ed. J. H. Channer (Exeter, England: Paternoster Press, 1985), 9–10.

13. Joseph Fletcher, "The 'Right' to Live and the 'Right' to Die," *Beneficent Euthanasia*, ed. Marvin Kohl (Buffalo: Prometheus Books, 1975), 46–47.

14. Beverly Wildung Harrison, *Our Right to Choose: Towards a New Ethic of Abortion* (Boston: Beacon Press, 1983), 108, 112–13.

15. Helga Kuhse, *The Sanctity-of-Life Doctrine in Medicine: A Critique* (Oxford: Clarendon Press, 1987), 12.

16. John J. Haldane, "The Ethics of Life and Death," *Scottish Journal of Theology* 38 (1985): 609.

17. Kuhse, *Sanctity-of-Life Doctrine in Medicine*, 5.

18. Ibid., 7.

2. THE BIBLICAL ORIGINS

1. Pope John Paul II, *Sacred in All Its Forms*, 335–36.

2. Ibid. Also see John Paul II, *Gospel of Life*, 70.

3. Ibid.

4. Stott, *Decisive Issues Facing Christians Today*, 309. Also see C. Ben Mitchell and Michael K. Whitehead, *The Sanctity of Life—A Time to Live, A Time to Die: Advance Directives and Living Wills* (Nashville: Christian Life Commission of the Southern Baptist Convention, n.d.), 4–6.

5. J. Kerby Anderson, "Euthanasia: A Biblical Appraisal," *Bibliotheca Sacra* 144 (April–June 1987): 215.

6. David Cairns, *The Image of God in Man* (London: SCM Press, 1953), 7–8, 21, 28.

7. Ibid., 132.

8. Ibid., 28–29.

9. Kass, "Death with Dignity and the Sanctity of Life," 35. Also published in Barry S.

Kogan, ed., *A Time to Be Born and a Time to Die: The Ethics of Choice* (New York: Aldine de Gruyter, 1991), 122–23.

10. W. T. Purkiser, *Sanctification and Its Synonyms* (Kansas City, Mo.: Beacon Hill Press, 1961), 15.

11. J. Robert Nelson, *Human Life: A Biblical Perspective for Bioethics* (Philadelphia: Fortress Press, 1984), 74–75.

12. Joseph V. Sullivan, "The Immorality of Euthanasia," in *Beneficent Euthanasia*, ed. Marvin Kohl (Buffalo: Prometheus Press, 1975), 22.

13. James M. Childs Jr., *Christian Anthropology and Ethics* (Philadelphia: Fortress Press, 1978), 86.

14. Ibid., 90–92, 95, 112.

15. Gerhard von Rad, "The Prohibition of Image in the Old Testament," *Theological Dictionary of the New Testament*, ed. Gerhard Kittel, trans. Geoffrey W. Bromiley (Grand Rapids, Mich.: Eerdmans, 1964), 387–90; Anders Nygren, *Agape and Eros*, vol. 1 (London: SPCK, 1953), 181; Cairns, *Image of God in Man*, 18, 29.

16. Childs, *Christian Anthropology and Ethics*, 87.

17. Cairns, *Image of God in Man*, 22–23.

18. Albert Gelin, *The Concept of Man in the Bible* (London: Geoffrey Chapman, 1968), 33.

19. Childs, *Christian Anthropology and Ethics*, 8. Also see Joseph Fichtner, *Theological Anthropology* (Notre Dame, Ind.: University of Notre Dame Press, 1963), 9–10.

20. Childs, *Christian Anthropology and Ethics*, 96.

21. Ibid., 97–99.

22. Ibid., 87.

23. Cairns, *Image of God in Man*, 45; Childs, *Christian Anthropology and Ethics*, 87.

24. Richard B. Brandt, "Defective Newborns and the Morality of Termination," in *Infanticide and the Value of Life*, ed. Marvin Kohl (Buffalo: Prometheus Books, 1978), 47.

25. See, for instance, Paul D. Simmons, *Birth and Death: Bioethical Decision-Making* (Philadelphia: Westminster Press, 1983), 145–46; Kuhse, *Sanctity-of-Life Doctrine in Medicine,* 157; and K. Danner Clouser, "'The Sanctity of Life': An Analysis of a Concept," *Annals of Internal Medicine* 78 (1973): 123.

26. Glanville Williams, *The Sanctity of Life and the Criminal Law* (London: Faber & Faber, 1958), 279.

27. Karl Barth, *Church Dogmatics*, vol. 3:4, ed. G. W. Bromiley and T. F. Torrance (Edinburgh: T. & T. Clark, 1961), 344.

28. Ibid., 412.

29. Ibid., 399.

30. Bruce Kaye, "The Value of Life and the Ethical Practice of Medicine," *St. Mark's Review* 142 (winter 1990): 27–28.

31. 1 Samuel 15:3 (NRSV).

32. J. W. Rogerson, "Using the Bible in the Debate about Abortion," in *Abortion and the Sanctity of Life*, 82.

33. See, among others, Northrup Frye, *The Great Code: The Bible and Literature* (San Diego: Harvest/HBJ Book, Harcourt Brace Jovanovich, 1983), 219–20.

34. Barth, *Church Dogmatics*, vol. 3:4, 399–400.

35. John Paul II, *Gospel of Life*, 86, 94, 96.

36. Barth, *Church Dogmatics*, vol. 3:4, 399–400; Nelson, *Human Life*, 82–113.

37. John Paul II, *Gospel of Life*, 82.

38. Bernard Häring, *Medical Ethics*, ed. Gabrielle L. Jean (Slough: St. Paul Editions, 1972), 14, 49–50. Also see José Comblin, *Retrieving the Human: A Christian Anthropology*, trans. Robert R. Barr (Maryknoll, N.Y.: Orbis Books, 1990), 58.

39. James M. Gustafson, *Ethics from a Theocentric Perspective*, vol. 2 (Chicago: University of Chicago Press, 1984), 292.

40. Kaye, "The Value of Human Life and the Ethical Practice of Medicine," 28.

41. Ibid. Also see John 15:13.

42. Wayne A. Meeks, *The Origins of Christian Morality: The First Two Centuries* (New Haven, Conn.: Yale University Press, 1993), 132–33. Also see Frederick C. Grant, *An Introduction to New Testament Thought* (New York: Abingdon Press, 1950), 168–69.

43. Meeks, *Origins of Christian Morality*, 132–33.

44. See Romans 12:1; 2 Corinthians 4:10. Also see discussion of Romans 12:1 and Colossians 3:5 in Barth, *Church Dogmatics*, vol. 3:4, 410.

45. W. Norman Pittenger, *The Christian Understanding of Human Nature* (Philadelphia: Westminster Press, 1964), 54–56. Also see Grant, *Introduction to New Testament Thought*, 168–69.

46. Harrison, *Our Right to Choose*, 66–67. Also see Elaine Pagels, *Adam, Eve, and the Serpent* (New York: Random House, Vintage Books, 1989), xxii–xxiii.

47. John Paul II, *Gospel of Life*, 78, 81. Also see Robert N. Wennberg, *Terminal Choices: Euthanasia, Suicide, and the Right to Die* (Grand Rapids, Mich.: Eerdmans and Paternoster Press, 1989), 46.

48. John Paul II, *Gospel of Life*, 51, 55, 70–71, 96.

49. See Robert L. Wilken, *The Myth of Christian Beginnings: History's Impact on Belief* (Garden City, N.Y.: Anchor Books, Doubleday, 1972), 158; and Simmons, *Birth and Death*, 67.

50. Barth, *Church Dogmatics*, vol. 3:4, 437.

51. Ibid., 446.

52. Ibid., 408. Also see Gustafson, *Ethics from a Theocentric Perspective*, vol. 2, 189.

53. Williams, *Sanctity of Life and the Criminal Law*, 225.

54. Simmons, *Birth and Death*, 124–25.

55. Kass, "Death with Dignity and the Sanctity of Life," 35.

56. Paul D. Simmons, *Personhood, the Bible, and the Abortion Debate* (Washington, D.C.: Religious Coalition for Abortion Rights Educational Fund, Inc., 1987), 23.

57. John Paul II, *Gospel of Life*, 108. Also see John T. Noonan Jr., "An Almost Absolute Value in History," in *The Morality of Abortion: Legal and Historical Perspectives*, ed. John T. Noonan Jr. (Cambridge: Harvard University Press, 1970), 6.

58. John Paul II, *Gospel of Life*, 108–13. Also see Noonan, "An Almost Absolute Value in History," 7–9.

59. Rogerson, "Using the Bible in the Debate about the Sanctity of Life," 77–78.

60. Stott, *Decisive Issues*, 315.

61. Rogerson, "Using the Bible in the Debate about the Sanctity of Life," 78. Also see Roy J. Enquist, "Abortion and the Image of God," *Dialog* 23: 200–201, and Simmons, *Birth and Death*, 174–75.

62. Rogerson, "Using the Bible in the Debate about the Sanctity of Life," 83.

63. Ibid., 85.

64. Ibid., 81.

65. Ibid.

66. Ibid., 87. Also see Barth, *Church Dogmatics*, vol. 3:4, 433.

67. Dennis Hollinger, "Can Bioethics Be Evangelical?" *Journal of Religious Ethics* 17 (fall 1989): 163.

68. Enquist, "Abortion and the Image of God," 200–201.

69. Simmons, *Birth and Death*, 124–25. Also see Allen Verhey, "Scripture and Medical Ethics: Psalm 51:10A, the Jarvik VII, and Psalm 50:9," *Religious Methods and Resources in Bioethics*, ed. Paul Camenisch (Dordrecht: Kluwer Academic Publishers, 1994), 262.

70. Harrison, *Our Right to Choose*, 65. Also see Elizabeth Adell Cook, Ted G. Jelen, and Clyde Wilcox, *Between Two Absolutes: Public Opinion and the Politics of Abortion* (Boulder, Colo.: Westview Press, 1992), 98–99, 105.

3. THE THEOLOGICAL ORIGINS

1. William K. Frankena, "The Ethics of Respect for Life," *Respect for Life in Medicine, Philosophy, and the Law* (Baltimore: Johns Hopkins University Press, 1977), 31.

2. Kuhse, *Sanctity-of-Life Doctrine in Medicine*, 15, 17, 19–20. Also see Norman St. John-Stevas, "Law and Moral Consensus," in *Life and Death: Ethics and Options*, with an introduction by Daniel H. Labby (Portland and Seattle: Reed College and University of Washington Press, 1968), 45.

3. Anderson, "Euthanasia: A Biblical Appraisal," 208.

4. Frankena, "Ethics of Respect for Life," 35.

5. William E. H. Lecky, *History of European Morals from Augustus to Charlemagne*, vol. 2, 3d ed. (New York: D. Appleton & Co., 1883). The first printing of Lecky's work may have been as early as 1869. See Frankena, "Ethics of Respect for Life," 35.

6. Lecky, *History of European Morals*, vol. 2, 20.

7. Ibid., 11.

8. Ibid., 11, 17–18.

9. Ibid., 17–18.

10. Ibid., 20.

11. Ibid., 34.

12. Sallie McFague, *The Body of God: An Ecological Theology* (Minneapolis: Fortress Press, 1993), 163.

13. Grant, *Introduction to New Testament Thought*, 170–76. Also see J. G. Davis, *The Early Christian Church: A History of Its First Five Centuries* (Grand Rapids, Mich.: Baker Book House, 1965), 48–52.

14. Cairns, *Image of God in Man*, 56, 102–3. Though 2 Peter 1:4 was cited in support, Patristic divinization doctrine had little biblical basis.

15. Paul Ramsey, *Basic Christian Ethics* (New York: Charles Scribner's Sons, 1950), 261. Also see Childs, *Christian Anthropology and Ethics*, 86. The image-likeness distinction is also discussed in Enquist, "Abortion and the Image of God," 199.

16. Justo L. González, *A History of Christian Thought: From the Beginnings to the Council of Chalcedon*, vol. 1 (Nashville: Abingdon Press, 1970), 202–3.

17. Jaroslav Pelikan, *Christianity and Classical Culture: The Metamorphosis of Natural*

Theology in the Christian Encounter with Hellenism (New Haven, Conn.: Yale University Press, 1993), 8–9.

18. Ibid., 285.

19. Ibid., 281.

20. Ibid.

21. *De Beatitudinibus*, Oratio VII: 44, 1280. Also cited in John Paul II, *Gospel of Life*, 144.

22. Pelikan, *Christianity and Classical Culture*, 281.

23. Lecky, *History of European Morals*, 17–18.

24. Pagels, *Adam, Eve, and the Serpent*, 55–56, 81, 96.

25. Dimitru Staniloae, "Image, Likeness, and Deification in the Human Person," trans. Ioan Ionita and R. Barringer, *Communario* (US) 13 (spring 1986): 73–74.

26. Pagels, *Adam, Eve, and the Serpent*, 116.

27. Cairns, *Image of God in Man*, 77.

28. Staniloae, "Image, Likeness, and Deification in the Human Person," 71.

29. Daniel E. Scuiry, "The Anthropology of St. Gregory of Nyssa," *Diakonia* 18 (1983): 40.

30. Margaret Ruth Miles, *Augustine on the Body* (Missoula, Mont.: Scholars Press, 1979), 85.

31. Pelikan, *Christianity and Classical Culture*, 290.

32. Ibid., 291–92.

33. Ibid.

34. Cairns, *Image of God in Man*, 103, 108–9.

35. Childs, *Christian Anthropology and Ethics*, 85–86.

36. Charles N. Cochrane, *Christianity and Classical Culture: A Study of Thought and Action from Augustus to Augustine* (New York: Oxford University, Galaxy Book, 1957), 406–7.

37. Miles, *Augustine on the Body*, 97. Also see Childs, *Christian Anthropology and Ethics*, 54.

38. Enquist, "Abortion and the Image of God," 199.

39. Childs, *Christian Anthropology and Ethics*, 52.

40. Ibid., 52–53.

41. Pagels, *Adam, Eve, and the Serpent*, 113.

42. Augustine, "On the Trinity, XII, II," *Basic Writings of St. Augustine*, ed. Whitney J. Oakes (New York: Random House, 1948), (I) 329–30, (II) 818. Also cited in Ramsey, *Basic Christian Ethics*, 256.

43. Cochrane, *Christianity and Classical Culture*, 453.

44. Ibid.

45. Ibid., 453–54.

46. Childs, *Christian Anthropology and Ethics*, 55.

47. Augustine, *Epistula*, CXXXVII. 2, as cited in Miles, *Augustine on the Body*, 94–95.

48. Ibid., 95.

49. Ibid., 43.

50. But see Enquist, "Abortion and the Image of God," 199. Enquist states: "Augustine describes the *imago* as an immanent trinity defined as a unity of meaning, understanding and will. Again a negation of the body is implied."

51. Cochrane, *Christianity and Classical Culture*, 444. Also see Miles, *Augustine on the Body*, 133.

52. Cochrane, *Christianity and Classical Culture*, 449.

53. Childs, *Anthropology and Christian Ethics*, 55.

54. Cochrane, *Christianity and Classical Culture*, 452.

55. Pagel's negativity toward Augustine is quite pronounced. See Pagels, *Adam, Eve, and the Serpent*, 106, 109, 113, 117–18, 125–26. Also see Lecky, *History of European Morals*, 5–6.

56. Enquist, "Abortion and the Image of God," 199.

57. Pagels, *Adam, Eve, and the Serpent*, 125–26.

58. Cairns, *Image of God in Man*, 120.

59. Ibid., 112–13.

60. Ibid., 122.

61. Ibid.

62. Martin Luther, *Martin Luther's Works: Sermons*, vol. 51, ed. and trans. John V. Doberstein (Philadelphia: Muhlenberg Press, 1959), 152.

63. See, for instance, Martin Luther, *Luther's Works: Table Talk*, vol. 54, ed. and trans. Theodore G. Tappert (Philadelphia: Fortress Press, 1967), 65, no. 408. Also see "Large and Small Catechisms of Martin Luther," in Theodore G. Tappert, ed. and trans., *The Book of Concord: The Confessions of the Evangelical Lutheran Church* (Philadelphia: Fortress Press, 1987), especially 343, 389–90.

64. Enquist, "Abortion and the Image of God," 200.

65. Helmut Thielicke, *Theological Ethics: Foundations*, vol. 1, ed. William H. Lazareth (Philadelphia: Fortress Press, 1966), 212. Also see extended discussion, ibid., 167–70.

66. John Calvin, *Calvin: Commentaries*, vol. 23, trans. and ed. Joseph Haroutunian and Louise Smith (Philadelphia: Westminster Press, 1958), 327.

67. John Calvin, *Institutes of the Christian Religion*, vol. 1, 3.7.6., trans. John Allen (Philadelphia: Presbyterian Board of Christian Education, 1936), 758.

68. Ibid., vol. 1, 2.8.39, 437.

69. Jean Calvin, *Instruction in Faith (1537)*, trans. Paul T. Fuhrmann (Philadelphia: Westminster Press, 1949), 30.

70. Jean Calvin, *Calvin: Theological Treatises*, vol. 22, trans. J. K. S. Reid (Philadelphia: Westminster Press, 1954), 117.

71. See, for instance, Jean Calvin, *Calvin's Commentary on Seneca's De Clementia* (Leiden: E. J. Brill, 1969). For a more general account of Calvin's early humanism and Stoic leanings, see William J. Bouwsma, *John Calvin: A Sixteenth Century Portrait* (New York: Oxford University Press, 1988), 113–27; plus Quirinus Breen, *John Calvin: A Study in French Humanism*, 2d ed. (Hamden, Conn.: Archon Books, 1968), 67–85.

72. Bouwsma, *John Calvin*, 143. The translation of the Calvin passage appears to be Bouwsma's own.

73. Calvin, *Institutes*, vol. 1, 5.5., 67

74. See discussion in Thomas F. Torrance, *Calvin's Doctrine of Man* (Westport, Conn.: Greenwood Press, 1977), 90.

75. John Calvin, "Sermon 17: The Authority and Reverence We Owe to God's Word," *Sermons from Job* (Grand Rapids, Mich.: Baker Book House, 1979), 252.

76. John Calvin, *Sermon on Deuteronomy* 24:19. Cited by Torrance, *Calvin's Doctrine of Man*, 88.

77. Bouwsma, *John Calvin*, 142. Also see Torrance, *Calvin's Doctrine of Man*, 19.

78. Bouwsma, *John Calvin*, 141.

79. Cairns, *Image of God in Man*, 138.

80. Torrance, *Calvin's Doctrine of Man*, 93.

81. Ibid. Also see Cairns, *Image of God in Man*, 144–45.

82. Calvin, *Institutes*, 1.3.6.5., 748.

83. John Calvin, *Commentaries*, vol. 23, 318–19.

84. For a brief account of the dispute between Erasmus and the Protestant Reformers on the human condition and Protestant soteriological concepts as a disincentive for moral virtue, see Stevie Davies, *Renaissance Views of Man* (New York: Barnes & Noble/Harper & Row, 1979).

85. Torrance, *Calvin's Doctrine of Man*, 7–9.

86. Suzanne Selinger, *Calvin against Himself: An Inquiry into Intellectual History* (Hamden, Conn.: Archon Books, 1984), 109–13.

87. The deletion of any sanctity of life affirmation from the creeds and confessions of the Reformed Church following Calvin's death is not the only instance where Calvin's followers determined that a larger faithfulness to their theological master required digression from his stated convictions. In lectures delivered at the University of Bonn immediately after the Second World War, Karl Barth expressly stated that "in Calvin we have a delightful example before our eyes, of pupils of a great master often seeing better than he." Barth went on to commend Olevian and Ursin, Calvin's pupils and authors of the Heidelberg Catechism, for not adhering to Calvin's catechism in its heterodox account of Christ's suffering. See Karl Barth, *Dogmatics in Outline* (New York: Harper & Row/Harper Torchbooks, 1959), 101.

88. See, for example, the discussion of the sixth commandment in *The Heidelberg Catechism* (New York: United Church Press, 1962), 105–8, where sacredness or sanctity of life rhetoric would in all likelihood have appeared if the Catechism had been disposed to invoke it. Yet not one word about the sanctity or sacredness of life surfaces.

89. A review of fifty-six privately penned English-language catechisms from the sixteenth to nineteenth centuries failed to turn up more than three instances where sanctity or sacredness of life language was either directly or indirectly employed. The two pre-nineteenth-century catechisms which allude to the sacredness of life cite non-Christian sources as their authority. For a bibliographic list of catechisms reviewed, as well as further discussion, see Geoffrey G. Drutchas, Appendix, *Is Life Sacred? The Incoherence of the Sanctity of Life as a Moral Principle within the Christian Churches* (Ann Arbor, Mich.: Dissertation Services, 1998).

4. EARLY CHRISTIAN PRACTICES

1. Comblin, *Retrieving the Human*, 50.

2. Noonan, "An Almost Absolute Value in History," 7.

3. John Paul II, *Gospel of Life*, 109–10.

4. Gustafson, *Ethics from a Theocentric Perspective*, vol. 2, 140–50. Also see brief discussion in Allen Verhey, "On James M. Gustafson: Can Medical Ethics Be Christian?" *Theological Voices in Medical Ethics*, ed. Allen Verhey and Stephen E. Lammers (Grand Rapids, Mich.: Eerdmans, 1993), 37.

5. Timothy A. Byrnes and Mary C. Segers, Introduction, *The Catholic Church and the Politics of Abortion*, ed. Timothy A. Byrnes and Mary C. Segers (Boulder, Colo.: Westview Press, 1992), 2.

6. Noonan, "An Almost Absolute Value in History," 58.

7. Albert Felling; Jan Lammers; and Leo Spruit, "Church Membership, Religion, and Attitude towards Abortion in the Netherlands," *Journal of Empirical Theology* 5 (1992): 56–57.

8. Williams, *The Sanctity of Life and the Criminal Law*, 58; Pagels, *Adam, Eve, and the Serpent*, 78–97, 130, 143; Simmons, *Birth and Death*, 68.

9. John Connery, *Abortion: The Development of the Roman Catholic Perspective* (n.p.: Loyola University Press, 1977), 176.

10. Ibid., 37. For Connery's summary of Clement's views, see 160–240.

11. Ibid., 40, 42.

12. Ibid., 52–53.

13. Daniel A. Dombrowski, "St. Augustine, Abortion, and *Libido Crudelis*," *Journal of the History of Ideas* 49 (January–March 1988): 152.

14. Ibid., 153.

15. Connery, *Abortion*, 58, 85, 90, 106.

16. Williams, *Sanctity of Life and the Criminal Law*, 57–61. Also see McFague, *Body of God*, 35. But see John T. Noonan Jr., "Aquinas on Contraception," *St. Thomas Aquinas on Politics and Ethics*, trans. and ed. Paul E. Sigmund (New York: W. W. Norton, 1988), 232, where Noonan claims that Thomas Aquinas regarded sexual pleasure as good even though he treated it as unlawful and a venial sin.

17. Connery, *Abortion*, 59–61. Also see Noonan, "An Almost Absolute Value in History," 38.

18. Pope Pius XI, *Casti Connubii: Encyclical Letter of His Holiness Pope Pius XI on Christian Marriage in View of the Present Conditions, Needs, Errors, and Vices That Affect the Family and Society,* comm. Vincent McNabb (New York: Sheed & Ward, 1933), 25–26.

19. Gustafson, *Ethics from a Theocentric Perspective*, vol. 2, 53.

20. Ibid., 56.

21. Lecky, *History of European Morals*, 23.

22. Connery, *Abortion*, 215. Also see 122–23, 173, 179, 182–83.

23. Noonan, "An Almost Absolute Value in History," 24.

24. Connery, *Abortion*, 122–23.

25. See discussion in Dombrowski, "St. Augustine, Abortion, and *Libido Crudelis*," 152.

26. G. Bonner, "Abortion and Early Christian Thought," *Abortion and the Sanctity of Human Life*, ed. J. H. Channer (Exeter, England: Paternoster Press, 1985), 97–98.

27. Dombrowski, "St. Augustine, Abortion, and *Libido Crudelis*," 153. Also see John Boswell, *The Kindness of Strangers: The Abandonment of Children in Western Europe from Late Antiquity to the Renaissance* (New York: Pantheon Books, 1988), 147–49.

28. Connery, *Abortion*, 50.

29. Ibid., 58.

30. Noonan, "An Almost Absolute Value in History," 15.

31. Ibid., 27.

32. Connery, *Abortion*, 85, 90, 106.

33. Thomas A. Shannon and Allan B. Wolter, "Reflections on the Moral Status of the Pre-Embryo," *Theological Studies* 51 (1990): 618.

34. Connery, *Abortion*, 111; Haring, *Medical Ethics*, 76.

35. Connery, *Abortion*, 10.

36. Ibid., 21.

37. Ibid., 306–7.

38. Ibid.

39. Ibid., 23.

40. Ibid., 80.

41. Ibid., 93.

42. Ibid., 96–97.

43. Ibid., 111.

44. Ibid., 148.

45. Ibid.

46. Ibid., 148, 166. Also see Noonan, "An Almost Absolute Value in History," 32–33.

47. Ibid., 34; Connery, *Abortion*, 38.

48. Ibid., 187. Also see Noonan, "An Almost Absolute Value in History," 33–35, and Shannon and Wolter, "Reflections on the Moral Status of the Pre-Embryo," 605–6.

49. Byrnes and Segers, *The Catholic Church and the Politics of Abortion*, 2. Also see Kristin Luker, *Abortion and the Politics of Motherhood* (Berkeley: University of California Press, 1984), 58–60.

50. Connery, *Abortion*, 307. Also see Carol A. Tauer, "The Tradition of Probabilism and the Moral Status of the Early Embryo," *Theological Studies* 45 (1984): 8–9.

51. Connery, *Abortion*, 291.

52. Ibid., 308.

53. Noonan, "An Almost Absolute Value in History," 37.

54. Even today, not all Roman Catholic writers are in accord with their church's position on immediate animation as a historically or medically sanctioned doctrine. See, for instance, Joseph Donceel, "Animation and Hominization," *Theological Studies* 31 (March 1970): 76–105. Also see Peter Byrne, "The Moral Status of the Embryo: The Relevance of the Animation Tradition in Light of Contemporary Philosophy," *Nederlands Theologisch Tijdschrift* 41 (April 1987): 149, 151; and Häring, *Medical Ethics*, 83, on the development of the cerebral cortex and personhood.

55. Luker, *Abortion and the Politics of Motherhood*, 60–62; James C. Mohr, *Abortion in America: The Origins and Evolution of National Policy*, 1800–1900 (New York: Oxford University Press, 1978), 186–87.

56. Luker, *Abortion and the Politics of Motherhood*, 20, 60–61; Mohr, *Abortion in America*, 183–84, 190–91.

57. Harrison, *Our Right to Choose*, 20. Also see an account of the disagreement between two Lutheran denominations on the proper moral approach to abortion in Enquist, "Abortion and the Image of God," 198.

58. Bonner, "Abortion and Early Christian Thought," 94–95.

59. John Paul II, *Gospel of Life*, 109–10.

60. Boswell, *Kindness of Strangers*, 136, 138–79.

61. See, for example, Pagels, *Adam, Eve, and the Serpent*, 5, where it appears assumed that "exposure" or abandonment led to certain death.

62. Boswell, *Kindness of Strangers*, 429.

63. Ibid.

64. Ibid., 161.

65. Ibid., 162–63.

66. Ibid., 135.

67. Ibid., 177.

68. Ibid.

69. Ibid., 69.

70. Ibid., 178.

71. Ibid., 415–17.

72. Ibid., 421. Also see Peter Singer, *Rethinking Life and Death: The Collapse of Our Traditional Ethics* (New York: St. Martin's Press, 1994), 129–30.

73. Boswell, *Kindness of Strangers*, 424.

74. Laila Williamson, "Infanticide: An Anthropological Analysis," in *Infanticide and the Value of Life*, 69.

75. Lecky, *History of European Morals*, 17–18.

76. Peter Brown, *The World of Late Antiquity, A.D. 150–750* (New York: Harcourt Brace Jovanovich, 1980), 110.

77. Ibid., 104.

78. Marvin Kohl, "Voluntary Beneficent Euthanasia," in *Beneficent Euthanasia*, ed. Marvin Kohl (Buffalo: Prometheus Books, 1975), 138.

79. Aquinas, *St. Thomas Aquinas on Politics and Ethics*, 69–71; Gustafson, *Ethics from a Theocentric Perspective*, vol. 2, 47–48, 52.

80. William A. Clebsch, *Christianity in European History* (New York: Oxford University Press, 1979), 139.

81. Williams, *Sanctity of Life and the Criminal Law*, 25.

82. Barth, *Church Dogmatics*, vol. 3:4, 437–38.

83. Ibid.

84. Ibid.

85. Ibid. Also see Ernst Troeltsch, *The Social Teachings of the Christian Churches*, vol. 2, trans. Olive Wyon (Chicago: University of Chicago Press, Midway Reprint, 1976), 533.

86. Alister E. McGrath, *A Life of John Calvin: A Study in the Shaping of Western Culture* (Cambridge, Mass.: Basil Blackwell, 1990), 115–16. Also see Roland Bainton, *Hunted Heretic: The Life and Death of Michael Servetus, 1511–1553* (Boston: Beacon Press, 1953), 210, 214–15. Ironically, apologies for John Calvin in both biographical works only serve to highlight the general lack of commitment to the sanctity of life in Western society.

87. Barth, *Church Dogmatics*, vol. 3:4, 437–38.

88. Ibid.

89. Ibid.

90. Robert L. Wilken, *The Christians As the Romans Saw Them* (New Haven, Conn.: Yale University Press, 1984), 307.

91. Williams, *Sanctity of Life and the Criminal Law*, 229.

92. Ibid.

93. Barth, *Church Dogmatics*, vol. 3:4, 412.

94. Williams, *The Sanctity of Life and the Criminal Law*, 232.

95. Sullivan, "The Immorality of Euthanasia," 19.

96. Wennberg, *Terminal Choices*, 53, 66.

97. Lecky, *History of European Morals*, 43–45.

98. Augustine, *De civitate Dei*, Lib. I 20 (CSEL 40), 38, as cited in Sullivan, "The Immorality of Euthanasia," 19–20.

99. Williams, *Sanctity of Life and the Criminal Law*, 230–31. Also see Wennberg, *Terminal Choices*, 53, 66.

100. Williams, *Sanctity of Life and the Criminal Law*, 231.

101. Ibid., 232.

102. Gustafson, *Ethics from a Theocentric Perspective*, vol. 2, 193.

103. Williams, *Sanctity of Life and the Criminal Law*, 237.

104. Here Aquinas may have been indebted to Pythagoras and Plato. See Simmons, *Birth and Death*, 116, and J. David Bleich, "Assisted Suicide Is Contrary to Judeo-Christian Beliefs," in *Euthanasia: Opposing Viewpoints*, ed. Carol Wekesser (San Diego: Greenhaven Press, 1995), 42–43.

105. This argument is borrowed from Simmons, *Birth and Death*, 103. Although Simmons invokes it to express his own abhorrence of Christians who believe that a pregnancy resulting from rape should still be viewed as God's will, it is equally apt in critiquing Aquinas's stance against suicide.

106. See, for example, Daniel Cronin, *Conserving Human Life* (St. Louis: Pope John Center, 1989), 33–65, and Simmons, *Birth and Death*, 117.

107. Williams, *Sanctity of Life and the Criminal Law*, 278–80. Also see Cronin, *Conserving Human Life*, 8, 12–13.

108. See related discussion in Barth, *Church Dogmatics*, vol. 3:4, 404, 408, 411.

109. See similar argument in Gustafson, *Ethics from a Theocentric Perspective*, vol. 2, 215, and Simmons, *Birth and Death*, 108.

110. Williams, *Sanctity of Life and the Criminal Law*, 232.

111. Ibid.

112. Philippe Ariès, *Western Attitudes toward Death from the Middle Ages to the Present*, trans. Patricia Ranum (Baltimore: Johns Hopkins University Press, 1974), 28.

113. Alexander Solzhenitsyn, *Cancer Ward*, trans. Nicholas Bethell and David Burg (New York: Farrar, Straus and Giroux, 1969), 100. Cited by Ariès, *Western Attitudes toward Death*, 13.

114. Ibid.

115. Ibid., 22.

116. Vitoria, *Reflectio de Temperantia*, n. 1, as cited in Daniel Cronin, *Conserving Human Life*, 35.

117. Ibid., 85.

118. Ibid., 35.

119. *Relectio de Homicidio*, n. 35, as cited in Cronin, *Conserving Human Life*, 37.

120. Ibid.

121. Ibid., 131, 262.

122. Gregory Sayrus, *Clavis Regia Conscientiae* (Venetiis, 1625), Cap. IX, n. 38, as cited in Cronin, *Conserving Human Life*, 41.

123. See discussion of amputation among Roman Catholic moralists in Cronin, *Conserving Human Life*, 41, 44, 46, 48, 56–58, 61.

124. Ibid., 45–46.

125. Ibid., 71.

126. Sanchez, *Consilia*, Tom. II, Lib. V, Cap. 1, dub. 33, as cited in Cronin, *Conserving Human Life*, 42. Also see Vitoria, *Relectio de Temperantia*, n. 9, as cited in Cronin, *Conserving Human Life*, 36.

127. C. La Croix, *Theologia Moralis*, vol. 1 (Ravennae, 1761), Lib. III, Pars I, Tract IV, Cap. 1, dub. I, n. 3, as cited in Cronin, *Conserving Human Life*, 62.

128. C. Billuart, *Summa S. Thomae* (Parisiis, 1852), Tom. VI, Dissert. X, Art III, Consect. n. 3, as cited in Cronin, *Conserving Human Life*, 64.

129. J. De Lugo, *De Justitia et Jure*, Disp. 10, Sect. I, n. 29, as cited in Cronin, *Conserving Human Life*, 53.

130. John Paul II, *Gospel of Life*, 83.

131. Ibid., 82–86.

132. 2 Corinthians 4:11 (NRSV).

133. Robert M. Veatch and Carol G. Mason, "Hippocratic vs. Judeo-Christian Medical Ethics: Principles in Conflict," *Journal of Religious Ethics* 15 (spring 1987): 93–94.

134. Timothy F. Sedgwick, "A Moral Matrix: Religious Practices and Health Care," in *Religious Methods and Resources in Bioethics*, 295.

135. John Howard Yoder, "What Would You Do If?" *Journal of Religious Ethics* 2 (fall 1974): 90. Cited by Stanley Hauerwas, *The Peaceable Kingdom: A Primer in Christian Ethics* (Notre Dame, Ind.: University of Notre Dame Press, 1983), 125.

136. See Stanley Hauerwas, *Naming the Silences: God, Medicine, and the Problem of Suffering* (Grand Rapids, Mich: Eerdmans, 1990), 49.

137. See Hauerwas, *Peaceable Kingdom*, 124–27.

138. Jeff Lyon, "Sanctity of Life vs. Quality of Life: The Ethics of Neonatal Care," *Playing God in the Nursery* (New York: W. W. Norton, 1985), 223–24. For similar sentiments, see Cronin, *Conserving Human Life*, 132, 257.

5. THE NON-CHRISTIAN ORIGINS

1. Clouser, "'The Sanctity of Life,'" 119.

2. Frankena, "Ethics of Respect for Life," 35–36.

3. Kuhse, *Sanctity-of-Life Doctrine in Medicine*, 20.

4. Ludwig Edelstein, *Ancient Medicine: Selected Papers of Ludwig Edelstein*, ed. Owsei Temkin and C. Lilian Temkin (Baltimore: Johns Hopkins University Press, 1967), 6, 14. Also cited in Frankena, "Ethics of Respect for Life," 37–38.

5. Paul Carrick, *Medical Ethics in Antiquity: Philosophical Perspectives on Abortion and Euthanasia* (Dordrecht: D. Reidel Publishing Co., 1985), 151.

6. John Paul II, *Gospel of Life*, 158.

7. Veatch and Mason, "Hippocratic vs. Judeo-Christian Medical Ethics," 93.

8. Ibid.

9. Carrick, *Medical Ethics in Antiquity*, 151, 154, 156.

10. Ibid., 39.

11. The Stoic philosophy was an important influence on the Roman mind as personified by the emperor Marcus Aurelius. See Bonner, "Abortion and Early Christian Thought," 98–99.

12. Edelstein, *Ancient Medicine*, 6, 14. Also cited in Frankena, "Ethics of Respect for Life," 37–38.

13. Cairns, *Image of God in Man*, 64.

14. Ibid.

15. Ramsey, *Basic Christian Ethics*, 250.

16. Frederick Copleston, *A History of Philosophy: Greece and Rome*, vol. 1:2 (Garden City, N.Y.: Doubleday, Image Books, 1962), 132.

17. Ibid., 132–33.

18. Ibid., 139.

19. Ibid., 132.

20. Ernst Troeltsch, *The Social Teachings of the Christian Churches*, vol. 1, trans. Olive Wyon (Chicago: University of Chicago Press, Midway Reprints, 1960), 65–66. For an acknowledgment of the impact that Stoicism also had upon Christianity with regard to "basic assumption[s] of the equality of human lives," see Noonan, "An Almost Absolute Value in History," 3.

21. Copleston, *A History of Philosophy*, vol. 1:2, 142.

22. Ibid., 143–44.

23. On the ambivalence of the early Christians toward embodied, earthly life and their attraction to Platonic and neo-Platonic otherworldliness as they affirmed the "inestimable value" of the human soul, see Lecky, *History of European Morals*, 34. With regard to the two-tiered mind-set of the Christian churches, separating the temporal from the spiritual, which permitted the emergence of the cosmopolitan Renaissance and the resurfacing of Stoic notions, including the sanctity of life, see Troeltsch, *Social Teachings of the Christian Churches*, vol. 1, 376–78. Also see Roland Bainton, "Luther's Attitudes on Religious Liberty," *Studies on the Reformation* (Boston: Beacon Press, 1963), 21.

24. For an extended discussion of Stoicism's revival during the Renaissance, as well as its significant influence upon the Protestant reformers, see Breen, *John Calvin*, 67–74. Also see Agnes Heller, *Renaissance Man*, trans. Richard E. Allen (London: Routledge & Kegan Paul, 1978), 101–38; and Antonio Poppi, "Fate, Fortune, Providence, and Human Freedom," *The Cambridge History of Renaissance Philosophy*, ed. Charles B. Schmitt (Cambridge: Cambridge University Press, 1988), 647.

25. Marsilio Ficino, *Theologica Platonica*, first published in 1474, various editions, III, 2, and XVI, 3. Cited in Singer, *Rethinking Life and Death*, 167.

26. See, for example, Davies, *Renaissance Views of Man*, 13–15. But see discussion of the Reformation and Counter Reformation impact on art, splitting spirituality from physicality, in Selinger, *Calvin against Himself*, 133–43.

27. Ariès, *Western Attitudes toward Death*, 28.

28. Ibid., 51.

29. Ibid.

30. Ibid., 46–47.

31. Ibid.

32. Ibid., 70. For additional descriptions of the charnel houses see Caroline Walker Bynum, *The Resurrection of the Body in Western Christianity, 200–1336* (New York: Columbia University Press, 1995), 203–4, 212–13; and Paul Binski, *Medieval Death: Ritual and Representation* (Ithaca, N.Y.: Cornell University Press, 1996), 55–56.

33. Ariès, *Western Attitudes toward Death*, 39–40.

34. Ibid., 57–58.

35. Ibid., 67.

36. Ibid., 65.

37. Ibid., 40, 105–6.

38. Ibid., 81.

39. For a brief account of the ferment of the age, see Frederic Seebohm, *The Oxford Reformers* (London and New York: J. M. Dent & Sons/E. Dutton, 1929), 2–8.

40. For a brief account of Martin Luther's highly ambivalent stance towards the Renaissance, see Roland Bainton, "Interpretations of the Reformation," *Studies on the Reformation* (Boston: Beacon Press, 1963), 111–12. Also see "Luther's Attitudes on Religious Liberty," 22, in the same volume.

41. For an informative description of the Council of Trent as a simultaneous reaction to the Protestant Reformation and Renaissance humanism, see Adolf Harnack, *Outlines in the History of Dogma*, trans. Edwin Knox Mitchell (Boston: Beacon Press, 1957), 510–18.

42. *The Encyclopedia of Philosophy*, reprint ed., 1972, s.v. "Reformation," by B. A. Gerrish, vol. 7, 100–101. For a similar view, see Bainton, "Interpretations of the Reformation," 106, 112–13.

43. Leroy E. Loemker, *Struggle for Synthesis: The Seventeenth Century Background of Leibniz's Synthesis of Order and Freedom* (Cambridge: Harvard University Press, 1972), 250, 100.

44. Ibid., 235.

45. Ibid., 234–35.

46. Ibid., 16.

47. Carl L. Becker, *The Heavenly City of the Eighteenth Century Philosophers* (New Haven, Conn.: Yale University Press, 1969), 102–3.

48. Ibid., 157–58.

49. H. Shelton Smith, Robert Handy, and Lefferts A. Loetscher, *American Christianity: An Historical Interpretation with Representative Documents*, vol. 2 (New York: Charles Scribner's Sons, 1963), 125.

50. Becker, *Heavenly City*, 157.

51. Ibid., 64. Also see Sterling Lamprecht, Introducton, *Locke Selections*, ed. Sterling Lamprecht (New York: Charles Scribner's Sons, 1956), xxviii.

52. Carole Pateman, *The Problem of Political Obligation: A Critique of Liberal Theory* (Berkeley: University of California Press, 1985), 63.

53. Immanuel Kant, *The Moral Law or Kant's Groundwork of the Metaphysics of Morals*, trans. H. J. Paton (London: n.p., 1950), 421; and Immanuel Kant, *Kant's Critique of Practical Reason and Other Works on the Theory of Ethics*, 6th ed., trans. T. K. Abbott (London: n.p., 1909), 38–39. Also cited in Copleston, *A History of Philosophy: Modern Philosophy, Kant*, vol. 6:2, 116, 120.

54. *Encyclopedia Americana*, 1974 ed., "Kant, Immanuel," by W. H. Werkmeister, vol. 16, 306. Also see discussion in Gustafson, *Ethics from a Theocentric Perspective*, vol. 2, 121.

55. Immanuel Kant, *Critique of Judgement*, trans. and intro. J. H. Bernard (New York: Hafner Publishing Co., 1951), 268. Also cited by Gustafson, *Ethics from a Theocentric Perspective*, vol. 2, 121–22.

56. Ibid., 121.

57. Copleston, *A History of Philosophy*, vol. 6:2, 136.

58. Ibid., 134.

59. Ibid., 137. On Kant's pietistic upbringing, refer to summary biography in *Encyclopedia Americana*, "Kant, Immanuel," 304.

60. Gustafson, *Ethics from a Theocentric Perspective*, vol. 2, 122.

61. Immanuel Kant, *Religion within the Limits of Reason Alone*, trans. and intro. Theodore M. Greene and Hoyt H. Hudson (New York: Harper Torchbooks, 1960), 54.

62. Ibid., 55.

63. Gustafson, *Ethics from a Theocentric Perspective*, vol. 2, 123n.

64. Ibid., 124.

65. Immanuel Kant, *The Metaphysical Principles of Virtue*, trans. James Ellington and intro. Warner Wick (Indianapolis: Bobbs-Merrill, 1964), 83–84.

66. Gustafson, *Ethics from a Theocentric Perspective*, vol. 2, 119.

67. Ibid.

68. Copleston, *A History of Philosophy*, vol. 6:2, 109.

69. See, for instance, McFague, *Body of God*, 84, 119.

70. Byrne, "The Moral Status of the Embryo," 140.

71. For example, see Bernard Häring, *Ethics of Manipulation: Issues in Medicine, Behavior Control, and Genetics* (New York: Seabury Press, 1975), 54–55.

72. Kenneth Vaux, *Birth Ethics: Religious and Cultural Values in the Genesis of Life* (New York: Crossroad, 1989), 84–85.

73. *Encyclopedia Americana*, "Kant, Immanuel."

74. See discussion in Christopher Lasch, *The True and Only Heaven: Progress and Its Critics* (New York: W. W. Norton, 1991), 198–201. Also see *The Encyclopedia of Philosophy*, 1972 ed., "Locke, John" by James G. Clapp. For an excellent account of the evolution of church-state separation under liberal aegis, see Guido de Ruggiero, *The History of European Liberalism*, trans. R. G. Collingwood (Boston: Beacon Press, 1966), 396–406.

75. Michel Foucault, "Right of Death and Power over Life," *The History of Sexuality: An Introduction*, vol. 1, trans. Robert Hurley (New York: Random House, Vintage Books, 1990), 135–59. See esp. 141–42.

76. Robert Nisbet, *History of the Idea of Progress* (New York: Basic Books, 1980), 172–73.

77. See, for example, Theodore Parker, "The Permanent and Transient in Christianity," in *American Christianity*, vol. 2, 144.

78. Lecky, *History of European Morals*, 5–6, 11–12.

79. Such tolerance which helped to avert undue conflict and controversy was not accidental. Instead, it was a demonstration of a quintessentially liberal virtue. See Anthony Arblaster, *The Rise and Decline of Western Liberalism* (Oxford: Basil Blackwell, 1985), 66–70.

80. William R. Hutchison, *The Modernist Impulse in American Protestantism* (Oxford: Oxford University Press, 1982), 3, 13.

81. Earl Morse Wilbur, *A History of Unitarianism in Transylvania, England, and America* (Boston: Beacon Press, 1969), 423–36.

82. Robert Leet Patterson, *The Philosophy of William Ellery Channing* (New York: Bookman Associates, 1952), 52–56, 110–13. Channing's affinity for both Stoicism and John Locke's philosophy is particularly evident in his own exposition of natural rights doctrine. Ibid., 108–9, 111–13.

83. Wilbur, *A History of Unitarianism*, 424–25. Also see Andrew Delbanco, *William Ellery Channing: An Essay on the Liberal Spirit in America* (Cambridge: Harvard University Press, 1981), xi; and Daniel Walker Howe, *The Unitarian Conscience: Harvard Moral Philosophy, 1805–1861* (Cambridge: Harvard University Press, 1970), 100–101.

84. William Ellery Channing, "Unitarian Christianity: Discourse at the Ordination of Rev. Jared Sparks," *The Works of William E. Channing, D. D.*, 3d complete ed., vol. 3 (Boston: James Monroe & Co., 1843), 93–94.

85. William Ellery Channing, "Likeness to God: Discourse at the Ordination of F. A. Farley," *The Works of William E. Channing, D. D.*, vol. 3, 228.

86. Ibid., 243–44.

87. Patterson, *Philosophy of William Ellery Channing*, 100–103.

88. Hutchison, *Modernist Impulse*, 17–19.

89. Perry Miller, ed., *The Transcendentalists: An Anthology* (Cambridge: Harvard University Press, 1971), 192, 210–13.

90. Ralph Waldo Emerson, "The Divinity School Address," *Concord Idealism: Ralph Waldo Emerson [and] Henry David Thoreau*, ed. Randall Stewart and Dorothy Bethurum (Chicago: Scott, Foresman, 1954), 29.

91. Ibid., 24–25.

92. For discussion of Emerson's Stoic proclivities, see Lasch, *True and Only Heaven*, 243–46.

93. Perry Miller, Introduction, *The Transcendentalists*, 8–9.

94. Conrad Wright, "'At Morning Blest and Golden-Browed,' Unitarians, Transcendentalists, and Reformers, 1835–1865," *A Stream of Light: A Sesquicentennial History of American Unitarianism*, ed. Conrad Wright (Boston: Unitarian Universalist Association, 1975), 39.

95. See Joan Von Mehren, *Minerva and Muse: A Life of Margaret Fuller* (Amherst: University of Massachusetts Press, 1974); and Henry Steele Commager, *Theodore Parker: Yankee Crusader* (Boston: Beacon Press, 1962), esp. chapters 8–11.

96. Wright, "'At Morning Blest and Golden-Browed,'" 38–39. Also see E. I. F. Williams, *Horace Mann: Educational Statesman* (New York: Macmillan Co., 1937), 72–73.

97. See Smith, Handy, and Loetscher, eds., *American Christianity*, 259. For further discussion of Christian Personalism or humanism, see Hutchison, *Modernist Impulse*, 206–25.

98. Alexis de Tocqueville, *Democracy in America*, ed. Phillip Bradley (New York: Knopf, 1945).

99. John Stone and Stephen Mennell, Introduction, *Alexis de Tocqueville on Democracy, Revolution, and Society: Selected Writings* (Chicago: University of Chicago Press, 1980), 4–7. Also see Alexis de Tocqueville and Gustave de Beaumont, *On the Penitentiary System in the United States and Its Application to France*, trans. Francis Lieber (Carbondale and Edwardsville: Southern Illinois University Press, 1964).

100. Lasch, *True and Only Heaven*, 59–60.

101. Barth, *Church Dogmatics*, vol. 3:4, 438.

102. Ibid.

103. Daniel C. Callahan, "Religion and the Secularization of Bioethics," *Theology, Religious Traditions, and Bioethics, Hastings Center Report: A Special Supplement*, ed. Daniel C. Callahan and Courtney S. Campbell (July/August 1990), 3; and Robert Veatch, *A Theory of Medical Ethics* (New York: Basic Books, 1981), 45–46.

104. See especially Gustave Flaubert, *Madame Bovary*, trans. Eleanor Marx Aveling (New York: Random House, Modern Library), 210, where the practice of the physician is referred to as a "sacred office, although the ordinary practitioners dishonoured it."

105. See Mohr, *Abortion in America*; Luker, *Abortion and the Politics of Motherhood*.

106. Luker, *Abortion and the Politics of Motherhood*, 19.

107. Mohr, *Abortion in America*, 50.

108. Luker, *Abortion and the Politics of Motherhood*, 20.

109. Mohr, *Abortion in America*, 36. One of the earliest and loudest abortion opponents was Harvard medical professor Walter Channing, brother of the famous Unitarian divine William Ellery Channing. Ibid., 105.

110. Luker, *Abortion and the Politics of Motherhood*, 21.

111. Ibid., 27–35; Mohr, *Abortion in America*, 184–85.

112. Ibid., 160–64.

113. Ibid., 184–85.

114. Luker, *Abortion and the Politics of Motherhood*, 22.

115. Ibid.

116. Copleston, *A History of Philosophy*, vol. 1:2, 176.

117. Winslow Ayer, *The Great Crime of the Nineteenth Century and Perils to Child Life, Physical and Moral* (Grand Rapids, Mich.: Central Publishing Co., 1880), 52. Cited in Luker, *Abortion and the Politics of Motherhood*, 23.

118. Carl Degler, *At Odds: Women and Family in America from the Revolution to the Present* (New York: Oxford University Press, 1980), 247. Cited in Luker, *Abortion and the Politics of Motherhood*, 28.

119. See discussion of late-nineteenth-century legislative movement against abortion in Williams, *The Sanctity of Life and the Criminal Law*, 24–25.

120. James Bentley, *Albert Schweitzer: The Enigma* (New York: HarperCollins, 1992), 132–33; and Albert Schweitzer, *The Teaching of Reverence for Life*, trans. Richard and Clara Winston (New York: Holt, Rinehart and Winston, 1965), 59.

121. Ibid., 26.

122. Ibid., 47.

123. Ibid., 41. Also see Albert Schweitzer, *Out of My Life and Thought* (New York: Holt, 1949), 261, 130–31; and Jackson Lee Ice, *Schweitzer: Prophet of Radical Theology* (Philadelphia: Westminster Press, 1971), 39, 83–84, 157.

124. See, for example, Karl Barth, *Ethics*, ed. Diedrich Braun and trans. Geoffrey Bromiley (New York: Seabury Press), 120–21, 139. Also see Ice, *Schweitzer*, 33–46.

125. Nisbet, *History of the Idea of Progress*, 247. Also see Foucault, *History of Sexuality*, vol. 1, 138, 144–45.

126. See, for instance, Mary McCarthy, *Birds of America* (New York: Harcourt Brace Jovanovich, 1971), and Norman Mailer, *Why Are We in Vietnam?* (New York: Putnam, 1967).

127. Daniel Callahan, "The Abortion Debate: Is Progress Possible?" in *Abortion: Understanding Differences*, ed. Sidney Callahan and Daniel Callahan (New York: Plenum Press, 1984), 318–19.

128. Daniel Labby, Introduction, *Life or Death: Ethics and Options* (Portland and Seattle: Reed College and University of Washington Press, 1968), viii–ix.

129. Edward Shils, "The Sanctity of Life," in *Life or Death*, 5.

130. Ibid., 6.

131. Ibid.

132. Daniel Callahan, "The Sanctity of Life," in *The Religious Situation: 1969*, ed. Donald R. Cutler (Boston: Beacon Press, 1969).

133. Ibid., 299.

134. Julian R. Pleasants, "Commentary on 'The Sanctity of Life,'" in *The Religious Situation: 1969*, 342–43.

135. Hans Jonas, "Contemporary Problems in Ethics from a Jewish Perspective," *Journal of Central Conference of American Rabbis* (January 1968): 34–35. Cited in Leon Kass, *Toward a More Natural Science: Biology and Human Affairs* (New York: Macmillan, Free Press, 1985), 38n.

136. Kass, *Toward a More Natural Science*, 39n.

137. Shils, "The Sanctity of Life," 3.

138. Ibid., 5.

139. Callahan, "The Sanctity of Life," 325.

140. Ibid., 331–32.

141. Ibid., 360.

142. Ibid., 306.

143. Ibid., 330.

144. Ibid., 331–32.

145. Edward Keyserlingk, *Sanctity of Life or Quality of Life in the Context of Ethics, Medicine, and Law* (Ottawa: Law Reform Commission of Canada, Protection of Life Series, 1979).

146. Ibid., 36.

147. See, for example, the theologies of Paul Tillich, Alfred North Whitehead, Henry Nelson Wieman, and Karl Rahner. For further discussion of this issue, see Richard A. McCormick, "The Consistent Ethic of Life: Is There a Historical Soft Underbelly?" in *The Critical Calling: Reflections on Moral Dilemmas Since Vatican II* (Washington, D.C.: Georgetown University Press, 1989), 217–18.

148. Shils, "Sanctity of Life," 9.

149. Ibid., 12.

150. Ibid. Also see Callahan, "The Sanctity of Life," 307.

151. Abraham Kaplan, "Social Ethics and the Sanctity of Life," in *Life or Death*, 166–67.

152. See Mary Meehan, "More Trouble Than They're Worth? Children and Abortion," in *Abortion: Understanding Differences*, 149.

153. Kass, "Death with Dignity and the Sanctity of Life," 38.

154. Ibid., 35.

155. Frankena, "Ethics of Respect for Life," 30–33.

156. Callahan, "Sanctity of Life," 300.

157. Ibid., 363.

158. Ibid., 301.

159. Ibid., 363, on impact of education.

160. Ibid., 319.

161. Ibid., 334. For original Fletcher citation, see Joseph Fletcher, "The Right to Die," *Atlantic Monthly*, April 1968, 63.

162. Callahan, "Sanctity of Life," 335.

163. Ibid.

164. Baruch Brody, *Abortion and the Sanctity of Human Life: A Philosophical View* (Cambridge: M.I.T. Press, 1975), 30, 38.

165. Ibid., 48, 56.

166. Ibid., 39, 74–76, 79.

167. Ibid., 80, 116.

168. Ibid., 50–55, 66, 132–33.

169. Ibid., 132–33.

170. Shils, "Sanctity of Life," 29.

171. Sissela Bok, "Who Shall We Count as a Human Being? A Treacherous Question in the Abortion Discussion," *Abortion, Pro and Con*, ed. Robert L. Perkins (Cambridge, Mass.: Shenkman, 1974), 94.

172. Kass, "Death with Dignity and the Sanctity of Life," 34.

173. Ibid.

174. Ibid., 40.

175. Keyserlingk, *Sanctity of Life or Quality of Life*, 4.

176. Ibid., 17.

177. Ibid., 60.

178. Ibid., 57.

179. Ibid., 76–79.

180. Ibid., 100. Also see H. Tristram Engelhardt, "Medicine and the Concept of Person," a paper delivered at the Kennedy Institute, Georgetown University, Washington, D.C., November 19, 1974, 16.

181. Keyserlingk, *Sanctity of Life or Quality of Life*, 100.

182. Ibid., 44–45.

183. Frankena, "Ethic of Respect for Life," 25.

184. Ibid., 34.

185. Ibid., 51.

186. Ibid.

187. Ibid., 53.

188. Ibid., 54.

189. Ibid., 52–53.

190. Ibid., 58.

191. Callahan, "Sanctity of Life," 327.

192. Ibid., 315.

193. Ibid., 311–12.

194. Callahan, "The Abortion Debate," 312.

195. Kuhse, *Sanctity-of-Life Doctrine in Medicine*, 20–21.

196. Daniel Callahan, *Setting Limits: Medical Goals in an Aging Society* (New York: Simon & Schuster, Touchstone Books, 1988); and Daniel Callahan, *The Troubled Dream of Life: Living with Mortality* (New York: Simon & Schuster, 1993).

6. THE RECENT POLITICS OF SANCTITY

1. Dietrich Bonhoeffer, *Prisoner for God: Letters and Papers from Prison*, ed. Eberhard Bethge and trans. Reginald H. Fuller (New York: Macmillan, 1953), 146.

2. James M. Burtness, *Shaping the Future: The Ethics of Dietrich Bonhoeffer* (Philadelphia: Fortress Press, 1985), 11–14. Also see discussion of Bonhoeffer's stance in Franklin Sherman, "The Lutheran Ethos and Biomedical Ethics Today," *Currents in Mission and Theology* 15 (December 1988): 568–69.

3. For discussion and criticism of this trend, see John H. Yoder, *The Original Revolution: Essays on Christian Pacifism* (Scottdale, Pa.: Herald Press, 1971), 152–59.

4. See Hutchison, *Modernist Impulse*, generally, for a narrative account of how some Christian churches responded to the challenge of modernity. The typology of response outlined above has some affinity to the "Christ against culture," "Christ above culture," and "Christ of culture" stances outlined by H. Richard Niebuhr, *Christ and Culture* (New York: Harper & Row, Harper Colophon Books, 1951), 45–161.

5. Hutchison, *Modernist Impulse*, 206–25; and Smith, Handy, and Loetscher, *American Christianity*, vol. 2, 259.

6. Hutchison, *Modernist Impulse*, 121–22.

7. Clebsch, *Christianity in European History*, 260.

8. Connery, *Abortion*, 291–92.

9. Willard L. Sperry, *The Disciplines of Liberty: The Faith and Conduct of the Christian Freeman* (New Haven, Conn.: Yale University Press, 1921), 59–61. Cited in Hutchison, *Modernist Impulse*, 252.

10. Pope Pius XI, *Casti Connubii*, 49, 30, 37.

11. Ibid., 10, 26, 30, 32.

12. Ibid., 28–29.

13. Joan E. O'Donovan, "Man in the Image of God: The Disagreement between Barth and Brunner Reconsidered," *Scottish Journal of Theology* 39 (1986): 437.

14. Cairns, *Image of God in Man*, 155. Also see Emil Brunner, *The Divine Imperative: A Study in Christian Ethics*, trans. Olive Wyon (Philadelphia: Westminster Press, 1947), 159. Following his public 1934 disagreement with Karl Barth over imago Dei doctrine, Brunner chose to forgo use of the terms "formal" and "material" because of the possible confusion they generated. See, for instance, Emil Brunner, "Appendix I," *The Divine Imperative* (New York: Macmillan, 1937). Nevertheless, Brunner's twofold imago Dei doctrine remained basically unchanged.

15. Cairns, *Image of God in Man*, 162.

16. Ibid., 154. But see J. Edward Humphrey, *Makers of the Modern Theological Mind: Emil Brunner*, ed. Bob E. Patterson (Peabody, Mass.: Hendrickson, 1976), 163–64, where it is asserted that Brunner was not as biblically grounded in his statements about the imago Dei as he sometimes claimed.

17. Brunner, *Divine Imperative*, 163.

18. Ibid., 172–73.

19. Ibid., 171–72.

20. Ibid.

21. Ibid.

22. Ibid., 172–73.

23. Ibid.

24. Ibid., 172. Also see Purkiser, *Sanctification and Its Synonyms*, 15–16.

25. O'Donovan, "Man in the Image of God," 434.

26. On the ambiguity and confusion generated by Karl Barth's dialectical style, see Dennis Voskuil, "Neoorthodoxy," in *Reformed Theology in America: A History of Its Modern Development*, ed. David F. Wells (Grand Rapids, Mich.: Eerdmans, 1985), 252.

27. Barth, *Church Dogmatics*, vol. 3:4, 324. Also see Barth, *Ethics*, 120–21, 139.

28. Ibid., 117.

29. Ibid., 119–20.

30. Ibid., 124.

31. Ibid., 139–40.

32. Ibid., 140

33. Ibid., 142.

34. Ibid., 143. Also see Brunner, *Divine Imperative*, 171–72.

35. Barth, *Ethics*, 143–44.

36. Ibid., 161.

37. Barth, *Church Dogmatics*, 324.

38. Barth, *Ethics*, 131.

39. Barth, *Church Dogmatics*, 327.

40. Ibid., 336.

41. Ibid., 343.

42. Ibid., 341.

43. Ibid., 338–39.

44. Ibid., 339.

45. Ibid.

46. Ibid.

47. Ibid.

48. Ibid., 328–29.

49. Barth, *Dogmatics in Outline*, 101.

50. Barth, *Church Dogmatics*, 414.

51. Ibid., 418.

52. Ibid., 397–98.

53. See, for example, ibid., 346, 384.

54. Ibid., 342.

55. Ibid., 343.

56. Ibid., 363.

57. Ibid., 367.

58. Ibid., 357, 371.

59. Ibid., 417.

60. Ibid.

61. Ibid., 418.

62. Ibid., 418, 417.

63. Ibid., 422.

64. Ibid., 421. Barth recoiled, for instance, at the Vatican demand that seven nuns, raped by German soldiers during the Second World War, carry their pregnancies to full term.

65. Ibid., 422–23.

66. See discussion of Karl Barth's attitude towards abortion in Gustafson, *Ethics from a Theocentric Perspective*, vol. 2, 32. Barth's nuanced approach to abortion prompted Paul Ramsey, otherwise a great admirer of Barth, to criticize him for an inconsistent sanctity of life position and a possibly pro-abortion stance. See Paul Ramsey, "Reference Points in Deciding about Abortion," in *The Morality of Abortion*, 91–93.

67. Barth, *Church Dogmatics*, 403.

68. Ibid., 423.

69. Ibid., 424.

70. Ibid., 425.

71. Ibid., 427.

72. Ibid.

73. Ibid., 400–401.

74. Perhaps not without cause, many orthodox Reformed Christians were profoundly suspicious of Karl Barth's neo-orthodoxy, believing that it bore "the corrupted stain of liberalism." See Voskuil, "Neoorthodoxy," 257–58.

75. John Hersey, *Hiroshima* (New York: Alfred Knopf, 1946). Hersey's acclaimed account of Hiroshima's bombing had its genesis as an extended article written for the *New Yorker* magazine, August 31, 1946.

76. Jean Bethke Elshtain, "Reflections on Abortion, Values, and the Family," in *Abortion: Understanding Differences*, 66, 72.

77. Nelson, *Human Life*, 4.

78. Ibid., 3–4.

79. Häring, *Ethics of Manipulation*, 53.

80. Ibid., 209.

81. O'Donovan, "Man in the Image of God," 433.

82. Langdon Gilkey, "Theological Frontiers: Implications for Bioethics," *Theology and Bioethics: Exploring the Foundations and Frontiers*, ed. Earl E. Shelp (Dordrecht: D. Reidel Co., 1985), 119.

83. C. S. Lewis, *The Abolition of Man* (New York: Macmillan, 1965), 41.

84. John Paul II, *Gospel of Life*, 29.

85. Ibid., 29–30.

86. The phrase is borrowed from Richard Hofstadter, *The Paranoid Style in American Politics* (New York: Knopf, 1965).

87. In attending ordination and installation services during the early 1980s, the present author used to wager with colleagues as to whether one of the presiding clergy would once again invoke Pogo's immortal words. Invariably, someone did.

88. See, for example, the discussion in Gilkey, "Theological Frontiers," 117–18.

89. Ibid.

90. Ibid., 123.

91. John Paul II, *Gospel of Life*, 100–101.

92. Häring, *Ethics of Manipulation*, 13.

93. Ibid., 30.

94. Ibid., 156, 33–34.

95. Ibid., 44–45, 210–11.

96. See, for example, Jacques Ellul, *The Technological Society*, trans. John Wilkinson (New York: Random House, Vintage Books, 1964), 434–36.

97. George Hunston Williams, "The Sacred Condominium," in *The Morality of Abortion*, 171.

98. Comblin, *Retrieving the Human*, 69.

99. Ibid., 74.

100. Ibid., 68, 74–75.

101. Cairns, *Image of God in Man*, 10.

102. Ibid., 108.

103. Ibid., 232.

104. Robert Wennberg, "The Right to Life: Three Theories," *Christian Scholars Review* 13 (1984): 316.

105. This changed orientation is evident in the humanism of the eminent Anglican evangelical John Stott. See, for instance, Roy McCoughry, "Basic Stott: Candid Comments on Justice, Gender, and Judgment," *Christianity Today* 40 (January 8, 1996): 26.

106. But see John Paul II, *Gospel of Life*, 49–50, 146, 151, 158, 163, and, especially, 180, where the Roman Catholic pontiff is quite explicit about his desire to cooperate with those who, otherwise beyond the Christian pale, share his convictions about the need to uphold life's sanctity.

107. Häring, *Ethics of Manipulation*, 184.

108. Luke 9:50.

109. 1 Corinthians 9:19–22.

110. Williams, "Sacred Condominium," 171.

111. Paul Ramsey, *The Patient as Person* (New Haven, Conn.: Yale University Press, 1970), xiii.

112. Gilkey, "Theological Frontiers," 125.

113. John Paul II, *Sacred in All Its Forms*, 28.

114. Cairns, *Image of God in Man*, 221–22.

115. Ibid., 7–8.

116. John Paul II, *Gospel of Life*, 100. For a congruent evangelical Protestant claim, see Anderson, "Euthanasia: A Biblical Appraisal," 215.

117. With regard to claims about the latency of the sanctity of life doctrine within Christianity see, for example, John Paul II, *Gospel of Life*, 46, 77–78, 81–82, 97, 108.

118. Childs, *Christian Anthropology and Ethics*, 63.

119. Paul Ramsey, "The Morality of Abortion," in *Life or Death*, 78.

120. O'Donovan, "Man in the Image of God," 435.

121. Ibid., 436–39, 445, 450.

122. Ramsey, *Basic Christian Ethics*, 250, 254–58, 277.

123. Paul Ramsey was also a participant in the Reed College symposium on the sanctity of life and apparently delivered his *Dublin Review* article as a paper. The *Dublin Review* article was thus republished as Ramsey, "The Morality of Abortion," 71–76. For a publishing history of the article see Ramsey, "Reference Points in Deciding about Abortion," 90.

124. Lennart Nilsson's photographs were first published in *Life* magazine on April 30, 1965, and then in Axel Ingelman-Sundberg and Claes Wirsen, *A Child Is Born: The Drama of Life before Birth in Unprecedented Photographs*, photo. Lennart Nilsson (New York: Dell Publishing Co., 1966), as well as in *The Terrible Choice: The Abortion Dilemma* (New York: Bantam Books, 1969).

125. Ramsey, "Reference Points in Deciding about Abortion," 74–75.

126. For an interesting account of Paul Ramsey's evolving vocation as a bioethicist, see Leroy Walters, "Religion and the Renaissance of Medical Ethics," in *Theology and Bioethics*, 11.

127. Ramsey, "The Morality of Abortion," 70.

128. Ibid., 71.

129. Ibid., 72.

130. Ibid., 75.

131. Ibid.

132. See, for example, Ramsey, "Reference Points in Deciding about Abortion," 91.

133. Ibid., 92–93.

134. James M. Wall, "Editorials: Suicide, Responsibility, and the Sacredness of Life," *Christian Century* 108 (October 30, 1991): 987–88.

135. See, for instance, "Is Every Life Worth Living?," 987–88; Sharon Anderson, "Sanctity of Life Issues Bring a Variety of Demonstrators to Washington, D.C.," *Christianity Today* 29 (July 12, 1985): 40; National Conference of Catholic Bishops' Committee for Pro-Life Activities and the American Jewish Conference, "Treatment of Handicapped Newborns," *Origins NC Documentary Service* 15 (September 5, 1985): 192; Ramsey Colloquium on Religion and Public Life, "Always to Care, Never to Kill: A Declaration on Euthanasia," *First Things* 20 (February 1992): 45–47; Richard D. Land, *Sanctity of Human Life* (Nashville: Christian Life Commission, 1991); Colson and Neuhaus, eds., *Evangelicals and Catholics Together*, xv–xxxiii; and Ronald Geschwendt, "Editorial: Life Is Still Sacred," *Sunday School Guide* 75 (March 3, 1996): 1. For denominational resolutions on the sacredness of life by the Missouri Synod Lutheran Church, the Southern Baptist Convention, the Orthodox Church in America, the Episcopal Church, and the United Methodist Church, see Gerald LaRue, *Playing God: 50 Religions' Views on Your Right to Die* (Wakefield, R.I.: Moyer Bell, 1996), 131, 208–10, 126–27, 159, and 183–84.

136. William Temple, *Christianity and Social Order*, intro. Ronald H. Preston (New York: Crossroad Book, Seabury Press, 1977), 87–88.

137. See, for example, Richard A. McCormick, "The Quality of Life, the Sanctity of Life," *Hastings Center Report* 8 (February 1978): 30; Harrison, *Our Right to Choose*, 112–13; and Lewis B. Smedes, "On Reverence for Life and Discernment of Reality," *Reformed Journal* (July 1987): 16–17.

138. For a discussion of Pope John Paul II's understanding of the human person, see James J. McCartney, "Some Roman Catholic Conceptions of Person and Their Implications for the Ontological Status of the Unborn," in *Abortion and the Status of the Fetus*, ed. William B. Bondeson et al. (Dordrecht: D. Reidel Co., 1983), 323. With regard to Paul Ramsey's views on personhood and his support for a traducian perspective, see Ramsey, "Reference Points in Deciding about Abortion," 64–79. True to his "medical indications" approach, Ramsey believes that modern genetic science has vindicated the traducian perspective, which holds that the human person begins with the fertilization of the ovum. Ibid., 67.

139. See, for example, Paul Ramsey, *Ethics at the Edges of Life*, 268–99.

140. Wennberg, "The Right to Life," 317.

141. For additional discussion of contending sacralities and the gap between them, see Harrison, *Our Right to Choose*, 255; and Richard A. McCormick, "The Consistent Ethic of Life," 212.

142. Wennberg, "The Right to Life," 330.

143. Paul Lauritzen, "On Being Medieval without Menace: Catholic Magisterial Teaching as a Source for Bioethics," in *Religious Methods and Resources in Bioethics*, 306–7.

144. Troeltsch, *Social Teachings of the Christian Churches*, vol. 2, 554–60, 615–16.

145. Veatch, *Theory of Medical Ethics*, 46.

146. Ibid., 47.

147. Williams, *The Sanctity of Life and the Criminal Law*, 182.

148. James R. Kelly, "Learning and Teaching Consistency," 165.

149. John Paul II, *Sacred in All Its Forms*, 20.

150. John Paul II, *Gospel of Life*, 10.

151. Ibid., 11.

152. Ibid., 51.

153. Ibid., 53.

154. John Paul II, *Sacred in All Its Forms*, 12.

155. John Paul II, *Gospel of Life*, 31.

156. Ibid., 33.

157. Comblin, *Retrieving the Human*, 448–49.

158. Ibid., 46–47.

159. John Paul II, *Gospel of Life*, 130–31.

160. John Paul II, *Sacred in All Its Forms*, 11.

161. John Paul II, "Encyclical: *Veritas Splendor*," *Origins NC Documentary Service* 23: 310.

162. John Paul II, *Gospel of Life*, 127.

163. Ibid., 127–28.

164. Ibid., 129.

165. Ibid., 131.

166. Ibid., 133.

167. See, for example, James G. Hanink, "On Germain Grisez: Can Ethics Give Answers?"

in *Theological Voices in Medical Ethics*, 175; and Benedict M. Ashley, "Birth Issues: Pro-Life Evangelization," 89–90.

168. Ramsey, "The Morality of Abortion," 74.

169. Ibid., 77–78.

170. Ramsey, *Ethics at the Edges of Life*, 205.

171. Simmons, *Birth and Death*, 37.

172. Ibid., 48.

173. Harrison, *Our Right to Choose*, 225.

174. Vaux, *Birth Ethics*, 79, 81–82.

175. John Paul II, *Gospel of Life*, 93.

176. Ibid., 95.

177. Ibid., 69.

178. Ibid., 94.

179. Häring, *Ethics of Manipulation*, 60–61.

180. Häring, *Medical Ethics*, 67, 69.

181. Barth, *Church Dogmatics*, 328, 330–31, 336, 340. Barth conflates "gift" and "loan" language in discussing the ownership of human life.

182. Brunner, *Divine Imperative*, 172.

183. For different Protestant denominational statements on the stewardship of human life, see LaRue, *Playing God*, 185–86, 188, 216, 234, 242, 283, 319. Also see Daniel B. McGee's discussion of a "value of life" or sanctity of life stance, ibid., 221.

184. Ibid., 216. Here Baptist theologian William M. Tillman cites Deuteronomy 5:26, Joshua 3:10, Matthew 16:16, and John 5:26 as support for the idea that human life is a "sacred trust" requiring our proper stewardship.

185. See Genesis 1:26–28. Human autonomy is also implied by Genesis 2:19–20, where the first created human being is authorized to name the other creatures brought forth by God.

186. Pagels, *Adam, Eve, and the Serpent*, xxiii.

187. See, for example, Genesis 15:18, Exodus 24, and Samuel 7:4–16.

188. For a concise discussion of the nature of the freedom and autonomy implied in the covenantal relationship with God in the context of Old Testament tradition and precedent, see Paul D. Hanson, *Dynamic Transcendence: The Correlation of Confessional Heritage and Contemporary Experience in a Biblical Model of Divine Activity* (Philadelphia: Fortress Press, 1978), 30, 51–52, 77–80.

189. *The International Standard Bible Encyclopedia* (Grand Rapids, Mich.: Eerdmans, 1988), "Steward," by T. M. Dorman.

190. For gospel parables involving stewardship, see Matthew 24:45–51, Luke 12:35–48, and Luke 16:1–9.

191. Romans 12:1 (NRSV).

192. For instance, 1 Peter 4:10 states: "Like good stewards of the manifold grace of God, serve one another with whatever gift each of you has received" (NRSV). Akin to certain verses of the apostle Paul's epistles (Romans 12:6–8; Ephesians 4:11; 1 Corinthians 12:8–10, 13:1–3, 14:6, 26), Peter's statement appears to refer to spiritual gifts—special talents and blessings made possible through the grace of God for the common good, rather than for the benefit of the individual upon whom any particular grace-gift has come to rest. Because every spiritual gift depends upon God's continuing grace from moment to moment and the gift-giving is always ongoing and unfinished, human "ownership" is elusive or not completely possible. Thus, it becomes appropriate to speak in an exceptional way, as Peter does, of the

human stewardship of spiritual "gifts." See discussion of spiritual gifts in *The International Standard Bible Encyclopedia*, q.v. "Spiritual Gifts," by R. Spittler. Also see *Harper's Bible Dictionary*, "Spiritual Gifts" (San Francisco: Harper & Row, 1985), 989–90. There is no indication, however, that the apostles Peter or Paul regard embodied physical life as a spiritual gift or charism in the highly particular way they conceive these terms.

193. In the custom and law of Western society the effectuation of a gift has consistently involved a transfer of ownership usually signified by appropriate possession of the gift item by the donee. See Ashbel Green Gulliver et al., *Cases and Materials on Gratuitous Transfers: Wills, Intestate Succession, Trusts, Gifts, and Future Transfers* (St. Paul, Minn.: West, 1967), 359, 361.

194. Paul F. Camenisch, "Gift and Gratitude in Ethics," *Journal of Religious Ethics* 9 (spring 1981): 1.

195. Ibid., 8.

196. Ibid.

197. *Interpreter's Dictionary of the Bible* (Nashville and New York: Abingdon Press, 1962), "Steward, Stewardship," by C. U. Wolf. Also see *Harper's Dictionary*, "Steward."

198. John Paul II, *Gospel of Life*, 27.

199. John Paul II, *Sacred in All Its Forms*, 302.

200. Ibid., 321.

201. Ibid., 324–25.

202. Ramsey, *Ethics at the Edges of Life*, 139–42.

203. Ibid., 203.

204. Ramsey, "The Morality of Abortion," 61. Also see Ramsey, *Ethics at the Edges of Life*, 188.

205. Häring, *Medical Ethics*, 179. Also see ibid., 70–71, concerning attitude towards suicide on the part of those disposed to sacralize nature.

206. John Paul II, *Sacred in All Its Forms*, 33, 138.

207. John Paul II, *Gospel of Life*, 74.

208. Ibid., 42.

209. Ibid., 76. Pope John Paul II's stress on coitus open to procreation reinvigorated a centuries-old sex ethic which gives primacy to procreation "over other meanings of sexual expression." The sheer durability of this sex ethic was a source of surprise and dismay to some in the Roman Catholic Church who, rightly or wrongly, believed that it has been "publicly and definitively abandoned" by the Second Vatican Council. See Richard A. McCormick, "The Ethics of Reproductive Technology," in *The Critical Calling*, 339. Also see John Mahoney, *Bioethics and Belief* (London: Sheed & Ward, 1984), 28.

210. John Paul II, *Gospel of Life*, 172.

211. Ibid., 107. Of course, what John Paul II regarded as obvious was not so apparent to other Roman Catholic theologians such as Karl Rahner and Richard A. McCormick. See McCormick, "Ethics of Reproductive Technology," 343–44.

212. Kristin Luker, "Abortion and the Meaning of Life," in *Abortion: Understanding Differences*, 33. Also see Luker, *Abortion and the Politics of Motherhood*, 164–65.

213. John Paul II, *Sacred in All Its Forms*, 137–38.

214. Introducing a collection of addresses by John Paul II, editor James V. Schall indicated the seriousness with which a "pro-life" pope and church hierarchy embraced the idea of divinely ordained gender roles when he, amid a more encompassing discussion of the sanctity of life, wrote: "Women who follow masculine models or men who follow feminine ones—both male

and female are rooted in nature, not merely in culture—end up threatening sex itself, and with it, the way the race reproduces itself and cares for itself." Ibid., 25–26.

215. Williams, "Sacred Condominium," 150–55, 169.

216. David Smith, "On Paul Ramsey," 21. Smith notes that Ramsey, taking exception to the notion that "the essentially human is simply the socially relational," came "close to affirming that the image of God is bodily." Ibid., 19.

217. Ramsey, *Ethics at the Edges of Life*, 203–4.

218. Stott, *Decisive Issues Facing Christians Today*, 324–25.

219. J. Kerby Anderson, "Artificial Reproduction: A Biblical Appraisal," *Bibliotheca Sacra* 143 (January–March 1986): 64–66.

220. T. H. Milby, "Natural Law, Evolution, and the Question of Personhood," *Quarterly Review* 39 (summer 1986): 40, 42, 46; Karl Rahner, *Theological Investigations: Writings of 1965–67*, vol. 9, trans. Graham Harrison (New York: Herder & Herder, 1972), 226n; Charles Hartshorne, "Scientific and Religious Aspects of Bioethics," in *Theology and Bioethics*, 33.

221. Kuhse, *Sanctity-of-Life Doctrine in Medicine*, 195.

222. Luker, *Abortion and the Politics of Motherhood*, 190, 193, 199–215.

223. Kohl, "Voluntary Beneficent Euthanasia," 138. Of course, consistency arguments could and did cut more than one way. Abortion foes berated liberal opponents of capital punishment and nuclear war who displayed remarkable tolerance when it came to the "mass murder of fetuses." See Haldane, "The Ethics of Life and Death," 611; and Williams, "Sacred Condominium," 171.

224. Hanink, "On Germain Grisez," 158.

225. Smedes, "On Reverence for Life and Discernment of Reality," 17.

226. Cardinal Joseph Bernardin, "Cardinal Bernardin's Call for a Consistent Ethic of Life," *Origins NC Documentary Service* 13 (December 29, 1983): 491.

227. Ibid., 492.

228. Ibid., 493.

229. Ibid., 493–94.

230. Cardinal Joseph Bernardin, "Cardinal Bernardin's St. Louis Address: Enlarging the Dialogue on a Consistent Ethic of Life," *Origins* (April 5, 1984): 707–8.

231. Ibid., 709.

232. Stephen D. Johnson and Joseph B. Tamney, "Factors Related to Inconsistent Life-Views," *Review of Religious Research* 30 (September 1988): 40.

233. Kelly, "Learning and Teaching Consistency," 162.

234. Ibid.

235. Ibid.

236. John Paul II, *Gospel of Life*, 101.

237. Ibid., 99.

238. Ibid., 49.

239. Ibid., 155, 160.

240. Ibid., 161.

241. Ibid., 162.

242. John Connery, "A Seamless Garment in a Sinful World," *America* 151 (1984): 5–8.

243. McCormick, "The Consistent Ethic of Life," 211.

244. Ibid., 221. Also see discussion in Lisa Sowle Cahill, "On Richard McCormick: Reason and Faith in Post–Vatican II Catholic Ethics," in *Theological Voices in Medical Ethics*, 99.

245. McCormick, "The Consistent Ethic of Life," 231. Also, Cahill, "On Richard McCormick," 100.

246. McCormick, "The Consistent Ethic of Life," 221. Also see McCormick, "The Quality of Life, the Sanctity of Life," 34; and Cahill, "On Richard McCormick," 98.

247. Hauerwas, *Peaceable Kingdom*, 88.

248. Marvin Kohl, *The Morality of Killing: Sanctity of Life, Abortion, and Euthanasia* (London: Peter Owen, 1974), 3.

249. Bernardin, "Cardinal Bernardin's St. Louis Address," 709. Also see Kelly, "Learning and Teaching Consistency," 163.

250. J. Stephen Cleghorn, "Respect for Life: Research Notes on Cardinal Bernardin's 'Seamless Garment,'" *Review of Religious Research* 28 (December 1986): 138–39.

251. Ibid.

252. Cook, Jelen, and Wilcox, *Between Two Absolutes*, 124, 122.

253. Ibid., 101.

254. Ibid., 101, 105.

255. Henri Hilhorst, "Religion and Euthanasia in the Netherlands: Exploring a Diffuse Relationship," *Social Compass* 30 (1983): 498.

256. Ibid., 500.

257. Ibid.

258. Felling, Lammers, and Spruit, "Church Membership, Religion, and Attitude towards Abortion in the Netherlands," 63–64.

259. Ibid., 64–65.

260. Dorie Giles Williams, "Religion, Beliefs about Human Life, and the Abortion Decision," *Review of Religious Research* 24 (September 1982): 46.

261. Harrison, *Our Right to Choose*, 192. Also see Ronald Dworkin, *Life's Dominion: An Argument about Abortion, Euthanasia, and Individual Freedom* (New York: Knopf, 1993), 101.

262. Harrison, *Our Right to Choose*, 54, 118, 128.

263. Cleghorn, "Respect for Life," 136.

264. Cook, Jelen, and Wilcox, *Between Two Absolutes*, 108.

265. Johnson and Tamney, "Factors Related to Inconsistent Life-Views," 41, 44. Also see Eric Woodrum and Beth L. Davison, "Reexamination of Religious Influences in Abortion Attitudes," *Review of Religious Research* 33 (March 1992): 234.

266. Susan Teft Nicholson, *Abortion and the Roman Catholic Church* (Knoxville: Religious Ethics, JRE Studies in Religious Ethics 2, 1978), 3.

267. Williams, "Religion, Beliefs about Human Life, and the Abortion Decision," 45. Also see earlier, more limited research, based in the Washington, D.C., area, reaching a similar conclusion in E. Patricia McCormick, *Attitudes towards Abortion: Experience of Selected Black and White Women* (Lexington, Mass.: Lexington Books, 1975), 67.

268. Anthony Shaw, "Who Should Die and Who Should Decide," in *Infanticide and the Value of Life*, 103–4, 110n–11n.

269. David J. Doukas, David Waterhouse, David W. Gorenflo, and Jerome Seid, "Attitudes and Behaviors on Physician-Assisted Death: A Study of Michigan Oncologists," *Journal of Clinical Oncology* 13 (May 1995): 1055–56, 1060; Jerald G. Bachman, Kirsten H. Alcser, David J. Doukas et al., "Attitudes of Michigan Physicians and the Public towards Legalizing Physician-assisted Suicide and Voluntary Euthanasia," *New England Journal of Medicine* 334 (February 1, 1996): 303, 306; Jonathan S. Cohen, Stephen D. Fihn, Joseph J. Boyko et al., "Attitudes towards Assisted Suicide and Euthanasia among Physicians in Washington State,"

New England Journal of Medicine 331 (July 14, 1994): 89, 93–94. In Oregon, 60 percent of polled physicians felt that physician-assisted suicide should be legal in some cases. See Melinda A. Lee, Heidi D. Nelson, Virginia Tilden et al., "Legalizing Assisted Suicide—Views of Physicians in Oregon," *New England Journal of Medicine* 334 (February 1, 1996): 310–15; Michelle Reisner and Anthony N. Damato, "Attitudes of Physicians Regarding Physician-assisted Suicide," *New Jersey Medicine* 92 (October 1995): 663–66; Peter Baume and Emma O'Malley, "Euthanasia: Attitudes and Practices of Medical Practitioners," *Medical Journal of Australia* 161 (July 18, 1994): 140; and Courtney S. Campbell and Bette-Jane Crigger, eds., *Mercy, Murder and Morality*, 1.

270. David A. Asch, "The Role of Critical Care Nurses in Euthanasia and Assisted Suicide," *New England Journal of Medicine* 334 (May 23, 1996): 1374.

271. Bachman, Alcser, and Doukas, "Attitudes of Michigan Physicians and the Public towards Legalizing Physician-assisted Suicide and Voluntary Euthanasia," 303, 306.

272. Nelson, *Human Life*, 141.

7. RESPECT FOR LIFE AS AN ALTERNATIVE TO SANCTITY

1. Barth, *Church Dogmatics*, vol. 3:4, 342. In spite of his sanctity of life stance, Barth openly expressed concern about the possible dangers of "an idolatry that has nothing whatever to do with Christian obedience." Ibid. Anticipating trends to come, Barth warned that health consciousness could end up as an idolatry. Barth, *Ethics*, 130. Typical of the disclaimers of idolatry by sanctity of life advocates is the statement by Pope John Paul II that life on earth is "not an 'ultimate' but 'penultimate' reality" and that one's own death can be a "supreme act of obedience to the Father." See Pope John Paul II, *The Gospel of Life*, 4, 123. But what one hand giveth, the other repeatedly takes away. Elsewhere in the same document, as discussed in chapters above, John Paul II emphatically declares that human life "remains a *sacred* reality entrusted to us." Ibid., 4. An absolutizing of human life is further clear in the "Declaration on Euthanasia" issued by the Sacred Congregation for the Doctrine of the Faith (June 26, 1980), which plainly asserts, as Brian Johnstone has noted, that "human life is sacred and no one may dispose of it at will." Brian Johnstone, "The Sanctity of Life, the Quality of Life, and the New Baby Doe Law," *Linacre Quarterly* 52 (August 1985): 264.

2. Richard A. McCormick, "Theology and Bioethics: Christian Foundations," in *Theology and Bioethics*, 106.

3. Ibid., 110.

4. Ibid., 97, 111.

5. Ibid., 97.

6. Ibid. For a critical view of Richard McCormick's stance which puts it in still sharper relief from a sanctity of life position, see Paul Ramsey, *Ethics at the Edges of Life*, 174.

7. Ron Hamel, "On Bernard Häring: Construing Medical Ethics Theologically," *Theological Voices in Medical Ethics*, ed. Allen Verhey and Stephen E. Lammers, 222.

8. Ibid.

9. Ibid., 223. The desacralization of nature is a major leitmotif of Häring's work. See Häring, *Medical Ethics*, xii, 5–6, 13, 20–22.

10. Ibid., 140–41.

11. Ibid., 142–43.

12. For remarks on Kenneth Vaux's part that seem to affirm the sanctity of life concept, see Vaux, *Birth Ethics*, 143. For joint declaration decrying idolatry, see Jan Van Eys and Ken-

neth Vaux, "A Declaration of Faith and Health," *Christian Century* (July 3–10, 1985), 643–44.

13. Howard Moody, "Life Sentence: Individual Autonomy, Medical Technology, and the 'Common Good,'" *Christianity and Crisis* 47 (October 12, 1987): 335–36.

14. Ibid., 336.

15. Ivan Illich, *Medical Nemesis: The Expropriation of Health* (Toronto: Bantam Books, 1977), 202–3.

16. Ibid. Also see Pierre Delooz, "Who Believes in the Hereafter?" in *Death and Presence*, ed. Andre Godin (Brussels: Lumen Vitae Press, 1972), 17–38.

17. Stanley Hauerwas, *Suffering Presence: Theological Reflections on Medicine, the Mentally Handicapped, and the Church* (Notre Dame, Ind.: University of Notre Dame Press, 1986), 91.

18. Ibid., 92–93. With regard to Hauerwas's critique of Paul Ramsey's use of covenant language, see ibid., 72.

19. Hauerwas, *Peaceable Kingdom*, 88.

20. Yoder, *The Original Revolution*, 42. Cited by Hauerwas, *Peaceable Kingdom*, 88.

21. Hauerwas, *Suffering Presence*, 92.

22. Verhey, "On James M. Gustafson," 43.

23. James M. Gustafson, *The Contribution of Theology to Medical Ethics* (Milwaukee: Marquette University Press, 1975), 63. Cited by Verhey, "On James M. Gustafson," 42.

24. Harrison, *Our Right to Choose,* 222.

25. Hartshorne, "Scientific and Religious Aspects of Bioethics," 34.

26. Charles Birch and John Cobb, *The Liberation of Life* (Cambridge: Cambridge University Press, 1981), 166. Birch and Cobb join in the objection to obsessive life-extension efforts. Ibid., 168.

27. Callahan, *Troubled Dream of Life*, 70–71.

28. Ibid., 86.

29. For example, see Social Concerns Committee of the Commission on Theology and Church Relations for Missouri Synod Lutheran Church, "Report on Euthanasia with Guiding Principles," in LaRue, *Playing God*, 134. Also see Paul D. Simmons, "Baptist-Evangelical Biomedical Ethics," *Bioethics Yearbook* (Dordrecht: Kluwer, 1991), n.p. Cited by LaRue, *Playing God*, 223.

30. See Bernardin, "Cardinal Bernardin's Call for a Consistent Ethic of Life," 494; and Cardinal Joseph Bernardin, "Cardinal Bernardin's Georgetown Address: Religion and Politics—The Future Agenda," *Origins NC Documentary Service* 14 (November 8, 1984): 328.

31. In the year after "Cardinal Bernardin's Call for a Consistent Life Ethic," in which the prelate advocated public civility, twenty abortion clinics were bombed across the United States. See discussion of bombings by a concerned "pro-life" advocate in "Abortion Bombings," *America* 151 (December 22, 1984): 413–14. Also see the more recent, highly spirited debate on civility and civil language between James Dobson and John D. Woodbridge in James Dobson, "Why I Use 'Fighting Words': A Response to John Woodbridge's Culture War Casualties," *Christianity Today* 39 (June 19, 1995): 27–30, and John D. Woodbridge, "Why Words Matter: A Response to James Dobson," *Christianity Today* 39 (June 19, 1995): 31–32.

32. Pope Pius XI, *Casti Connubii*, xiii.

33. Hauerwas, *Peaceable Kingdom*, 60–61.

34. See, for example, John Paul II, *Gospel of Life*, 6–8, 16, 21, 43.

35. Sullivan, "The Immorality of Euthanasia," 23.

36. Ibid., 22.

37. Harrison, *Our Right to Choose*, 90.

38. Ibid., 92.

39. Gustafson, *Ethics from a Theocentric Perspective*, vol. 2, 9.

40. Ibid., 32–33.

41. Ibid., 111–12.

42. Ibid., 249.

43. Sullivan, "The Immorality of Euthanasia," 28.

44. Hauerwas, *Peaceable Kingdom*, 60–61. Also see Hauerwas, *Suffering Presence*, 72.

45. Ibid.

46. Courtney S. Campbell, "On James F. Childress: Answering That of God in Every Person," in *Theological Voices in Medical Ethics*, 133–34, 138.

47. Nelson, *Human Life*, 125.

48. Campbell, "On James F. Childress," 139.

49. Hartshorne, "Scientific and Religious Aspects of Bioethics," 42.

50. Ibid., 43.

51. H. Tristram Engelhardt Jr., "Fashioning an Ethic for Life and Death in a Post-Modern Society," in *Mercy, Murder, and Morality*, 7.

52. H. Tristram Engelhardt Jr., *The Foundations of Bioethics* (New York: Oxford University Press, 1986), 385.

53. Lawrence H. Tribe, "Forward: Toward a Model of Roles in the Due Process of Life and Law," *Harvard Law Review* 87 (1973): 21–23. See discussion regarding Tribe's article in Virginia Abernathy, "Children, Personhood, and a Pluralistic Society," in *Abortion: Understanding Differences*, 133.

54. Clouser, "'The Sanctity of Life,'" 120–23.

55. Stanley Hauerwas, *A Community of Character: Towards a Constructive Christian Social Ethic* (Notre Dame, Ind.: University of Notre Dame Press, 1981), 108.

56. Basil Mitchell, "The Role of Theology in Bioethics," in *Theology and Bioethics*, 76.

57. See, for example, Charles Meyer, "Is Suicide Ever an Acceptable Option for Christians?" *Episcopal Life* (January 1992): 28. Also cited by LaRue, *Playing God*, 162–63.

58. Gustafson, *Ethics from a Theocentric Perspective*, vol. 2, 281.

59. Ibid., 277.

60. Ibid., 58.

61. See chapters 13 and 14 in Rahner, *Theological Investigations*, vol. 9.

62. Ibid., 210–11.

63. Ibid.

64. Ibid., 218–19, 221. Not surprisingly, Paul Ramsey was intensely critical of Karl Rahner's view of human self-transcendence with its attendant possibilities for intervention into nature and human nature. It "sounds remarkably," Ramsey said, "like a priestly blessing over everything." Paul Ramsey, *Fabricated Man: The Ethics of Genetic Control* (New Haven, Conn.: Yale University Press, 1970), 139–40. Also see discussion of Rahner's stance and Ramsey's dim view of it in Gustafson, *Ethics from a Theocentric Perspective*, vol. 2, 77. Nevertheless, when it suited his own sanctity of life outlook, Ramsey even acknowledged that human beings were capable of modifying what was "natural." As Helga Kuhse has observed, Ramsey saw some omissions in medical care as killing because interventions in such cases had become "second nature." See Kuhse, *Sanctity-of-Life Doctrine in Medicine*, 55.

65. Häring, *Ethics of Manipulation*, 35.

66. Ibid., 51–52.

67. Ibid., 70.

68. Hamel, "On Bernard Häring," 225.

69. Häring, *Ethics of Manipulation*, 64. Also cited in Hamel, "On Bernard Häring," 225.

70. Häring, *Ethics of Manipulation*, 69. For a remarkably similar perspective from a Protestant theologian, see Simmons, *Birth and Death,* 220.

71. Häring, *Ethics of Manipulation*, 67.

72. Simmons, *Birth and Death*, 139, 136–37.

73. Callahan, *Troubled Dream of Life*, 63.

74. Ibid., 64.

75. Ibid., 85.

76. Ibid., 71, 84.

77. Ibid., 72.

78. Ibid., 72–73.

79. Kuhse, *Sanctity-of-Life Doctrine in Medicine*, 200–205.

80. Cahill, "On Richard McCormick," 98.

81. Ibid., 91.

82. Richard McCormick, "Theology in the Public Forum," in *The Critical Calling*, 202. Cited in Cahill, "On Richard McCormick," 91–92.

83. Ibid., 92.

84. Ibid., 93.

85. Ibid., 96.

86. Ibid., 97.

87. Gustafson, *Ethics from a Theocentric Perspective*, vol. 2, 249.

88. Ibid., 213.

89. Ibid., 214.

90. Ibid., 56.

91. Ibid., 11.

92. Ibid., 60.

93. Ibid., 245.

94. Ibid.

95. Ibid., 246.

96. Verhey, "On James M. Gustafson," 52.

97. Ibid., 50. Also see Gustafson, *Ethics from a Theocentric Perspective*, vol. 2, 247, 275.

98. See, for example, McFague, *Body of God*, 73.

99. Verhey, "On James M. Gustafson," 41.

100. Harrison, *Our Right to Choose*, 191.

101. Ibid.

102. Ibid.

103. Ibid., 208.

104. Pittenger, *The Christian Understanding of Human Nature,* 9.

105. For a similar "sacramental" perspective, see remarks by the Reverend Lord Soper, former president of the Methodist Conference in Great Britain, while in attendance at the International Conference on Euthanasia and Suicide at Oxford, England, September 1980, as reported in LaRue, *Playing God*, 179.

106. Barth, *Church Dogmatics*, vol. 3:4, 414–15.

107. Paul Ramsey, *Ethics at the Edges of Life*, 211.

108. Anderson, "Euthanasia: A Biblical Appraisal," 214.

109. Germain Grisez, "A New Formulation of Natural Law Argument against Contraception," in *St. Thomas Aquinas on Politics and Ethics*, 239.

110. National Conference of Catholic Bishops' Committee for Pro-Life Activities, "Statement by NCCB Pro-Life Committee: No Alternative Teaching on Abortion," *Origins NC Documentary Service* 15 (October 17, 1985): 312.

111. Mark Siegler and Alan J. Weisbard, "Against the Emerging Stream: Should Fluids and Nutritional Support Be Discontinued?" *Archives of Internal Medicine* 145 (1985): 129–31, 145. Also see Mark Siegler and Alan J. Weisbard, "On Killing Patients with Kindness: An Appeal for Caution," in *By No Extraordinary Means: The Choice to Forgo Life-Sustaining Food and Water*, ed. Joanne Lynn (Bloomington and Indianapolis: Indiana University Press, 1989), 113–14.

112. Daniel Callahan, "Public Policy and the Cessation of Nutrition," in *By No Extraordinary Means*, 66.

113. See Wibren van der Burg, "The Slippery Slope Argument," *Ethics* 102 (October 1991): 43–44, 63–65; and Frederick Schauer, "Slippery Slopes," *Harvard Law Review* 99 (December 1985): 382.

114. Simmons, *Birth and Death*, 119.

115. Ibid.

116. Hollinger, "Can Bioethics Be Evangelical?," 165.

117. Gustafson, *Ethics from a Theocentric Perspective*, vol. 2, 314–15.

118. Marc Gellman, "On Immanuel Jakobovits: Bringing the Ancient Word to the Modern World," in *Theological Voices in Medical Ethics*, 186, 195.

119. James F. Childress, "When Is It Morally Justifiable to Discontinue Medical Nutrition and Hydration?" in *By No Extraordinary Means*, 74–76.

120. Ibid., 78.

121. See Cronin, *Conserving Human Life*, 79, 132, 268–69. Also see Arthur Dyck, "Beneficent Euthanasia and Benemortasia: Alternative Views of Mercy," in *Beneficent Euthanasia*, 127.

122. Kohl, *The Morality of Killing*, 106. Also see Fletcher, "The 'Right' to Live and the 'Right' to Die," 49–50; and Joseph Fletcher, *Personhood: Essays in Biomedical Ethics* (Buffalo: Prometheus Press, 1979), 152.

123. Singer, *Rethinking Life and Death*, 192–96.

124. Ibid., 195–96.

125. Daniel Callahan, "Can We Return Death to Disease?" in *Mercy, Murder, and Morality*, 5–6.

126. Ramsey, *Ethics at the Edges of Life*, 195. Also see Ramsey, *The Patient as Person*, 161–64.

127. H. Richard Niebuhr, *The Responsible Self* (New York: Harper & Row, 1963), 60–61.

128. Foucault, *History of Sexuality*, vol. 1, 142.

129. Dworkin, *Life's Dominion*, 148–71, 237.

130. Mitchell, "The Role of Theology in Bioethics," 76–77.

131. See James M. Gustafson, "All Things in Relation to God: An Interview with James M. Gustafson," *Second Opinion* 16 (March): 80–107.

132. Callahan, *Setting Limits*, 105.

133. Vaux, *Birth Ethics*, 141. Also see James P. Wind, "What Can Religion Offer Bioethics?" in *Theology, Religious Traditions, and Bioethics*, 18–20.

134. Hollinger, "Can Bioethics Be Evangelical?," 172, 175.

135. Hauerwas, *Peaceable Kingdom*, 30, 33.

136. Ibid., 30–34.

137. Ibid., 59, 61.

138. Ibid., 97.

139. Ibid., 99.

140. Gustafson, *Ethics from a Theocentric Perspective*, vol. 2, 299, 32–33.

141. Ibid., 319–20.

142. Ibid., 275.

143. Ibid., 283. Also see James M. Gustafson, *Can Ethics Be Christian?* (Chicago: University of Chicago Press, 1975), 93.

144. See, for instance, James M. Gustafson, *The Church as Moral Decision-Maker* (Philadelphia: Pilgrim Press, 1970), 83–95, 153–56. Also see Gustafson, *Ethics from a Theocentric Perspective*, vol. 2, 290–91.

145. Gustafson, *Can Ethics Be Christian?*, 62.

146. Ibid., 63.

147. Ibid., 129–30, 165.

148. Ibid., 168.

149. Gustafson, *Ethics from a Theocentric Perspective*, vol. 2, 290–91.

150. Ibid.

151. Yoder, *The Original Revolution*, 154–66.

152. Paul Ramsey, *Ethics at the Edges of Life*, 152.

Copyright Acknowledgments

From Karl Barth, *Church Dogmatics*, vol. 3:4, ed. G. W. Bromiley and T. F. Torrance (Edinburgh: T. & T. Clark, 1961). Reprinted by permission of T. & T. Clark Ltd.

From William K. Frankena, "The Ethics of Respect for Life," in *Respect for Life in Medicine, Philosophy, and Law* (Baltimore: Johns Hopkins University Press, 1977). Reprinted by permission of The Johns Hopkins University Press.

From Daniel A. Dombrowski, "St. Augustine, Abortion, and Libido Crudelis," *Journal of the History of Ideas* 49 (January–March 1988). Reprinted by permission of The Johns Hopkins University Press.

From Philippe Ariès, *Western Attitudes towards Death from the Middle Ages to the Present* (Baltimore: Johns Hopkins University Press, 1974). Reprinted by permission of The Johns Hopkins University Press.

From Daniel Cronin, *Conserving Human Life* (St. Louis: St. John Center/Franciscan Herald Press, 1980). Reprinted by permission of Franciscan Press.

From Benedict M. Ashley, "Birth Issues: Pro-Life Evangelization," in *The New Technologies of Birth and Death: Legal and Moral Dimensions* (St. Louis and Chicago: St. John Center/Franciscan Herald Press, 1980). Reprinted by permission of Franciscan Press.

From Howard Moody, "Life Sentence: Individual Autonomy, Medical Technology, and the Common Good," *Christianity and Crisis* 47 (October 12, 1987). Reprinted by permission of the author.

From Bruce Kaye, "The Value of Human Life and the Ethical Practice of Medicine," *St. Mark's Review* 42 (winter 1990). Reprinted by permission of St. Mark's Review.

From Leon Kass, "Death with Dignity and the Sanctity of Life," *Commentary* 89 (March 1990). Reprinted by permission of Commentary magazine.

From James M. Wall, "Suicide, Responsibility, and the Sacredness of Life," *The Christian Century* (October 30, 1991). Copyright Christian Century Foundation. Reprinted by permission.

From two addresses by Cardinal Joseph Bernardin, *Cardinal Joseph Bernardin's Call*

Index